Project Management

Project Management

Dr. Vinod N. Patel

Oxford Book Company
Jaipur ▪ New Delhi

Published By

Oxford Book Company

Regd. Off. "Bony Residency", Gate No. 2
Opp. Tilak Public School, Vishweswariya Nagar,
Gopalpura Road, Jaipur - 302018, India
Ph: 0141 - 2761280, Telefax: 2761381
email - oxfordbookjpr@gmail.com
website - oxfordbookcompany.com

Delhi Office: 102, 1st Floor, Satyam House,
4327/3, Ansari Road, Darya Ganj,
New Delhi - 110002, India
Ph: 011-45652440

Distributed By

KEYA INTERNATIONAL PRESS LLP
E-mail: keyainternationalpressllp@gmail.com

Published in India, 2025

ISBN : 9788189473419

Typeset by Shivangi Computers, Jaipur

Printed and bound in India by Thomson Press Ltd.,
New Delhi

Preface

A project is a temporary and one-time endeavour undertaken to create a unique product or service that brings about beneficial change or added value. The property of being a temporary and a one-time undertaking contrasts with processes or operations which are permanent or semi-permanent ongoing functional work to create the same product or service over and over again. The management of these two systems is often very different and requires varying technical skills and philosophy, hence requiring the development of project management.

The discipline of organising and managing resources in such a way that these resources deliver all the work required to complete a project with defined scope, time and cost constraint is known as project management. Certain people have an innate ability to do project management more efficiently than others. This is because some people are able to apply their skills and talents in whatever combination necessary to move projects forward and other cannot even if they have the same or superior individual skills. The ability to make things happen is a combination of knowing how to be a catalyst in a variety of different situation and having the courage to do so. The ability to be a catalyst is so important to some that it is used as a litmus test in hiring project managers. Making things happen is dependent on having a sense of which things are more important than others and applying that sense to every single interaction that takes place on the team.

The first challenge of project management is ensuring that a project is delivered within the defined constraints. The second, more ambitious challenge is the optimised allocation and integration of the inputs needed to meet those pre-defined objectives. How to face these challenges and how skills and techniques are inculcated in project managers is the domain of present book. The book makes detailed elaboration on all the stages, techniques, skills, concepts and many other aspects that are must towards making project managers expert in their field.

Dr. Vinod N. Patel

Contents

1

An Introduction

Meaning and History

The discipline of organising and managing resources in such a way that these resources deliver all the work required to complete a project within defined scope, time, and cost constraint is known as project management. A project is a temporary and one-time endeavour undertaken to create a unique product or service, that brings about beneficial change or added value. This property of being a temporary and a one-time undertaking contrasts with processes, or operations, which are permanent or semi-permanent ongoing functional work to create the same product or service over and over again. The management of these two systems is often very different and requires varying technical skills and philosophy, hence requiring the development of project management.

The first challenge of project management is ensuring that a project is delivered within the defined constraints. The second, more ambitious, challenge is the optimised allocation and integration of the inputs needed to meet those pre-defined objectives. The project, therefore, is a carefully selected set of activities chosen to use resources (time, money, people, materials, energy, space, provisions, communication, quality, risk, etc.) to meet the pre-defined objectives.

Almost any human activity that involves carrying out a non-repetitive task can be a project. So we are all project managers! We all practise project management.But there is a big difference between carrying out a very simple project involving one or two people and one involving a complex mix of people, organisations and tasks. This has been true for millennia, but large-scale projects like the Pyramids often used rather simple control and resource techniques including brute force to 'motivate' the workforce. The art of planning for the future has always been a human trait. In essence a project can be captured on paper with a few simple elements: a start date, an end date, the tasks that have to be carried out and when they should be finished, and some idea of the resources (people, machines, etc.) that will be needed during the course of the project. When the plan starts to involve different things happening at different times, some of which are dependent on each other, plus resources required at different times and in different quantities and perhaps working at different rates, the paper plan could start to cover a vast area and be unreadable. This was a problem facing the US Navy in the development of the Polaris missile system. There were so many aspects to the project that a new technique had to be invented to cope with it: the PERT technique. This and later developments led to mathematical techniques that can be used to find the critical path through a series of planned tasks that interconnect during the life of a project.

You could begin the story of modern project management from this time. But that would be unfair as project management is not only about planning but also about human attributes like leadership and motivation. Nevertheless, the idea that complex plans could be analysed by a computer to allow someone to control a project is the basis of much of the development in technology that now allow projects of any size and complexity not only to be planned but also modelled to answer 'what if?' questions. The original programmes and computers tended to produce answers long after an event had taken place. Now, there are many project planning and scheduling programs that can provide real time information, as well as linking to risk analysis, time recording, costing, estimating and other aspects of project control. But computer programmes are not project management: they are tools for project managers to use. Project management is all that mix of components of control, leadership, teamwork, resource management, etc., that goes into a successful project.

Project managers can be found in all industries. Their numbers have grown rapidly as industry and commerce has realised that much of what it does is project work. And as project-based organisations have started to emerge, project management is becoming established as both a professional career path and a way of controlling business. So opportunities in project management now exist not only in being a project manager, but also as part of the support team in a project or programme office or as a team leader for part of a project. There are also qualifications that can be attained through the professional associations. One reason for the rapid growth is the need to understand how to look after complex projects, often in hightech areas, which are critical to business success but also have to use scarce resources efficiently. Most people still want their projects to be on time, meet quality objectives, and not cost more than the budget. These form the classic time, quality, cost triangle. In fact, if you have an unlimited budget and unlimited time, project management becomes rather easy. For most people, however, time and money are critical and that is what makes project management so important today.

As a discipline, project management developed from several different fields of application, including construction, mechanical engineering, military projects, etc. In the United States, the forefather of project management is Henry Gantt, called the father of planning and control techniques, who is famously known for his use of the 'bar' chart as a project management tool, for being an associate of Frederick Winslow Taylor's theories of scientific management, and for his study of the work and management of Navy ship building. His work is the forerunner to many modern project management tools, including the work breakdown structure and resource allocation. The 1950s mark the beginning of the modern project management era. Again, in the United States, prior to the 1950s, projects were managed on an *ad hoc* basis using mostly Gantt Charts, and informal techniques and tools. At that time, two mathematical project scheduling models were developed: (1) the 'Program Evaluation and Review Technique' or PERT, developed as part of the United States Navy's (in conjunction with the Lockheed Corporation) Polaris missile submarine programme; and (2) the 'Critical Path Method' (CPM) developed in a joint venture by both DuPont Corporation and Remington Rand Corporation for managing plant maintenance projects. These mathematical techniques quickly spread into many private enterprises.

In 1969, the Project Management Institute (PMI) was formed to serve the interest of the project management industry. The premise of PMI is that the tools and techniques of project management are common even among the widespread application of projects from the software industry to the construction industry. In 1981, the PMI Board of Directors authorised the development of what has become the The Guide to the Project Management Body of Knowledge, containing the standards and guidelines of practice that are widely used throughout the profession.

The Project Manager

Project management is quite often the province and responsibility of an individual project manager. This individual seldom participates directly in the activities that produce the end result, but rather strives to maintain the progress and productive mutual interaction of various parties in such a way that overall risk of failure is reduced. A project manager is often a client representative and has to determine and implement the exact needs of the client, based on knowledge of the firm he/she is representing. The ability to adapt to the various internal procedures of the contracting party, and to form close links with the nominated representatives, is essential in ensuring that the key issues of cost; time, quality, and, above all, client satisfaction, can be realised.

In whatever field, a successful project manager must be able to envisage the entire project from start to finish and to have the ability to ensure that this vision is realised. Any type of product or service—buildings, vehicles, electronics, computer software, financial services, etc.—may have its implementation overseen by a project manager and its operations by a product manager.

Triple Constraints of Project Management

Projects need to be performed and delivered under certain constraints just as other human activities. Traditionally, these constraints have been listed as scope, time, and cost. This is also referred to as the *Project Management Triangle*, where each side represents a constraint. One side of the triangle cannot be changed without impacting the others. A further refinement of the constraints separates product 'quality' or 'performance' from scope, and turns quality into a fourth constraint. The time constraint refers to the amount of time available to complete a project. The cost constraint refers to the budgeted amount available for the project. The scope constraint refers to what must be done to produce the project's end result. These three constraints are often competing constraints. Increased scope typically means increased time and increased cost, a tight time constraint could mean increased costs and reduced scope, and a tight budget could mean increased time and reduced scope.

The discipline of project management is about providing the tools and techniques that enable the project team (not just the project manager) to organise their work to meet these constraints.

Time Constraint

Broken down for analytical purposes into the time required to complete the components of the project, which is then further broken down into the time required to complete each task contributing to the completion of each component. When performing tasks using project management, it is important to cut the work into several smaller pieces so that it is easy to follow.

Cost Constraint

Cost to develop a project depends on several variables including (chiefly): labour rates, material rates, risk management, plant (buildings, machines, etc.), equipment, and profit. When hiring an independent consultant for a project, cost will typically be determined by the consultant's or firm's per diem rate multiplied by an estimated quantity for completion.

Scope Constraint

The overall definition of what the project is supposed to accomplish, and a specific description of what the end result should be or accomplish. A major component of scope is the quality of the final product. The amount of time put into individual tasks determines the overall quality of the project. Some tasks may require a given amount of time to complete adequately, but given more time could be completed exceptionally. Over the course of a large project, quality can have a significant impact on time and cost (or *vice versa*).

Activities in Project Management

Project management is composed of several different types of activities such as:

- Planning the work or objectives
- Analysis and design of objectives
- Assessing and controlling risk (or risk management)
- Estimating resources
- Allocation of resources
- Organising the work
- Acquiring human and material resources
- Assigning tasks
- Directing activities
- Controlling project execution
- Tracking and reporting progress
- Analysing the results based on the facts achieved
- Defining the products of the project
- Forecasting future trends in the project
- Quality management
- Issues management
- Issues solving
- Defect prevention
- Project closure meet.

Project Management Artifacts

All successful projects adequately document objectives and deliverables. These documents are a mechanism to align sponsors, clients, and project team's expectations.

- Project charter
- Business case/feasibility study
- Scope statement/terms of reference
- Project management plan/project initiation document
- Work breakdown structure
- Change control plan
- Risk management plan
- Communications plan

- Governance model
- Risk register
- Issue log
- Action item list
- Resource management plan
- Project schedule
- Status report
- Responsibility assignment matrix
- Database of risks
- Database of lessons learned
- Stakeholder analysis.

These documents are normally hosted on a shared resource (i.e., Intranet webpage) and are available for review by the project's stakeholders. Changes or updates to these documents are explicitly outlined in the project's configuration management (or change control plan).

Control Variables in Project Management

Project management tries to gain control over variables such as risk, potential points of failure, etc. Most negative risks (or potential failures) can be overcome or resolved, given enough planning capabilities, time, and resources. According to some definitions risk can also be categorised as positive—meaning that there is a potential opportunity, e.g., complete the project faster than expected. Customers (either internal or external project sponsors), external organisations (such as government agencies and regulators) can dictate the extent of three variables: time, cost, and scope. The remaining variable (risk) is managed by the project team, ideally based on solid estimation and response planning techniques. Through a negotiation process among project stakeholders, an agreement defines the final objectives, in terms of time, cost, scope, and risk, usually in the form of a charter or contract.

To properly control these variables a good project manager has a depth of knowledge and experience in these four areas (time, cost, scope, and risk), and in six other areas as well: integration, communication, human resources, quality assurance, schedule development, and procurement.

Approaches in Project Management

For managing project activities there me several approaches including agile, interactive, incremental, and phased approaches. Regardless of the approach employed, careful consideration needs to be given to clarify surrounding project objectives, goals, and importantly, the roles and responsibilities of all participants and stakeholders.

The Traditional Approach

A traditional phased approach identifies a sequence of steps to be completed. In the traditional approach, we can distinguish 5 components of a project (4 stages plus control) in the development of a project:

- Project initiation stage
- Project planning or design stage
- Project execution or production stage
- Project monitoring and controlling systems
- Project completion stage.

Not all the projects will visit every stage as projects can be terminated before they reach completion. Some projects probably don't have the planning and/or the monitoring. Some projects will go through steps 2, 3 and 4 multiple times.

Many industries utilise variations on these stages. For example, in bricks and mortar architectural design, projects typically progress through stages like Pre-planning, conceptual design, schematic design, design development, construction drawings (or contract documents), and construction administration. In software development, this approach is often known as 'waterfall development', i.e., one series of tasks after another in linear sequence. In software development many organisations have adapted the Rational Unified Process (RUP) to fit this methodology, although RUP does not require or explicitly recommend this practice. Waterfall development can work for small tightly defined projects, but for larger projects of undefined or unknowable scope, it is less suited. Because software development is often the realisation of a new or novel product, this method has been widely accepted as ineffective for software projects where requirements are largely unknowable up front and susceptible to change. While the names may differ from industry to industry, the actual stages typically follow common steps to problem solving—defining the problem, weighing options, choosing a path, implementation and evaluation.

Critical Chain Approach

In critical studies of project management, it has been noted that several of these fundamentally PERT-based models are not well suited for the multi-project company environment of today. Most of them are aimed at very large-scale, one-time, non-routine projects, and nowadays all kinds of management are expressed in terms of projects. Using complex models for 'projects' (or rather 'tasks') spanning a few weeks has been proven to cause unnecessary costs and low maneuverability in several cases. Instead, project management experts try to identify different 'lightweight' models, such as, for example, Extreme Programming for software development and Scrum techniques. The generalisation of Extreme Programming to other kinds of projects is extreme project management, which may be used in combination with the process modelling and management principles of human interaction management. Critical chain is an extension to the traditional critical path method.

Process-based Management

Also furthering the concept of project control is the incorporation of process-based management. This area has been driven by the use of maturity models such as the CMMI (Capability Maturity Model Integration) and ISO/IEC15504 (SPICE - Software Process Improvement and Capability Determination), which have been far more successful.

Agile project management approaches based on the principles of human interaction management are founded on a process view of human collaboration. This contrasts sharply with traditional approach. In the agile software development or flexible product development approach, the project is seen as a series of relatively small tasks conceived and executed as the situation demands in an adaptive manner, rather than as a completely pre-planned process.

Control Systems in Project Management

Project control begins early in the project with planning and ends late in the project with post-implementation review, having a thorough involvement of each step in the process. Project control is that element of a project that keeps it on-track, on-time, and within budget. Each project should be assessed for the appropriate level of control needed, too much control is too time consuming, too little control is too costly. Clarifying the cost to the business if the control is not implemented in terms of errors, fixes, and additional audit fees.

Control systems are needed for cost, risk, quality, communication, time, change, procurement, and human resources. In addition, auditors should consider how important the projects are to the financial statements, how reliant the stakeholders are on controls, and how many controls exist. Auditors should review the development process and procedures how they are implemented. The process of development and the quality of the final product may also be assessed if needed or requested. A business may want the auditing firm to be involved throughout the process to catch problems earlier on so that they can be fixed more easily. An auditor can serve as a controls consultant as part of the development team or as an independent auditor as part of an audit. Businesses sometimes use formal systems development processes. These help assure that systems are developed successfully. A formal process is more effective in creating strong controls, and auditors should review this process to confirm that it is well designed and is followed in practice. A good formal systems development plan outlines:

- A strategy to align development with the organisation's broader objectives
- Standards for new systems
- Project management policies for timing and budgeting
- Procedures describing the process.

Project Development Stages

Regardless of the methodology used, the project development process will have the same major stages.

There are two different lifecycles that work in conjunction with one another throughout the course of every project. The project lifecycle describes the tasks that must be completed to produce a product or service. Different project lifecycles exist for specific products and services. (For example, the lifecycle followed to build a house is very different from the lifecycle followed to develop a software package.) The project management lifecycle defines how to manage a project. It will always be the same, regardless of the project lifecycle being employed. One of a project manager's challenges is to understand how to align the specific project lifecycle with the project management lifecycle. Project tasks and project management tasks are concurrent and ongoing, and can be associated by project management deliverables. The Project Schedule, for example, contains both project and project management tasks. Phases in the two lifecycles will overlap, depending upon the project lifecycle being employed. The project manager needs to be aware of how the inputs and outputs of one lifecycle affect and shape the other.

The material in this section is organised according to the project management lifecycle. While no two projects are exactly alike, all projects should progress through the same five project management phases.

Project Origination

In this stage an individual proposes a project to create a product or develop a service that can solve a problem or address a need in the performing organisation. The performing organisation then submits the proposal to an evaluation and selection process. If selected, a budget or further management commitment for the project may also be required before a project manager is actually assigned and the project is authorised to progress to project initiation. Depending upon the standards and practices of the performing organisation, a time delay between the project's proposal and selection and its actual initiation may occur.

Initiation

The initiation stage determines the nature and scope of the development. If this stage is not performed well, it is unlikely that the project will be successful in meeting the business's needs. The key project controls needed here is an understanding of the business environment and making sure that all necessary controls are incorporated into the project. Any deficiencies should be reported and a recommendation should be made to fix them.

At the beginning of Project Initiation, a project manager is assigned. The project manager works with the project sponsor to identify the necessary resources and team members needed to further develop the key project parameters—cost, scope, schedule, and quality (CSSQ). The project team documents its charge in the form of a project charter, which is based on the project proposal, which includes the initial business case. approval of the project charter by the project sponsor authorises the designated team to begin the initial planning effort. The initial Project Plan resulting from Project Initiation differs in the level of detail and the validity of its estimates from project origination, and must be at a level sufficient to acquire any additional resources needed to progress to the next phase. The Project Plan also includes plans for involving and communicating with all the parties that are affected by the project, as well as identification of an initial set of foreseeable risks that can threaten the project. At the conclusion of Project Initiation, based on the initial planning documents, the business case is revised and re-evaluated and a decision is made to either halt the project, or proceed to project planning.

The initiation stage should include a cohesive plan that encompasses the following areas:

- Study analysing the business needs in measurable goals
- Review of the current operations
- Conceptual design of the operation of the final product
- Equipment requirement
- Financial analysis of the costs and benefits including a budget
- Select stake holders, including users, and support personnel for the project
- Project charter including costs, tasks, deliverables, and schedule.

Planning and Design

After the initiation stage, the system is designed. Occasionally, a small prototype of the final product is built and tested. Testing is generally performed by a combination of testers and end users, and can occur after the prototype is built or concurrently. Controls should be in place that ensure that the final product will meet the specifications of the project charter. Project Planning builds on the work done in Project Initiation, refining and augmenting CSSQ and Project Plan deliverables. Usually, additional members join the project team, and they assist the project manager in further elaborating the details of the cost, scope, schedule and quality. A number of key elements are added to the Project Plan, including project-specific items such as change control, acceptance management and issue management, as well as externally-focused items such as organisational change management and project transition. The initial list of project risks is augmented, and detailed mitigation plans are developed. Project planning marks the completion of the Project Plan—i.e., no work is left uncovered. However, some of the later phases of the project work may continue to be planned in more depth (e.g., Transition and Implementation details may not be developed until later in Project Execution). At the conclusion of Project Planning, the business case is revised and re-evaluated based on the completed planning documents and a decision is again made to either halt the project, or to commit the resources necessary for project execution and control. The results of the design stage should include a product design that:

- Satisfies the project sponsor, end user, and business requirements
- Functions as it was intended
- Can be produced within quality standards
- Can be produced within time and budget constraints.

Project Execution and Control

It includes the formal acceptance of the project and the ending thereof. Administrative activities include the archiving of the files and documenting lessons learned.

Project Execution and Control is where most of the resources are applied/expended on the project. A significant number of team members will join the project at the beginning of this phase. The primary task of the project manager during Project Execution and Control is to enable the project team to execute the tasks on the defined project schedule and develop the product or service the project is expected to deliver. The project manager uses the processes and plans prepared during project initiation and project planning to manage the project, while preparing the organisation for the implementation of the product/service and for transitioning the product/service responsibility from the project team to the performing organisation.

Maintenance is an ongoing process, and it includes:

- Continuing support of end users
- Correction of errors
- Updates of the software over time.

In this stage, auditors should pay attention to how effectively and quickly user problems are resolved.

Over the course of any construction project, the work scope changes. Change is a normal and expected part of the construction process. Changes can be the result of necessary design modifications, differing site conditions, material availability, contractor-requested changes, value engineering and impacts from third parties, to name a few. Beyond executing the change in the field, the change normally needs to be documented to show what was actually constructed. Hence, the owner usually requires a final record to show all changes or, more specifically, any change that modifies the tangible portions of the finished work. The record is made on the contract documents—usually, but not necessarily limited to, the design drawings.

Project Closure

In Project Closeout, the project team assesses the outcome of the project, as well as the performance of the project team and the performing organisation. This is accomplished primarily through soliciting and evaluating feedback from customers, project team members, consumers and other stakeholders. The primary purpose of this assessment is to document best practices and lessons learned for use on future projects. Key project metrics are also captured to enable the performing organisation to compare and evaluate performance measurements across projects.

Roles and Responsibilities in Project Management

There are many groups of people involved in the project lifecycle. The Project Team is a group that is responsible for planning and executing the project. It consists of a project manager and a variable number of project team members, who are brought in to deliver their tasks according to the project schedule.

(1) *Project Manager*: He is the person who is responsible for ensuring that the project team completes the project. The project manager develops the project plan with the team and manages the team's performance of project tasks. It is also the responsibility of the project manager to secure acceptance and approval of deliverables from the project sponsor and stakeholders.

(2) *Project Team Members*: There are responsible for executing tasks and producing deliverables as outlined in the project plan and directed by the project manager, at whatever level of effort or participation has been defined for them. On larger projects, some project team members may serve as *Team Leaders*, providing task and technical leadership.

(3) *Project Sponsor*: He is a manager with demonstrable interest in the outcome of the project who is responsible for securing spending authority and resources for the project. Ideally, the project sponsor should be the

highest-ranking manager possible, in proportion to the project size and scope. The project sponsor initiates the project proposal process, champions the project in the performing organisation, and is the ultimate decision-maker for the project. The project sponsor provides support for the project manager, approves major deliverables, and signs off on approvals to proceed to each succeeding project phase. The project sponsor may elect to delegate any of the above responsibilities to other personnel either on or outside the project team.

(4) *Performing Organisation Management (POM)*: It includes all members of the organisation's management team that may exert influence on project team members or be affected by and involved in the development and implementation of the product of the project. The committees that are formed to evaluate and select proposed projects for the performing organisation are comprised of members of the performing organisation management.

(5) *Project Proposal Team*: It is a group responsible for preparing the project proposal in the origination phase. It is organised by the project sponsor.

(6) *Project Selection Committee*: It comprises members of the performing organisation management team who meet on a regular basis to evaluate project proposals and select projects for initiation. They maintain the project proposal rating models and project selection criteria.

(7) *Customers*: These comprise the business units that identified the need for the product or service the project will develop. Customers can be at all levels of an organisation, from commissioner to entry-level clerk. Since it is frequently not feasible for all the customers to be directly involved in the project, the following roles are identified:

(a) *Customer Representatives:* Thse are members of the customer community that are identified and made available to the project for their subject matter expertise. Their responsibility is to accurately represent their business units' needs to the project team, and to validate the deliverables that describe the product or service that the project will produce. Customer representatives are also expected to bring back to the customer community the information about the project. Towards the end of the project, customer representatives will test the product or service the project is developing, using and evaluating it while providing feedback to the project team.

(b) *Customer Decision-makers:* These are those members of the customer community who have been designated to make project decisions on behalf of major business units that will use, or will be affected by, the product or service the project will deliver. Customer decision-makers are members of the POM responsible for achieving consensus of their business unit on project issues and outputs, and communicating it to the project team. They attend project meetings as requested by the project manager, review and approve process deliverables, and provide subject matter expertise to the project team. On some projects, they may also serve as customer representatives.

(c) *Consumers:* These include all the people that will use the product or service that the project is developing. Consumers internal to the performing organisations may also be customers.

(8) *Internal Stakeholders*: These include all the people that are in any way affected by the new product or service within the performing organisation. This may include the

project team, the performing organisation management, customers, as well as customer co-workers who will be affected by the change in customer work practices due to the new product or service; customer managers affected by modified workflows or logistics; customer correspondents affected by the quantity or quality of newly available information; and other similarly affected groups.

(9) *External Stakeholders*: These include all the people outside the performing organisation that are in any way affected by the new product or service. Consumers may also be external stakeholders.

(10) *Vendors*: These are contracted to provide additional products or services the project will require and may be members of the project team.

The following example illustrates how agency titles map to project roles on small, medium and large projects. Example includes project description, comparison of project roles and agency titles, and a project organisational chart.

Example 1: Small Project

Project Description:
The creation of a Security Research Lab is an example of a small project. The following is a summary of the roles filled on the Project Team:

Project Role	State Title
Project Sponsor	Deputy Commissioner for Policy/Standards, OFT
Project Manager	Emergency Response Team (ERT) Manager (Person responsible for development and implementation of the Security Research Lab)
Team Members: Technical Member	Program Technology Analyst

Team Members: Purchasing Unit Staff Member	Purchasing Assistant
Team Member: Space Planning Staff Member	Office Services Manager
Customers	OFT Security, Network and Application units and other state agencies.
Customer Representatives	State Agency Information Security Officers (ISO's)
External Stakeholders	The purpose of the project is to provide an environment for the Emergency Response Team (ERT) to simulate attacks with viruses and hacker tools so that appropriate countermeasures may be developed. Thus, stakeholders include the Legislature, the Executive Chamber, the citizens, and all agencies within NYS.
Internal Stakeholders	Emergency Response Team

2

Project Origination/Initiation

Introduction

Evaluation of projects proposed for the next planning cycle and to reach a consensus on the projects to be selected is done during project origination. During this phase, the strength of a project's business case is tested, and the viability of the proposed solution is explored. A determination is made as to whether the project is consistent with the agency's strategic plan and affordable within budget guidelines. The project proposal process may actually be part of the budget cycle, serving as the justification for budget requests. In this case, project proposals may need to be created a full budget cycle prior to the project's anticipated initiation. Other factors that impact project origination include statutory requirements, regulations, legislative restrictions, and civil service rules. Each organisation has its own approach to green-lighting desired projects. The approach outlined below is only one of many possible variations of the evaluation and selection process. There are some general principles, however, that apply to any effective evaluation and selection process:

(1) The deciding body must have enough information about the merits of the project's business case and the viability of its proposed solution to make a meaningful evaluation.
(2) The competing projects' merits must be evaluated and compared using a consistently applied methodology.
(3) The selection process must take into consideration the project's fit with the organisational mission and strategic plan.

Processes

The three major processes in this phase of the project management lifecycle are:

(1) *Developing project proposal*, where the initial business case is made, and initial project parameters are defined.
(2) *Evaluate project proposals*, where cost/benefit analysis is performed, and the projects are evaluated against a set of specific business criteria.
(3) *Select projects*, where a consensus is reached on the project's feasibility and relative importance in comparison to other proposed projects, and a decision is formally made regarding the project proposal.

Role Performers

The following roles are involved in carrying out the processes of this phase. The detailed descriptions of these roles can be found in Chapter 1.

- Project Sponsor
- Project Proposal Team
- Project Selection Committee.

Categories of Deliverables

Since a project manager is not usually assigned to the project at this time, members of the performing organisation management prepare and review project origination deliverables.

Processes	Tasks	Task Deliverables (Outcomes)
Develop Porject Proposal	Develop Business Case	Business Case
	Develop Proposed Solution	Proposed Solution
Evaluation Project Proposal	Present Project Proposal	Project Proposal Understanding
	Screen Project Proposal	Proposals Removed from Further Consideration
	Rate Project Proposals	Evaluation Ratings
Select Project	Prioritise Project Proposals	Prioritised Proposasl
	Choose Projects	Selected Projects
	Notify Project Sponsor	Proposal Decision Notice

Figure 1: Project Origination Tasks and Their Deliverables (or outcomes)

Developing Project Proposal

Introduction

In developing a proposal for preject, a persuasive case must be made for its viability given current organisational priorities. The initial business case for the project is formulated, and all information required for project selection is formalised in the proposed solution. A proposal for a project may come from any place in the performing organisation, but someone must be identified as the 'owner' of the proposal, and must serve as project sponsor, at least through the evaluation and selection process. The project sponsor may be in executive management, in a specific functional program area, or a representative of the customers or the consumers within the performing organisation. Since information from the business case is included in the proposed solution—and *vice versa*—the tasks to develop those documents should be performed not consecutively, but concurrently, with one document informing and influencing the other.

Role Performers

- Project sponsor
- Project proposal team.

Tasks in Developing Project Proposal

Developing Business Case

It one of the defining documents of the project, providing information necessary to support the decision to launch the project at the end of project origination and to continue the project in subsequent phases. The business case must identify an existing business need and lay the foundation for developing a potential solution to meet that need. The cost of implementing the solution must be estimated and compared to the benefits gained, and justification for the potential project should also depend on whether the project is consistent with the organisation's mission. For a sample business case template, see Figure 2, the Project Business Case. The business case must provide a compelling case for the project. A careful study should be made of expected benefits to the organisation implementing the project. An analysis of the costs, benefits and risks associated with the proposed approach can be made, and the justification necessary to obtain the proper level of commitment from the decision-maker(s) can be formulated. Once an original cost estimate for the project is derived during develop proposed solution. The business case can

State Project Business Case

Project Identification

Project Name :......................................Date.......................
Agency : ....
Business Unit/Programme Area : ....
Project Sponsor : ....Project Manager :...............

Enter the Project Name
Enter the current Date
Enter the name of the Business Unit of Programme Area
Enter the name of the Project Sponsor and the Project Manager (if known)

Business Need/Problem:

Briefly describe the Need or Problem diriving the proposed project

Solution (as described in Proposed Solution):

Brief describe the product of the project that would resolve the Business Need or Problem and the Solution proposed to crete it

Consistency/Fit with Organisation's Mission:

Describe how the project is consistent with the mission or provide rationale if it is not

(Continued)

Anticipated Benefits: (both qualitative and quantitative)

List all Anticipated Benefits resulting directly from the project. Specify the ways there will be measurable improvement of new capabilities. Consider the implication of not doing the project—what benefits would be missed?

Original Cost Estimate: (from Proposed Solution)

Provide Cost Estimate for project from proposal.

Cost/Benefit Analysis:

Briefly the Cost for the identified Benefits. Include quantitative analysis, e.g., calculations of anticipated savings, cost avoided, return on investment, etc.

Special Fund Sources:

List and describe any Sources for project funding. Are there grants that will be applied for? Are federal funds available? Is a charge-back to the Customers planned?

Figure 2: State Project Business Case

also identify special funding sources available for the proposed initiative, and should align the project's costs with the agency budget cycle. If the project is going to span multiple budget cycles, a multi-year strategy for project funding should be discussed with the agency fiscal officer, who may find it useful to review the business case with another constituency—the Division of the Budget (DoB).

During project origination, any estimates are acknowledged to be high-level at best. As the project progresses through the initiation and planning phases, those estimates will become more precise as more is learned about the true parameters of the project, and additional go/no go decisions will be made based on the latest information. It is also important to note that, in order to define project parameters with adequate precision, initiation and planning will require substantial resources, and initial estimates should reflect that fact. Before presenting the proposal for evaluation, the project sponsor should have the business case reviewed by the people most intimately familiar with its imperatives—customer secision-makers. The business case will continue to be a critical component of the decision-making process throughout the entire project management lifecycle—from the initial decision to proceed with the project to the decisions made at periodic project reviews to continue, modify or terminate the project. At the end of each project management phase and whenever there is a significant change to the project or the business function, the business case will be reviewed and re-validated.

Developing Proposed Solution

A proposal solution defines the optimal solution to address the need starts with the summary of the business need, and describes how the solution fits into the organisation's strategic plan. The proposed solution should include an evaluation of all alternatives considered, and a justification of the solution selected. The basis of time and cost estimates for the proposed solution (expert judgement, availability of historical data on similar projects, Request For Information (RFI) responses, etc.), as well as the accuracy of the estimates (+/- 100%, +/- 50%, etc.), should be documented. Some initial risk factors should be considered, along with strategies for mitigation. An initial assessment of the project's impact on the organisation is made, laying a foundation for a successful transition at the end of project execution and control. It may be advisable to include a description of the project's profile/visibility, documenting, for example, whether the project is required as a result of federal or state legislative action, gubernatorial or executive mandates, or agency programme priorities. In general, highly visible projects will receive higher priority. If the performing organisation uses standard evaluation forms/formats, the proposed solution may include a 'self-assessment' performed by the project sponsor or the project proposal team.

Such a self-assessment may assist the project sponsor to realize weaknesses in the proposal before formal submission for evaluation and selection. The proposed solution should also identify legislative, regulatory, and policy systems that will facilitate, compel, or constrain the project. For example, the project may be funded by a specific line item in the recently passed state budget, or the project may be constrained by necessary interfaces to state or federal funding and/or control/oversight agencies. All affected stakeholders should be identified. It is highly advisable to have an independent party verify the proposed solution and associated estimates. The completed proposed solution is combined with the business case to complete the project proposal, which will be presented to the project evaluation and selection process.

Deliverable

Project Proposal—a document describing the project that is submitted by the project sponsor to the selection process. It comprises the business case and the proposed solution, which include such items as a description of the product, the benefit to the performing organisation, alignment with the organisation's mission and strategic plan, a high-level estimate of the required resources, costs and timeframes, and any other information specifically required by the performing organisation for selection consideration.

Evaluating Project Proposals

For various new initiatives many organisations generate multiple proposals on a continuing basis; however, budgetary and other constraints allow only a fraction of those efforts to occur. Choosing the right projects, which support the organisation's mission and assist with the implementation of its strategic plan, becomes a crucial activity, starting with an objective evaluation of proposed initiatives.

This process presents an approach to rating competing proposals in a methodical, impartial fashion; the results are indispensable to the success of the subsequent project selection process. Organisations may implement this process in a variety of ways—from relying on unilateral decisions of a chief executive or designee, to convening cross-functional deliberative councils. The tasks presented below are designed to illustrate the components of an effective proposal screening and evaluation process, and not to prescribe a particular format required to reach a desired objective. The frequency of an organisation's evaluation/selection process may be dictated by many factors, including the size of the proposed projects, the vacillations of the budget cycle, and the occurrence of external mandates and internal imperatives.

Role Performers

- Project sponsor
- Project selection committee.

Presenting Project Proposals

It is beneficial to allow the project sponsor to make a case for the project in person because the quality and level of detail among typical project proposals rends to vary a great deal. This also allows decision-makers to ask questions and gather additional information on the spot, without resorting to more formal—and slower—channels of communication. The presentation should be based on the proposed solution and the business case, but it can take many forms—from a formal slide presentation to an informal run-through of existing material. The objective is to allow the decision-makers to interact with those who best understand the business reasons for the initiative, and its proposed solution.

The tasks to evaluate project proposals are:

- Present project proposals
- Screen project proposals
- Rate project proposals.

Screening Project Proposals

It may be useful to screen competing proposals by asking some important questions before a great deal of effort is expended on rating, prioritising and selecting presented projects, such as:

(1) Does the project support the organisation's mission?
(2) Does the proposed solution align with the organisation's strategic plan/technical architecture?
(3) Is there an available/plausible funding source for this effort?
(4) Does the project's cost/benefit analysis justify its initiation?

Unless a project is legislatively (or otherwise) mandated, simply working through these questions will result in elimination of some proposals from further consideration. The project sponsor should be notified, and the decision should be documented on the proposal decision notice form.

Rating Project Proposals

It is generally performed by executive management or by a group designated by executive management (Project Selection Committee). The group may meet on a regular or an as-needed basis to perform this function, or the rating of proposals may be an integral part of the organisational strategic/tactical planning and budgeting process. The process is usually formal, with specific forms/formats and procedures. In smaller organisations, however, it may be more informal, and may even be combined with the selection process. In these cases, a brief presentation to the commissioner, director, or other organisation head may be all that is required to commit resources (funding, personnel, equipment, etc.) and initiate the project. Proposals are generally rated according to a set of specific business criteria. The process may include a broad technical review to determine if the proposal follows current agency standards and technical architectures. The funding associated with a project is also a critical component of the rating process. A performing organisation may have unique rules regarding funding for proposals.

During project origination, the project sponsor must identify whether funds are expected from the performing organisation's current/future operating budget, or whether additional funding sources are available. The level of approvals needed may vary depending on whether the project exceeds or falls below defined thresholds. Thresholds may be based on cost, involvement of more than one functional area, project needs within or outside of standards and procedures, or other areas specific to the performing organisation.

The rating process generally assigns a score to each project, to inform the selection process. See Figure 3 for a Sample Project Rating Matrix.

Sample Project Rating Matrix

Project Name	*Project Sponsor*	*Strategic Alignment*	*Risk*	*Cost/ Benefit*	*Total*
1					
2					
3					

Each of these categories would have a separate matrix or worksheet as supporting documentation, which would typically roll up to a single rating within each category. These worksheets should be standard across projects to provide comparative rankings.

Strategic Alignment

Mandatory Requirement:

0 Initiative not mandatory

1 Initiative inferred by or strongly suggested in law.

2 Initiative specifically required by law, regulation.

Alignment to Mission, Goals and Objectives:

-1 The initiative does not map to any mission, goal, or objectives.

0 Explicit documentation somewhat maps this initiative to missions, goals, and objectives.

1 Explicit documentation clearly maps this initiative to missions, goals, and objectives.

2 Accomplishment of mission, goals, and objectives is highly dependent on this initiative and clear documentation exists which supports this assertion.

Process Improvement:

-1 Initiative does not assist generate process improvements.

0 There is documented evidence that the initiative will assist or generate process improvements within a workgroup.

1 There is documented evidence that the initiative will assist or generate process improvements across a division.

2 There is documented evidence that the initiative will assist or generate process improvements across the agency.

Other categories that might be included within strategic alignment include:

-1 Consequences of not initiative
0 Impact on internal and/or external customers
1 Cross-functional/organisational impact
2 Scope of beneficiaries.

Risk:

-1 The initiative impact depends on another initiative not yet complete-and-scheduled risk mitigation a actions have hot been identified.
0 There are no predicted or foreseen adverse impacts on the initiative schedule-or-the initiatives impact does not depend significantly on any other initiative yet to be completed.
1 There are no predicted or foreseen adverse impacts on the initiative schedule-and- there are no major interfaces with other initiative or systems.

Cost/benefit:

-1 The cost estimate is highly dependent upon uncontrolled variables (e.g., availability of external funding sources, changes in component pricing or maintenance contracts) and is therefore subject to significant change (>10%).
0 Situation may arise which may cause this year's costs to vary by no more than 10% of estimates.
1 Measures to identify in a timely manner and reduce variances between the actual cost of work performed and the budgeted cost of work performed are clearly documented.
2 Measures to identify in a timely manner and reduce variances between the actual cost of work performed and the budgeted cost of work performed are clearly documented-and-cost estimates are not significantly dependent upon identifiable uncontrolled variables.

Figure 3: Sample Project Rating Matrix

Evaluation Ratings

A score assigned to each project as a result of the project evaluation process. The ratings are used during project selection to rank projects in terms of their overall benefit to the performing organisation.

Selecting Projects

It is necessary to prioritise project proposals once these have been uniformly and objectively rated to reflect how they compare to one another in various aspects, including supporting current organisational priorities, the mission and the strategic plan. At that point in the select projects process, a decision can be made as to how many of the top-rated proposals can be accommodated by the agency's budget, resources, and ability to absorb organisational change. Whether the project is approved, declined, or sent back for additional information, the project sponsor must be notified, and the decision documented.

Prioritising Project Proposals

Quantitative ratings derived through the evaluation process make the prioritisation process a simple matter of sorting the higher scores to the top. However, it may be useful to review the generic rating criteria once again and decide if some additional measurements are needed. Complying with legislative mandates or executive chamber initiatives, for example, may trump even well conceived process improvement opportunities. These are the factors evaluated to determine a project's feasibility and its relative importance in comparison to other proposed projects. Whatever the final set of criteria, they should be documented and applied equally to each competing proposal, to enable a fair and competent selection process.

Role Performers

- Project sponsor
- Project selection committee.

Choosing Projects

Project selection decisions are usually made by a committee of executives from the performing organisation. Even if the commissioner or other agency head (chairman, director, etc.) makes the final decision, a project selection committee generally reviews and develops recommendations. It may be useful to, once again, invite the project sponsor to make a presentation to the committee and answer questions. The project selection committee must choose projects that, in combination, will provide the best investment for the performing organisation. The committee considers competing priorities in determining what is best for the whole. All proposals must be evaluated in the context of other proposals, current projects and ongoing operations in order to set priorities and determine resource availability. This process may be accomplished through discussion and vote, or the committee may use specific tools (software, spreadsheets, etc.) designed to facilitate comparison of the proposals. The projects chosen as a result of this process may not necessarily reflect what is best for an individual employee or a single work unit.

Sometimes a lower-priority project will be approved simply because it is low-risk or low-cost, and can deliver needed benefits or services. Sometimes a project can be undertaken because it needs few resources, and can be performed while larger initiatives are delayed. Projects may be approved for immediate action or with a delay for obtaining resources. It is also possible that a proposal could be returned to the project sponsor for further development without approval or rejection. Choosing a project does not necessarily guarantee that the project will be undertaken by the performing organisation. That is generally dependent upon the availability of necessary funding. Each performing organisation may have a different process whereby chosen projects are actually authorised to proceed to project initiation.

Notifying Project Sponsors

It is imperative to document the decisions once they are made and to explain their rationale to the project sponsors and other stakeholders. One of three outcomes can occur:

(1) A decision is made to proceed with the project. In this case, a determination must be made when project initiation can begin. At that point a project manager must be assigned to the project. The finance office must be brought on board to ensure adequate funding for the project, and control agencies may be notified that the project is being initiated.

(2) A decision cannot be made on the project without some additional information. In this case, the specific information required for an informed decision should be documented, and communicated to the project sponsor, along with some guidelines for submitting the proposal again in the next evaluation/selection cycle.

(3) A decision is made to decline the proposal. In this case, a detailed explanation for the decision should accompany the message, outlining where the proposal came up short in the screening, evaluation, prioritisation and/or selection.

The purpose of project initiation is to begin to define the overall parameters of a project and establish the appropriate project management and quality environment required to complete the project. Development of the project charter is a pivotal starting point for the project, establishing the project definition that will serve as the foundation for all future efforts. The completion of this process is marked by the Project Kick-off Meeting, in which the project manager presents the project charter. Successful projects begin with a detailed project definition that is understood and accepted by stakeholders. Putting everything down in writing helps ensure a commitment among project team members and between the team and the stakeholders. As part of project initiation, an initial project plan is developed, which comprises the project charter, cost/scope/schedule/quality (CSSQ) documents, and preliminary risk identification list. These documents, once approved, ensure a consistent understanding of the project, help to set expectations, and identify resources necessary to move the project to the next level of detailed planning. Potential problems are identified so that they can be addressed early in the project.

Also during project initiation, a high-level project schedule is developed as the roadmap to more detailed project planning and project execution and control. This high-level schedule will be refined over time, and will serve as the primary source of information regarding project status and progress. An accurate, realistic, and complete schedule, rigorously maintained, is essential to the success of a project. Sponsorship of the project must be confirmed or gained during project initiation. Having a project sponsor, and securing approval early in the project management lifecycle, helps to ensure a commitment to the project.

Processes Involved

This phase consists of the following processes:

(1) *Prepare for the project*, where the project sponsor and initial project team are identified and work with the project manager to create the project charter.

(2) *Define cost/scope/schedule/quality (CSSQ)*, where the project manager, along with the project team define the scope of the project and identify the preliminary budget,

high-level schedule and quality standards to complete the project.

(3) *Perform risk identification*, where the project manager and project team begin to identify and document any risks associated with the project.

(4) *Develop initial project plan*, where the project manager and project team identify all stakeholders and document their involvement in the project, develop means of communicating with them, and compile all documentation created during project initiation to produce the initial project plan.

(5) *Confirm approval to proceed to next phase*, where the project manager reviews and refines the business case, secures resources required for project planning and prepares the formal acceptance package for review and approval by the project sponsor.

Role Performers

The following roles are involved in carrying out the processes of this phase:

- Project manager
- Project sponsor
- Project team members
- Customer
- Customer representatives
- Stakeholders
- Performing organisation.

Categories of Deliverables

Project deliverables for this phase fall into three categories of importance and formality:

(1) *Phase deliverables*—major deliverables approved by the project sponsor or a designated alternate that allows the project to proceed to the next phase.
(2) *Process deliverables*—drafts of major deliverables or minor deliverables that may or may not require a formal sign-off but nevertheless must be reviewed by project team members, customer decision-makers, and the project sponsor. The review validates the project's progress, and allows the project manager to move on to the next process in confidence.
(3) *Task deliverables*—drafts of process deliverables or works-in-progress that are verified within the project team, and may or may not be reviewed by the project sponsor or customer representatives. Each task culminates with the production of one or more tangible deliverables, which allows the project manager to monitor project progress using concrete and real results.

Preparing for the Project

The project is assigned to a project team after formal project approval whose first responsibility is to prepare for the project. The project manager must work to ensure that the performing organisation's expectations and all available project information are effectively conveyed to the project team. This can be done collaboratively with the performing organisation's management team.

Role Performers

- Project manager
- Project sponsor
- Project team members
- Stakeholders.

Tasks to be Performed

The tasks to prepare for the project are:

- Identify the Project Sponsor
- Identify the Initial Project Team
- Review Historical Information
- Develop the Project Charter
- Conduct Project Kick-Off Meeting
- Establish the Project Repository

Names of the individuals needed to complete project initiation tasks will be documented in the project charter. In selecting the project team, definition of the skills required to perform current tasks as well as skills for future project tasks is needed. Immediate project needs should be met first. After project team members have been identified, the project manager should provide them with a project orientation and review with individual team members their current and future roles on the project. This establishes a baseline understanding of team members' project responsibilities, which will be useful for conducting performance reviews later in the project. Some agencies hold a meeting at the beginning of project initiation, where all potential stakeholders come together to review the project proposal, discuss required roles, and assign project team members. In other agencies, establishing a project team is a less formal process. You should choose and use the method to identify your Initial project team that will work best for your project and within your organisation. Take the opportunity, from the outset, to establish the concept of a project team that comprises not only the folks reporting directly to you, but also your project sponsor, customer representatives, customer decision-makers, and all other players participating in the project schedule.

Identifying the Project Sponsor

If a project sponsor has not been identified, the project manager must work with performing organisation management to identify and formally appoint someone to that position. Because the project sponsor will champion the project within the organisation, secure spending authority and resources, and provide support to the project

Processes	Tasks	Task Deliverables (outcomes)
Prepare for the Project	Identify Project Sponsor Identify Initial Project Team Review Historical Information	Project Sponsor Project Team Information Reviewed
	Develop Project Charter Conduct Project Kick-off Meeting Establish Project Repository	Project Charter Kick-off Metting Project Repository
Define CSSQ	Define Project Scope Develop High-level Schedule Identify Quality Standards Establish Project Budget	Scope Statement High-level Project Schedule Quality Management Plan Preliminary Budget Estimate
Perform Risk Identification	Identify Risks Document Risk	Risks and Impacts List of Risks
Develop Initial Project Plan	Identify and Document Stakeholders' Involvement Develop Communications Plan Compile all Information to Produce the Initial Project Plan	Description of Stakeholder Involvement Communications Plan Initial Project Plan
Confirm Approval to Proceed to Next Phase	Review/Refine Business Case Prepare Formal Acceptance Package Gain Approval Signature from Project Sponsor	Refined Business Case Approval Form Signed Approval Form

Figure 4: Project Initiation Tasks Outcomes and Deliverables

manager, it is imperative that he/she be identified as early in the project management lifecycle as possible. Building the relationship between the project manager and the project sponsor is critical to project success.

Identifying the Initial Project Team

The extent to which the project team has been defined at this point may vary. At a minimum the manager for the project and certain individuals who can provide support in preparing for the project should be identified. During project origination, a project proposal was created. During project initiation, the proposal is reviewed to determine the roles required to staff the project. With the help of appropriate stakeholders, the project sponsor should take the lead in identifying the names of individuals within the performing organisation who could fill the roles and become project team

Reviewing Historical Information

Development of the project charter will require review of documentation compiled or presented during project origination. Materials and information reviewed may include:

(1) The strategic plan, a formal document produced by the performing organisation that outlines the business goals and direction over a designated number of years.
(2) The project proposal, including the initial business case, which describes the project objectives and how they support the performing organisation's strategic business direction.
(3) Project selection criteria, defining the parameters used in determining whether or not to undertake a project and identifying its business justification and measurements of its success.
(4) Information from a previous project similar in size, scope and objectives.
(5) Project knowledge and experience of the individuals.

Developing the Project Charter

The purpose of developing the project charter is to document critical success factors and define and secure commitment for the resources required to complete project initiation. The charter also documents the project's mission, history, and background, describes the business problem the project is intended to resolve, and lists the benefits to be realised by the performing organisation as a result of implementing the product or service. Information compiled during project origination is used and applied in the development of the project charter. To further understand how the project was selected and to write an effective, comprehensive charter, the project manager must work with the project sponsor and any appropriate subject matter experts and stakeholders. If issues or conflicting project expectations are uncovered while developing the project charter, the project manager must communicate with stakeholders to resolve the discrepancies, elevate the issues when appropriate, and obtain consensus. Decisions that impact project expectations significantly should be thoroughly documented.

The project charter contains the following sections:

- Background
- Objective
- Critical success factors
- Required resources
- Constraints
- Authority.

Developing the project charter is a collaborative effort. Working with the project sponsor, the project manager should document the outcomes that must be achieved in order for the project to be considered a success. These critical success factors should correlate with the goals and objectives of the project. An effective way to define a critical success factor is to complete the following sentence, "The project will be a success if . . ."

Various areas of the performing organisation may be required to provide resources to the project in order to complete project initiation. The project sponsor and project manager must determine specific resource requirements and effort estimates, and include them in the charter. The project sponsor must communicate with the affected areas of the performing organisation, proactively gaining agreement and securing the necessary resources.

Once the project charter has been developed, the project manager should schedule a meeting to review its contents, secure necessary resources, and gain formal approval. Meeting attendees should always include the project sponsor and the members of performing organisation management whose resources are affected. Attendees may also include other members of the performing organisation who are able to provide resources that will add value to the project. During the meeting, the project manager presents the project charter for review. Resources are formally secured by gaining the signatures of the appropriate performing organisation managers. At the conclusion of the meeting, the project sponsor will formally approve or reject the charter. Should the project sponsor reject the charter, he/she must provide the reasons for rejection to allow the project manager to make necessary adjustments. Based on the contents of the project charter, the project manager should have a general understanding of the amount of effort that will be required to complete project initiation and produce an initial project plan. It is imperative that the project manager begins to track the remaining project initiation efforts and communicate status. Items to discuss during status meetings include accomplishments, progress against schedules, work to be done, and any open issues that need resolution. As part of the communications plan for the project, a project status report should be prepared and reviewed during the meetings.

At this early stage in the project management lifecycle, the project manager needs to ensure that only project initiation resources are secured. Resources required in subsequent project management lifecycle phases will be determined and documented later, in the project plan.

Conducting Project Kick-off Meeting

When the project charter is complete, the project kick-off meeting is conducted. The project kick-off meeting is the event that formally marks the beginning of the project. It is most likely the first opportunity for the project sponsor to assemble the entire project team to discuss his/her vision of the project, demonstrate support, and advocate project success. Project team members are introduced to each other and given the opportunity to discuss their areas of expertise and how they will contribute to the project. The project charter is presented by the project manager and discussed in an open forum, to foster a mutual understanding of and enthusiasm for the project. At the conclusion of the meeting, project team members will understand their 'next steps', and will leave the meeting ready and excited to begin work. Prior to the meeting, an agenda and a presentation highlighting the contents of the project charter should be prepared by the project manager. The project manager should designate one of the project team members as the scribe for the session, to capture decisions, issues, and action items. The project charter and any applicable supporting materials are distributed to attendees for their review. The review of the charter contents ensures that expectations for the project and its results are in agreement. If not already done, the project manager must ensure that the project sponsor has provided his/her signature on the project charter, indicating his/her approval of the contents of the document. If the project sponsor does not approve the charter, he/she must indicate the reason, to allow the project manager to make necessary adjustments. Following the session, the notes and action items should be compiled into meeting minutes and distributed to all attendees.

Establishing the Project Repository

Maintaining information about the project in an organised fashion provides an audit trail documenting the history and evolution of the project and facilitates new team member transitions and creates a central point of reference for those developing project definition documents. All relevant project-related material, documents produced, decisions made, issues raised and correspondence exchanged must be captured for future reference and historical tracking. The project repository can be kept as hard copy in a binder or notebook, or as electronic files and email folders, or both, at the discretion of the project manager, in accordance with organisational records management policies. All files related to the project should be grouped by categories within project-specific folders. The structure should be intuitive so that anyone browsing the directory can easily locate needed information. Within the primary hard copy repository, information should be organised in indexed volume(s) to enable easy access. An index should provide reference to all material maintained electronically (e.g., a file directory or email folder by drive, directory, and filename). The most current hard copy of documentation should be kept in the primary hard copy repository, with earlier versions in the electronic file. By the end of the project, a project repository may include the following materials:

- Project Proposal and supporting documentation, including the business case
- Project description/definition documents such as the project charter, the CSSQ, and the project plan
- Any working documents or informal documents defining cost, scope, schedule and quality (CSSQ) of the project

- Project schedules (baseline and current)
- Project financials
- Project scope changes and requests log
- Project status reports
- Team member progress reports and timesheets
- Issues log and details (open and resolved)
- Project acceptance log by deliverable
- Products
- Risk identification/model documentation
- Audit results, if encountered
- Correspondence, including any pivotal or decision-making memos, letters, e-mail, etc.
- Meeting notes, results, and/or actions.

The project repository should be available to everyone involved in the project and must, therefore, be considered 'public information'. It is not advisable to keep sensitive information concerning individuals on the project, such as salaries or evaluations, in the project repository. Some project-related documents may also be regarded as confidential. A confidential project repository should be established in a separate location to secure sensitive information.

Project Charter

This is a document that provides authority to establish the project, broadly defining its purpose, goals, and objectives. Resources required to complete project initiation are also identified and secured. The charter serves as a contract between the project team and project sponsor. The project charter is the first in a series of project definition documents defining the business goals and objectives the project will meet. Information within the project charter is provided at a general level that will be further refined in documentation produced during subsequent project activities.

Defining CSSQ

It stands for a project's quadruple constraints: Cost, Scope, Schedule, and Quality. Because the constraints are interdependent, they are defined and managed together. The CSSQ concept is incorporated throughout all project management lifecycle phases. The CSSQ work products are first created during project initiation. The purpose of defining CSSQ is to:

(1) Develop a written project scope statement to define the project. The scope statement will be used as the foundation for scope and schedule refinement during project planning.
(2) Establish a preliminary project schedule to define, at a very high level, the activities that must be accomplished at certain points in the project in order to deliver the product described in the scope statement.
(3) Define the quality processes and standards that will be used throughout the project.
(4) Determine the appropriate approaches for staff and materials acquisition, and establish a preliminary budget for the project.

Role Performers

- Project manager
- Project sponsor
- Project team members
- Customer representatives
- Stakeholders
- Performing organisation
- Customer decision-maker.

Tasks to be Performed

Defining Project Scope

The written scope statement is a document that serves as input to future project planning efforts. The scope statement should include:

(1) The business need the project will address.
(2) What the project will accomplish, how it will be accomplished and by whom?
(3) What the end result of the project will be (e.g., a product, service, other)?
(4) A list of project deliverables, which, when produced and accepted, indicate project completion. Also included is a list of those items/deliverables that are not in scope for the project. The project manager must be specific about what is in scope and what is not in scope, as the weaker the boundaries between the two, the more difficult it will be to effect the change control process if required later in the project. Also, the details regarding what is in and what is out of scope are critical input to the creation of a detailed project schedule.
(5) Critical success factors (usually cost, schedule, and quality measurements) that determine whether or not a project was successful.

The project charter, including the project outcome description, provides necessary information for defining the project scope relative to the business need and benefit for the organisation undertaking the project. The scope statement will build on the outcome of the project described in the project charter by developing an approach to deliver that result, and by developing additional detailed information about the scope of work to be done. Interviews with other project managers who have had experience developing scope statements for similar projects can also be helpful.

While writing the project scope, the project manager and customer representatives must consider the effect the outcome of the project may have on the performing organisation. The organisation must be prepared to support the product once it is transitioned. If implementing the product will result in a change to the way the organisation will conduct business, the project manager, project sponsor, and customer must anticipate impacts and communicate them proactively to the consumer community. Sometimes people are resistant to change. Selling the positive aspects of the project and the benefits of its product throughout the project's duration will facilitate acceptance. If adaptation to the new environment requires new skills, the project manager will need to identify appropriate training opportunities and include them in the project scope and project plan. (for information regarding training and training plans, see developing project team) 'scope creep' is a major bane of project management. How do you combat it? By pre-empting it with a thorough, accurate, precise, and mutually agreed upon scope statement. Avoid words and statements that require judgement or invite interpretation, such as 'improve', 'enhance', 'better', 'more efficient' and 'effective'. Use numbers, facts, and concrete results. Use quantifiable terms, and provide target values or ranges. Emphasise outcome, not process. "We will work very hard for a long time to improve our response capability and enhance our effectiveness" belongs in a Dilbert cartoon.

Developing High-Level Schedule

A project schedule is a calendar-based representation of work that will be accomplished during a project. Developing a schedule means determining the start and end dates for all tasks required to produce the project's product, and the project management deliverables. At this early stage in the project management lifecycle, information required to complete a project schedule is known only at an overview level, often based solely upon the expert judgement of the project manager or other individuals with experience managing projects with similar lifecycles. Even at a high level, this information still provides insight into preparing the first draft of a project schedule. The activities documented in the schedule at this early stage will

System Development Lifecycle

Work Breakdown Structure

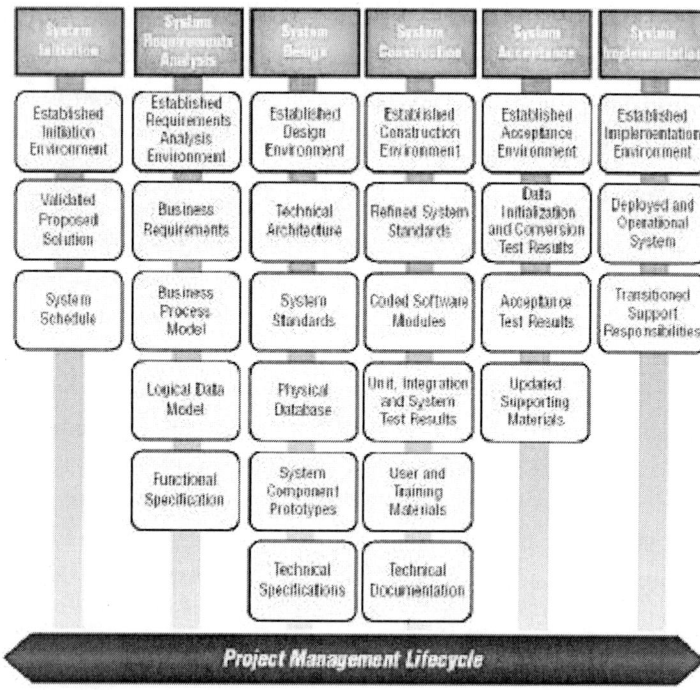

Figure 5: High-Level Work Breakdown Structure

be further broken down during project planning, when the schedule will be refined to include the specific individuals assigned and the amount of time required to complete the work. A Work Breakdown Structure (WBS) is a very useful work product that a project manager should create to facilitate development of a project schedule. A WBS is a graphical representation of the hierarchy of project deliverables and their associated tasks. As opposed to a project schedule that is calendarbased, a WBS is deliverable-based, and written in business terms. All tasks depicted are those focused on completion of deliverables. There are no dates or effort estimates in a WBS. Using a WBS, project team members are better equipped to estimate the level of effort required to complete tasks, and are able to quickly understand how their work fits into the overall project structure. The first hierarchical level of a WBS usually contains the phases that are specific to the lifecycle of the project being performed. (For example, the first level of the WBS for a software development project would most likely contain System Initiation, System Requirements Analysis, System Design, etc.)

For this reason, a WBS may be reused for other projects with the same lifecycle. Once the first level has been completed, it is broken down into more detailed sub-levels, until eventually all tasks are depicted. When defined to the appropriate level of detail, a WBS is very useful as input to both creating and refining a project schedule, including estimating required resources, level of effort, and cost. In project initiation, the information required to illustrate a complete WBS representing the entire project will not be known in sufficient detail. There will be enough information, however, to illustrate the tasks required to produce project initiation deliverables. The WBS is not static—the project manager should work with the project team during each project lifecycle phase to refine the WBS and use it as input to refining the project schedule. A preliminary list of the roles and skills required to perform the necessary work (e.g., architect, team leader) should be created at this stage in the project.

This list will be refined in subsequent phases, as more becomes known about the project. Additional constraints, such as completion dates for project deliverables mandated by the project sponsor, customer, or other external factors, will most often be known early in the project management lifecycle and should be noted. There may be financial, legal, or market-driven constraints that help dictate a project's high-level timeline. Using the information from the WBS as input, the project manager should begin to document effort estimates, roles and dependencies, in preparation for creating a project schedule using a project management tool. It may also be helpful to solicit input from past project managers, project team members and subject matter experts for insight into past project performance, and to help uncover required activities, dependencies, and levels of effort. Researching and documenting this information first will not only help organise thoughts on paper, but may bring new information to light.

Once the worksheet has been completed and reviewed, the project manager should enter the information into a project scheduling tool (e.g., Microsoft Project® or PlanView®) to produce the high-level project schedule. Information typically required for a project management tool includes activities, effort estimates to complete the activities, the role or individual assigned to them, and any known dependencies among them. The activities entered into the tool should be those required to complete the deliverables described in the project scope statement. Information will only be known at a very high level at this point, but will be refined during project planning.

Identifying Quality Standards

The project manager can reference the document containing the quality standards the organisation already has in place if the performing organisation has established quality standards. In most cases, however, this document does not exist, or the quality standards are not in place. The project manager and customer representatives must identify and document standards for each project deliverable during project initiation. If quality standards are not identified and documented, the project manager will have no way to determine if deliverables are being produced to an acceptable quality level. The project scope statement documents what the outcome of the project will be, and will help determine the appropriate quality standards to use. Additional information discovered when defining your project approach (e.g., your materials acquisition strategy) that is above and beyond that contained in the scope statement may aid in identifying quality standards.

Performance of a cost/benefit analysis can show whether the benefits of implementing the desired quality standards outweigh the cost of implementing them. Research of past projects that implemented quality standards similar to those that are candidates for the current project can also be helpful. Compliance to specific standards and regulations may be required and could dictate the quality standards to be measured against for a particular project. Preliminary standards should be reviewed again and modified or refined during project planning. The amasing thing about quality standards is that nobody has them available when the project starts, but everybody knows what they were supposed to be when the product is delivered. Do not accept lack of documentation as an excuse to skimp on your homework. On the contrary, dig down through organisational layers to discover what was used in the past (here's another way your historical data research pays off!) and what will be expected in the future. And if you can't find anything—create it, document it, publicise it, and put it in your project status report and your project repository.

Establishing Project Budget

The project manager calculates the preliminary budget by using available tools that will be required to complete project activities. All aspects of the project, including the cost of human resources, equipment, travel, materials and supplies, should be incorporated. At this point information will be presented at a summary level, to be refined during project planning, as more detailed information becomes known. However, the budget should be more detailed and more accurate now than it was during project origination. The project manager should use manual or automated tools to generate a preliminary budget estimate. The budgeting tools may be simple spreadsheets or complex mathematical modeling tools. For historical purposes, and to enable the budget to be refined, the project manager should always maintain notes on how this preliminary budget was derived. Cost estimating checklists help to ensure that all preliminary budgeting information is known and all bases are covered. The project manager must also have a general understanding of the cost of both the human resources and the equipment and materials required to perform the work. The method by which staff and products will be acquired for the project will directly affect the budgeting process. A number of constraints, financial, political, and organisational, may dictate the methods by which required individuals, equipment, and materials are acquired. The project manager needs to be aware of existing resource acquisition policies, guidelines, and procedures. In addition, the preferences of the performing organisation's management team and/or the In coming up with the project's budget, many project managers fall into either of the two extremes, depending on their temperaments and prior experience: those that are riskaverse or have been burned in the past 'aim high', inflating the project budget to protect against all eventualities; and those that are 'green', optimistic, or afraid of rejection 'aim low', underestimating the risks and realities. Neither approach, of course, is optimal: both put the whole project at risk, the former by either disqualifying the project in view of limited funds or inviting uninformed wholesale cuts, the latter by setting unrealistic expectations and guaranteeing multiple additional requests for more money.

The best approach is to use organisational experience, your own expertise, and the best advice you can muster, to predict with the greatest possible accuracy what the project will actually cost, and then set up a separate change budget. Above all, document the basis of your estimates! Customer representatives may influence acquisition decisions. In any case, the strategies defined should satisfy the needs of project stakeholders. Information from similar past projects can be used to gain an understanding of acquisition strategies; those that were successful and applicable may be considered for implementation on the current project. Once the project manager assesses the needs of the project, financial considerations, time constraints, and individual skills and availability, a method is defined for acquiring project staff. Depending on the way different organisations relate to one another, strategies used to acquire staff may vary. It is important for the project manager to understand the reporting relationships, both formal and informal, among different organisations, technical disciplines, and individuals.

Staff may be allocated from within an organisation or from an outside source using an established staff procurement procedure. The project manager should work with the project sponsor to determine staffing options.

The skills required for the project influence the means by which staff members are acquired. If there are limited qualified inhouse resources available to staff a project or if a project manager has had positive experiences with contract staff, for example, he/she may elect to retain contractors to fill the positions rather than allocating resources from within. If it is determined that it is necessary to recruit staff from outside the performing organisation, the project manager should work with the agency human resource office. The human resource office can assist in the recruitment of qualified staff in accordance with civil service rules. If the decision is made to utilise private consultants or contractors, the project manager should contact the agency contract management office for assistance regarding state contract vendors, and procurement guidelines. As is the case with human resources, a method is defined by which equipment, materials, and other non-human resources will be obtained. The project manager, in conjunction with the project sponsor, should determine the method to be used to acquire these resources. Regardless of how staff and products are acquired for the project, the project manager must add the estimated cost of all resources to the preliminary budget estimate.

Categories of Deliverables

(1) *Project scope statement*—documents a description of the project's deliverables, results, and critical success factors, and defines what is out of scope.

(2) *High-level project schedule*—a representation of tasks, durations, dependencies, and resources, to the extent that is currently known about the project. It should be produced using an automated project management tool. This schedule should be reviewed and approved by the project sponsor and customer decision-makers.

(3) *Quality management plan*—describes how the project team will implement the identified quality standards, the plan can be a very informal or highly detailed document, based on the needs of the project. It defines how project reporting will work, controls to be used in managing the project, audit needs, communication commitments, and any other quality processes that will be used throughout the course of the project. The quality management plan will become part of the final project plan created during project initiation and revised during project planning. At the end of project initiation, the quality management plan should include a description of the policy and standards the organisation has put in place to address quality. Any type of structured tool or checklist can be used to ensure that all quality measures have been considered. It may be a complex, industry-standard tool, or a simple 'To Do' list.

(4) *Preliminary budget estimate*—documents a preliminary estimate of the cost to complete the project.

Risk Identification

Risks are events that can potentially affect the cost, schedule, and/or efforts of a project. Risk identification begins during project initiation with the documentation of known project risks so that early planning can mitigate their effects. Throughout the duration of the project, risks must continue to be identified, tracked and analysed to assess the probability of their occurrence, and to minimise their potential impacts on the project.

Tasks to be Performed

Role Performers

- Project manager
- Project sponsor
- Project team members
- Customer representatives

Identifying Risks

The project manager solicits input from the project team, project sponsor, and from customer representatives, who try to anticipate any possible events, obstacles, or issues that may produce unplanned outcomes during the course of the project. Risks to both internal and external aspects of the project should be assessed. Internal risks are events the project team can directly control, while external risks happen outside the direct influence of the project team (e.g., legislative action). A list of risks is started, and as the scope, schedule, budget, and resource plan are refined during project planning, it is updated to reflect further risks identified.

The project should be analysed for risk in areas such as:

- culture of the performing organisation
- anticipated impact on the performing organisation of the resulting product or service

- the level to which the end result is defined (the more complete the definition, the lower the possibility of risk)
- technology used on the project (proven vs. new)
- relationships among team members
- impact on work units.

Documentation associated with project initiation can also be used to help identify risks. Some examples are:

- The project scope statement may uncover previously unidentified areas of concern (again, the more complete the scope definition, the lower the possibility of risk).
- Project constraints indicate likely risk sources.
- The high-level project schedule may produce extremely aggressive or unrealistic scheduling.
- Preliminary staffing requirements may be problematic if required resources have limited availability or unique skills that would be hard to find and/or replace should they leave the project.

Refer to the parts of this document concerning CSSQ and project charter information, to review for possible areas of risk. Historical information can be extremely helpful in determining potential project risks. Data and documentation from previous projects, or interviews with team members or other subject matter experts from past projects provide excellent insight into potential risk areas and ways to avoid or mitigate them.

Documenting Risks

The project manager documents identified risks to inform the risk identification and assessment process. Risk identification lists are typically organised by source of risk to help the project manager organize and record ideas. These lists may be generic or industry-specific. The project manager may even decide to create risk identification lists specifically geared toward the current project.

At this point, the project team is simply identifying and listing risks. During project planning, the items on the list will be transposed to a risk management worksheet, where they will be quantified and plans will be developed to mitigate them should they occur.

Developing Initial Project Plant

The project plan is a collection of information used to describe the environment that will govern the project. The work products previously produced during project initiation become part of the initial project plan. In addition to compiling these work products, developing the initial project plan involves identifying the stakeholders that will be involved in the project and establishing and documenting a plan for project communications. The project plan is an evolving set of documents—new information will continue to be added and existing information will be revised during project planning.

Role Performers

- Project manager
- Project sponsor
- Project team members
- Customer representatives.

Tasks to be Performed

Identifying and Documenting Stakeholders' Involvement

The organisation of the project team and outlines stakeholders' roles and responsibilities are defined by project managers. All stakeholders who will be involved in some capacity on the project should be identified. Some may be indirectly involved in an ancillary agency unit, a steering committee, or as external vendors or suppliers. Necessary contacts with agencies must be included. Members of these agencies are key stakeholders in many projects and interaction with them should be coordinated and planned. In defining the high-level schedule for defining CSSQ, a preliminary list of roles and skills required for the project was produced. This list may be useful when creating the list of stakeholder roles needed to perform the tasks leading to the desired project outcome and the responsibilities for each role. Even if the information is known only at a preliminary level, it is helpful to the project manager.

When documenting roles and responsibilities, the project manager should evaluate whether the individuals being assigned are in appropriate roles, if this information is known. If it is decided that assigned individuals may be weak in certain areas, or there are no individuals to fill certain roles, the project manager documents this information.

Developing a Communications Plan

It is a document describing the means by which project communications will occur. The communication process must be bi-directional. The project manager must receive input from project team members and stakeholders about their information and communications requirements, determine the best and most cost effective way in which the requirements can be met, and record the information in a formal, approved document. Similarly, the project manager must provide details to the team and the stakeholders regarding the communications he/she expects to receive, and document these requirements in the plan. The communications plan is developed early in the project management lifecycle. It must be reviewed regularly throughout the course of the project and updated as necessary to ensure it remains current and applicable. Some of the requirements the project manager and stakeholders will need to communicate and understand, and which should be documented in the communications plan include:

(1) How often and how quickly information needs to be disseminated?

(2) By what means the project manager and stakeholders prefer to receive information (via phone, email, paper)?

One of the greatest challenges in project management is getting the work done by individuals and business units that do not report to the project manager, or even to the project manager's entire chain of command. The earlier you can identify whom you need cooperation from, and the more detail you can provide as to the extent and outcome of that cooperation, the better your chances of actually influencing the work done. Make your case early and convincingly (emphasizing how the folks that DO have influence will benefit), and you may actually get them to do what your project requires.

(1) The communication mechanism currently used in the organisation, and how it might be leveraged or improved.
(2) The effectiveness of communications in past projects and whether specific improvements were recommended.

The methods and technologies used to communicate information may vary among departments or organisations involved in the project, and by stakeholders. These differences must be considered when creating a communications plan. For example, will all departments have access to email, or will exceptions need to be made? Are there any other considerations that may affect or limit communication? For example, there may be regulatory or contractual obligations that will affect the means by which communication can take place. A great way to communicate with the project sponsor and the customer representatives is to conduct a status meeting. Some items to discuss during the meeting include accomplishments, progress against schedules, work to be done, and any open issues that need resolution. A project status report should be prepared and reviewed during the meeting.

Compiling All Information to Produce the Initial Project Plan

All work products and deliverables from project initiation processes will be compiled for the initial project plan. At this point in the project management lifecycle, the project plan will consist of the following information:

- Project charter
- CSSQ
- List of risks
- Description of stakeholder involvement
- Communications plan.

This information will be refined and supplemented in later project phases as the project manager and team become more knowledgeable about the project and its definition. The project plan is not a static document; it requires iterative refinement.

Categories of Deliverables

(1) *Description of stakeholder involvement*—a document describing, to the level of detail currently known, the roles and responsibilities of all stakeholders, internal and external, who will in any way be involved in the project. This document is part of the project plan. This document will most likely be updated later as more about the project becomes known. "Don't judge the book by its cover." Hogwash! While we are not advocating style over substance, the format, style, and presentation do mean a lot. During the few minutes that most decision-makers will spend reviewing your written deliverables you want them to be well disposed towards you, and able to abstract the most information in the least amount of time. A professional-looking document will make a good first impression; a well-organised text that clearly and logically

builds your case will solidify that impression. So don't just slap some papers together, snap a rubber band around them, and submit it as the deliverable; treat your project plan as a repository of your brightest hopes for the future.

(2) *Communications plan*—a document written by the project manager that describes:

- How often and how quickly information will be needed by internal and external stakeholders
- How different types of information will be disseminated to the stakeholders (via email, phone, spreadsheets, formal documentation, etc.)
- The communications systems already in place and how they may be leveraged on the current project
- How the communications plan will be updated throughout the course of the project
- Any other information regarding the means by which information will be communicated to all project Stakeholders

(3) *Initial project plan*—the key deliverable produced during project initiation. The initial plan will be refined iteratively throughout the entire project management lifecycle and will serve as the main guide to follow during project execution and control. The initial project plan incorporates the deliverables above and is used to:

- Document project planning assumptions
- Document project planning decisions regarding alternatives chosen
- Facilitate communication among internal and external stakeholders
- Define key management reviews as to content, extent and timing

- Provide a baseline for progress measurement and project control.

Conforming for Continuance to Next Phase

This process is undertaken to formally acknowledge the completion, review and acceptance of all deliverables produced during project initiation. Formal acceptance and approval by the project sponsor or an authosised designee also signifies that the project can continue into its next phase, project planning. Acceptance and approval are ongoing. The project manager should review and gain approval from the project sponsor and customer decision-makers for all interim deliverables upon their completion. Interim acceptances should streamline final acceptance.

Role Performers

- Project manager
- Project sponsor
- Project team members
- Customer decision-makers.

Tasks to be Performed

Reviewing/Refining Business Case

At the completion of project initiation, the project manager must review the business case that was created during project origination. Because more information is now known about the project, the project manager will need to refine the business case to include the new information. The refined business case will be presented to the project sponsor as part of gaining approval to proceed.

Preparing for Formal Acceptance

At this time, the project manager should schedule a meeting to discuss and gain agreement to secure project planning resources.

Meeting attendees should always include the project sponsor and the members of performing organisation management whose resources will be affected. Attendees may also include members of other agencies who are able to provide resources that will add value during project planning. During the meeting, resources are formally secured by gaining the signatures of the appropriate performing organisation managers on the project deliverable approval form. In addition to reviewing the business case, all other deliverables produced during project initiation should be reviewed by the project manager to ensure that customer and project sponsor approvals have been received. Once the review has been completed, the project manager should organise the refined business case and all other deliverables into a cohesive package and prepare a formal approval form.

Gaining Approval Signature from Project Sponsor

The project manager must review the revised business case and the initial project plan with the project sponsor. Based upon changes to the business case and policies within the performing organisation, the project sponsor must decide if a project re-approval cycle is warranted. If project re-approval is necessary, the project manager should ensure the appropriate project origination processes are followed. At this point in time, the project sponsor may decide to terminate the project. This 'go/no-go' decision may be based upon factors outside the control of the project manager (i.e., the organisation may have new priorities that are in direct conflict with the project or increased risk may have been introduced to the project.) Realistically, termination of a project could happen at any point during the life of a project and is something a project manager should always keep in mind. At the end of this task, the project manager must present the deliverable acceptance package to the project sponsor or an authorised designee and obtain his/her signature on the project deliverable approval form, indicating approval to proceed to project planning. If the project sponsor does not approve the contents of the acceptance package, he/she should indicate the reason for rejecting it. It is then the responsibility of the project manager to resolve any issues regarding the deliverables and to present the updated package to the project sponsor again.

Key Elements of Project Initiation

Project initiation lays the foundation for the rest of the project management lifecycle. In the same way that a faulty foundation will result in an unstable and eventually unusable building, an incomplete or improperly executed initiation will result in a flawed project. What are some of the key elements of project initiation that require the most attention? The following processes and tasks are identified for this purpose:

No Sponsor no Champion

In prepare for the project, the first imperative is securing a project sponsor. Without the project sponsor to guide and support the project, the project manager has an impossible choice of either trying to take on the responsibilities of a project sponsor—for which he has no authority, or trying to secure the commitment of unwilling or uninterested executives—over whom he has little influence. Having one project sponsor who is high enough in the organisation to be of help, and interested enough in the outcome to be involved, is ideal. However, in many cases, the organisation insists on two people—usually managers from two main business functions involved in the project—serving as joint project sponsors. This situation is not a disaster—unless the managers are severely at odds with each other, especially about what the project ought to accomplish. In most cases, the project manager can sit down with the project sponsor(s) (as early as possible), and hammer out a common vision of what the project is supposed to do. Some of the useful questions to ask to gain consensus are:

(1) What are we trying to accomplish? What is the desired outcome?
(2) Who will benefit, and in what ways?
(3) Why is the project important to You?
(4) How is it going to change the way people do their work?
(5) How will the organisation adjust?

However, when the number of project sponsors exceeds two, trouble may be afoot. There will be so many more delays getting everyone to the same place, or chasing everyone down, so many more difficulties achieving a consensus, so many more corrections to deliverables, so many more minds to convince, so many more personalities to please. You'd better add lots of time to your schedule for securing necessary approvals! The effort you will expend in securing an interested, influential project sponsor now will pay dividends throughout the duration of the project. In some organisations, often those with a defined project selection method, projects may only be requested by someone willing to be the project sponsor.

Ineffective Kick-off Meeting

The importance of selecting an effective project team and writing a comprehensive project charter is self evident and well understood. However, the other key, but frequently overlooked or lightly regarded task in preparing for the project is the kick-off meeting. When conducted, the kick-off meeting is often wasted in a pro-forma, listless exercise of bringing unwilling participants together and stultifying them with boring recitations of project objectives, replete with industry buzzwords and technical jargon. Instead, you should look at the kick-off meeting as your opportunity to ignite interest in the project, secure enthusiastic participation in crucial activities later on, and set accurate expectations about what the project is—and is not—likely to accomplish. How? First of all, the kick-off meeting should be a creative, participatory exercise, involving all attendees. Second, it should emphasise and focus on how the project and its eventual product will benefit each attendee. And third, it should be a showcase for the performing organisation's commitment—and interest—in this project, and your team's enthusiasm for it. To make it a creative, joint exercise, you may consider asking the attendees to share ideas on why the project is important and how it will benefit the organisation as a whole. To involve self-interest, you may also want to ask participants to explain how the project will benefit each of them specifically, making their jobs better, easier or more fulfilling; and if they can't come up with anything, have the project sponsor make appropriate suggestions. To showcase executive commitment, develop a draft of 'talking points' for the project sponsor to use in a statement at the beginning of the kick-off meeting, explaining why the organisation is making a significant investment in this project, from both budgetary and human resource standpoints. Finally, this is a great opportunity to showcase yourself and your team, and demonstrate great enthusiasm for the project, which will be contagious and will set the tone for the activities to come.

Chicken before Egg, Schedule before Tasks

The task that gives project managers the most trouble is coming up with a project schedule before the project tasks are well defined and before many important project decisions are made. It is a lucky project manager who is not seized by 'analysis paralysis' at this stage of the game. How can I commit myself to an estimate (and let's not kid ourselves—the estimate you do put down will become a commitment, which the performing organisation will immediately embed in whatever budgetary or strategic plan they are developing) without knowing enough about the project? This paradox is easily resolved if you can estimate as you go along—one phase at a time. Unfortunately, that is a luxury afforded few, if any, project managers. The budgeting process demands answers well ahead of the game, and there is no avoiding it. The one thing that can help at this stage is experience—either personal, or in the form of organisational historical data. If you have been involved in similar projects in the past, you develop a feel for how long things take, and what obstacles—other than product-related—must be overcome and accounted for in the schedule. However, if you are new to project management, to the performing organisation, or to the technology, you need to fall back on organisational knowledge. If you are lucky, the organisation captured lessons learned from prior projects, and you can find out how long similar efforts have taken. More likely, no such knowledge base exists other than in people's heads, and your project sponsor can perform an important service in helping identify and recruit project managers who may have been involved in similar efforts. Make sure those efforts were actually successful—after all, you do not want to make the same mistake twice. Ask to see their initial and final project schedules. If they don't have either one (or worse, both) move along—anecdotal evidence is of very limited use in real life. Armed with all applicable knowledge, the moment finally comes to grab a mouse and start scheduling. Most of the time, the end date for the project will be pre-defined by some event outside your control—executive commitment, governmental mandate, or some physical constraint. In that case, 'backing into' an estimate is eminently reasonable. Walk through the entire project lifecycle backwards, making informed 'guesstimates' along the way, and see if you end up at the beginning with today's date.

In other cases, there is a budget limit that must be adhered to. Once again, you can back into your schedule by estimating how many weeks, months or years of effort by a reasonably-sized team the expected budget would support, and from there you can use the industry-standard percentages for product development lifecycles to approximate what your effort is going to be. Decide whether you will schedule according to effort, which is defined as the number of hours, days, or weeks per person, versus duration, which is defined as the number of work days or work weeks per task regardless of number of people. For a phase for which you have the most data (or experience), run a 'reasonableness' check to see if the estimate makes sense. Finally, you may have a completely blank slate—freedom to commit necessary resources over a reasonable time frame to get the job done in quality fashion. And when you wake up from that pleasant dream, you will go back to the first two options. But most of all, do not obsess over your preliminary schedule (that's why it's called 'high-level'). Document carefully all your estimating assumptions, and run it by as many experienced and knowledgeable people as you can—not the least, your project sponsor (that's also why it's called 'high-level').

Pretending Nothing will Go Wrong

The one process that shockingly few organisations engage in despite the fact that it can provide the most 'bang for the buck' is risk management, which consists of risk identification, assessment, and mitigation. Notice, there is nothing here that says 'risk avoidance'. You can't avoid risk—stuff will happen, and most of it will negatively impact your project, if you let it. What you can do is anticipate it, and be ready with a solution before the problem arrives. Once again, either your own experience, or organisational knowledge (captured as historical data in a repository, or as knowledge in people's heads) is the keep in mind that most early estimates tend to be on the optimistic side, before reality sets in. Consider your first attempt optimistic. Now make a second, more pessimistic attempt, assuming Murphy's law. This will provide you with the worst-case scenario. The truth is probably somewhere in the middle key. What obstacles, problems and disasters did other projects run into before? How were they dealt with? What was the impact on the schedule? Consider every aspect of your project. Ask yourself, what can possibly go wrong? What assumptions am I making that may not be accurate, or consistent? Then, for every risk factor that you identify, you need to determine how it can affect your project.

Not Enough Talk

Another activity that costs very little, but can provide enormous benefits, is communication. In fact, one of the few success factors consistently cited by the majority of agencies in analysing successful projects was frequent and comprehensive communication. Communication keeps all the players in the loop, avoids unpleasant surprises, and builds confidence in project progress and success. Nobody ever complains that they are being told too much, but they usually resent being told too little.

Building an effective communications plan starts with accurately accounting for all the players. Don't forget the project team, the project sponsor(s), all of the customers, and internal and external stakeholders. Anyone who will be in any way affected by the product or service that your project will develop must be communicated to at some point, and most likely throughout, the project lifecycle. For every player involved, determine how frequently the communication should occur (hint: early and often) and what it should contain (hint: the more the merrier). Of course, make sure it's OK with your project sponsor(s), but if you run into opposition on that front, remind them that even the old Soviet Union did end up discovering glasnost (openness).

Is the Project Official

Finally, you are all done with Initiation. Your schedule is a work of art. Your project charter inspires masses to commit great deeds. Your project plan is correct and complete. You think you are done? Not until you have a signature of someone that matters on a piece of paper that certifies that your opinion of your work is justified, and that you have authorisation to proceed to the next phase. Remember that unless you are in the highly unusual situation of being your own boss, you do not have the authority to certify your own work, or the clout to commit resources to continue. And unless you want to go very far out on that proverbial limb, you need to have proof that someone with proper authority—most likely, your project sponsor—is on board with what you have done, and what you are about to do. No matter how happy your customers and your project sponsor may be with your approach and your schedule, no matter how enthusiastic your project team, or your whole department, is with your plans, the only cover that you will have when things go terribly wrong (which, of course, if you've done everything correctly—including getting the approval form—will not happen) is that signature on that piece of paper. So please, do yourself a favor, and get that bulletproof vest before venturing into the shooting gallery known as the rest of the project.

3

Project Planning

Introduction

This stage define the exact parameters of a project and ensures that all the pre-requisites for project execution and control are in place. Project planning builds upon the work performed during project initiation. The project definition and scope are validated with appropriate stakeholders, starting with the project sponsor and customer decision-makers. Project scope, schedule and budget are refined and confirmed, and risk assessment activities advance to the mitigation stage. The initiation deliverables—CSSQ, and Initial project plan—are further developed, enhanced, and refined, until they form a definitive plan for the rest of the project. Additional project team members are brought on board and familiarised with the project objectives and environment, and additional resources are ready to be brought in following the finalised staff and material acquisition plans. Project planning is an opportunity to identify and resolve any remaining issues and answer outstanding questions that may undermine the goals of the project or threaten its success. It is an opportunity to plan and prepare, as opposed to react and catch up. Project sponsorship and commitment are re-confirmed at the end of the phase, with approval signifying authorisation to proceed and commit funds for project execution and control.

Processes Involved

This phase consists of the following processes:

(1) *Conducting project planning kick-off*, where the project manager conducts a meeting to formally begin the project planning phase, orient new project team members, andreview the documentation and current status of the project.

(2) *Refining CSSQ*, where the project team refines the cost, scope, schedule and quality components of the project to more accurately reflect the additional information is learned about the project.

(3) *Performing risk assessment*, where the project team and project manager review the list of risks identified in project initiation, identify new risks, evaluate each risk based on the likelihood of its occurrence and magnitude of its impact, and develop a plan to respond to each risk.

(4) *Refining project plan*, where additional management procedures and plans are developed and all updated documents created during project planning are compiled into the project plan to be utilised in project execution and control.

(5) *Confirming approval to proceed to next phase*, where the project manager reviews and refines the business case, secures resources required for the project execution and control phase and prepares the formal acceptance package for review and approval by the project sponsor.

Role Performers

The following roles are involved in carrying out the processes of this phase:

- Project manager
- Project sponsor
- Project team member
- Customer
- Customer decision-maker
- Customer representative
- Performing organisation management
- Stakeholders.

Categories of Deliverables

Project deliverables in this phase fall into three categories of importance and formality:

(1) *Phase deliverables*—major deliverables signed by the project sponsor or a designated alternate that allow the project to gain approval to proceed to the next phase.

(2) *Process deliverables*—drafts of major deliverables or minor deliverables that may or may not require a formal sign-off but nevertheless must be reviewed by project team members, customer decision-makers, and the project sponsor. The review validates the project's progress, and allows the project manager to move on to the next process in confidence.

(3) *Task deliverables*—drafts of process deliverables or works-in-progress that are verified within the project team, and may or may not be reviewed by the project sponsor or customer decision-makers. Each task culminates with the production of one or more tangible deliverables, which allows the project manager to monitor project progress using concrete and real results.

Starting with CSSQ, all task deliverables are eventually included as part of the project plan and the final acceptance package for this phase. Depending on available resources, some of these processes can be performed in parallel. The initial project schedule produced in project initiation will include the detailed schedule for the processes and tasks in project planning.

Conduct Project Planning Kick-off

It formally marks the beginning of project planning and facilitates the transition from project initiation. It ensures that the project remains on track and focused on the original business need. New project team members are thoroughly prepared to begin work, the current project status is reviewed, and all prior deliverables are re-examined. All deliverables produced during project initiation are used in project planning.

Role Performers

- Project manager
- Project sponsor
- Project team members
- Stakeholders.

Tasks to be Performed

Orienting New Project Team Members

The goal of orientation is to enhance the ability of new team members to contribute quickly and positively to the project's desired outcome. If individuals have recently joined the team, it is imperative they have adequate workspace, equipment, security access, and supplies necessary to perform their required tasks. The project manager (or team leader, if appropriate) must convey to each new team member, in a one-on-one conversation, what his/her role and responsibilities are related to the project. In order to streamline interaction among the team, new team members must also become familiar with the roles and responsibilities of all other Project Team members and stakeholders as soon as possible, and immediately receive copies of all project materials, including any deliverables produced so far. It is usually the project manager's responsibility to get new members of the team up to speed as quickly as possible. On large projects, however, if the team is structured with team leaders reporting to the project manager, it may be more appropriate to assign a team leader to 'mentor' the new individual.

Information that would be useful to new team members includes:

- All relevant project information from project origination and initiation
- Organisation charts for the project team and performing organisation
- Information on project roles and responsibilities
- General information about the customer and performing organisation
- Logistics (parking policy, work hours, building/office security requirements, user id and password, dress code, location of rest rooms, supplies, photocopier, printer, fax, refreshments, etc.)
- Project procedures (team member expectations, how and when to report project time and status, sick time and vacation policy) orientation sessions can be held for new members to ensure that they read and understand the information presented to them.

Reviewing Outputs of Project Initiation and Current Project Status

Before formally beginning project planning, the project charter and all components of the initial project plan should be reviewed. This is a checkpoint process—to recap what has been produced so far and analyse what will most likely be refined as project planning takes place. It is especially useful for any new members joining the team during this phase. The review of materials may spark innovative ideas from new team members since they bring different and varied experiences to the project. Some project managers make use of orientation checklists to ensure that nothing is forgotten during orientation sessions. It's a good idea to retain a package containing a checklist, an orientation meeting agenda, project materials and logistical information. Then, when a new member joins the project team, you can just copy its contents. Remember to keep the contents of the package current.

Kicking off Project Planning

As was the case for project initiation, a meeting is conducted to kick off project planning. At this meeting the project manager presents the main components of the initial project plan for review. Suggested items on the agenda to highlight during the project planning kick-off include:

- Introduction of new team members
- Roles and responsibilities of each team member
- Restating project background and objective(s)
- Most recent project schedule and timeline
- Identified risks
- Communications plan
- Current project status, including open issues and action items.

The goal of the kick-off meeting is to verify that all parties involved have consistent levels of understanding and acceptance of the work performed to date and to validate and clarify expectations of each team member in producing project planning deliverables. Attendees at the planning kick-off meeting should include the project manager, project team, project sponsor, and any other stakeholders with a vested interest in the status of the project. As in project initiation, the project sponsor should reinforce his/her support for the project and the value it will provide to the organisation. The project manager should also be sure one of the project team members in attendance is designated as the scribe for the session, to capture pertinent project decisions, issues, and action items. Following the session, the information captured should be compiled into meeting notes to be distributed to all attendees for review and approval. Meeting materials should be added to the project repository.

Refining CSSQ

During project initiation, the project team created the initial CSSQ, a set of formal documents defining the project and how its desired outcome(s) will be reached. During project planning, each section of the CSSQ will be refined as more information becomes known about the project. The CSSQ is not static—some of the components will continue to change throughout the life of the project. It should be noted that refining CSSQ occurs in parallel with other project-specific tasks. Project execution and control tasks are not put on hold while the project team waits for the plan to be finalized. In fact, the execution of project-specific tasks usually provides additional information necessary to further elaborate the planning efforts. The purpose of refining CSSQ is to use additional knowledge about the product of the project and the approach to be taken to:

(1) Improve the definition of project scope.

(2) Refine the project schedule by more accurately defining and sequencing project activities, estimating their durations, determining the dependencies among them, and assigning resources to them. The schedule will need to be adjusted according to the approach that will be used to produce the product and the availability of resources.

(3) Improve the understanding and definition of the processes and standards that will be used to measure quality during project execution and control.

(4) Refine the appropriate approaches for staff and material acquisition defined during project initiation, implement the plans, and more accurately define the budget required to produce the desired outcome of the project. The project budget will be affected based upon the approach that will be used to produce the product and the availability of resources.

Role Performers

- Project manager
- Project sponsor
- Project team members
- Customer
- Customer representative.

When refining CSSQ, the project manager should create a revised version of each document while maintaining the integrity of the original documents. This will provide an audit trail as to how CSSQ has evolved throughout the project lifecycle.

Tasks to be Performed

Refining Project Scope

The project scope must include discussions and interviews with the customer and other appropriate stakeholders. The scope document, therefore, will reflect a mutual agreement between all parties, which is more likely to ensure that buy-in is achieved. A clearly defined project scope is critical to the success of a project. Without a clear definition, work already performed may be subject to rework, resulting in lower team productivity. During project initiation, a scope statement was written to document a basic description of the project and its deliverables. Refining the project scope breaks deliverables into smaller pieces of work, allowing the scope and the existing project budget, schedule, and quality measurements to be more accurately defined. Where the initial project scope statement highlighted the deliverables to be produced in support of the desired project outcome, the revised project scope must go one step further. Using the information learned during project initiation, and based upon input gained by communicating regularly with the customer and other appropriate stakeholders, the project team must refine the scope statement to clearly define each deliverable—including an exact definition of what will be produced and what will not be produced.

The nature of the specific line of business associated with the product of each project will drive how the project scope is refined. For example, for building construction projects, architectural drawings will be completed; for application software projects, detailed requirements definition and design will be completed. Anything that impacts the team's ability to perform the work required by the project may be important to consider when refining the project scope. For example, impacts may occur due to a legislative decision. Both formal deliverables and less formal documents created during the project initiation, such as status reports, memos, and meeting minutes will be of assistance to the project team in revising the scope definition. Changes to a project scope document must be made using a defined change control process. This process should include a description of the means by which scope will be managed and how changes to scope will be handled. Once documented, the process becomes part of the project plan. It is vital to document a clear description of how to determine when there is a change in scope to facilitate change control during project execution and control. Documenting how to determine what constitutes change is a difficult process, but one that is critical to the change control management process. Additionally, while updating the project scope, the project manager and customer must consider the effect the updates may have on the organisation, anticipate impacts, and communicate them proactively to the user community. As in project initiation, selling the positive aspects of the project, the benefits of its product, and the value of changes to the scope during the entire duration of the project will facilitate acceptance down the road.

Refining Project Schedule

The work breakdown structure created during project initiation must be revised using the revised project scope. Deliverables illustrated in the work breakdown structure should be broken into smaller components, until each component is defined to the level of detail currently understood, or is small enough to allow the project manager to accurately estimate the time and cost required for its completion (using the project schedule worksheet). Using information from the project schedule worksheet as input, the project manager should update the project schedule to more accurately define required activities, dependencies, levels of effort, and deliverable due dates. You probably will not have sufficient information to break each and every component down into excruciating detail, especially if your project spans a long period of time. How can you predict the amount of work required to produce a deliverable that is scheduled to begin two years from now? You can, however, provide an estimate for the entire project at a high level, and should be able to provide accurate detail for the level of work required for the next 3 to 6 months. Describe the entire project to the level of detail you currently understand. Remember, as the project progresses, you will gain the information you need to break components down and provide estimates for the next 3 to 6 months! A good rule of thumb to follow is the 'eighty-hour rule': if the task requires more than two weeks duration to complete, it should be broken down further. This provides a solid basis for estimating level of effort, task planning, assignment of work, and measurement of performance in project execution and control. Use of the 'eighty-hour rule' not only greatly facilitates scheduling, but also lays a foundation for accurate tracking of actuals; reporting on progress is reduced to an objective, binary mode: each task (and its deliverable) is either done or not done.

On smaller projects a project manager works directly with project team members to obtain individual input on effort estimates. On larger projects with multiple components, the project manager most likely relies on the input of team leaders or individuals who are expert in the specific subject areas. In either case, the project manager should gain input from individuals who will actually perform the work or who have performed similar work in the past. This will not only make the effort estimates more accurate, but will help generate excitement and buy-in from the Project Team, as they will feel more a part of the process. Estimating the time to complete an activity is directly influenced by the capabilities of the individual assigned to perform it. The skill level of each person on the team should, therefore, be considered when doing effort estimates. A good practice is to base estimates on an assumed level of skill. This will allow the project manager to adjust his/her estimates up or down when the actual team is in place and the exact skill levels are known. It is imperative that all assumptions used in estimates are documented.

An experienced project manager also takes into account absenteeism, meetings, discussions, and staff interaction. A successful schedule builds in reality factors. Specific team members may have ongoing responsibilities occupying a portion of their time, and this must be factored into the schedule. Once effort estimates have been determined for each activity, the project schedule must be revised to reflect them. Any revisions or refinements that were made to the project scope will directly affect the project schedule and must be reviewed and incorporated into the schedule as needed.

Dependencies among tasks can be defined now, or adjusted as necessary.

Break each deliverable described in the project scope statement down into smaller, more manageable components. Repeat this until the components are small enough to be defined in the greatest possible detail. Questions to ask to determine if each deliverable has been broken down sufficiently are:

(1) Am I able to clearly define the component?
(2) Am I able to clearly state what will be done to complete the work and what will not be done?
(3) Am I able to estimate the time needed to complete the component? Am I able to assign an individual who will be responsible for completing the work?
(4) Am I able to assign a dollar value to the cost of completing the work?

If the answer to any of these questions is 'No', that particular component needs to be further broken down. This 'decomposition' exercise assists project staff to better understand and properly document the project scope. It also provides information needed for project schedule and budget revision.

(1) *discretionary dependencies*—those dependencies that are defined by the project team or customer that force the project manager to schedule tasks in a certain way. For example, the project team may be required to use an inhouse 'best practice' to complete an activity that forces other activities to be completed in a specific sequence.
(2) *external dependencies*—outside the realm of the project or outside the control of the project manager or customer, these dependencies may direct how portions of the project schedule must be defined. For example, a project activity may be dependent upon an outside vendor delivering a piece of equipment. This is something neither the project

team nor the customer can control, but it must be defined and considered when revising the schedule. Project schedule revision must also take into account:

- *Calendars*—the hours and days when project work is allowed, including seasonal restrictions, holidays, labor contract restrictions, vacation or training schedules.
- *Constraints*—completion dates for project deliverables mandated by the project sponsor, customer, or other external factors, which will most often be known early in the project. Additionally, there may be financial, legal, or legislative-driven constraints that help dictate a project's timeline.

Once the schedule has been revised to include tasks, effort estimates, resources, and dependencies, the project manager should study the schedule to determine its critical path. The critical path is the sequence of tasks in the schedule that takes the longest amount of time to complete. If any task on the critical path is delayed, the entire project will be delayed. A project manager can determine the critical path in a project schedule by looking at all tasks that run in parallel and computing the total amount of estimated time to complete them. The path that takes the most time to complete is the critical path. Tasks on the critical path that are completed late will delay the project, unless the project manager takes proactive steps to finish subsequent critical tasks ahead of schedule. Because of the important relationship between critical tasks and the project end date, the project manager must always be cognisant of the critical path and understand how it is affected when changes are made to the project schedule.

Refining/Defining Quality Standards and Quality Assurance Activities

The project manager and customer must determine if changes

have occurred to the project scope, customer requirements, external standards or regulations, or any other aspect of the project that will affect the quality standards established for each deliverable during project initiation. If the standards are no longer valid, the quality policy must be changed appropriately to refine existing standards or define additional ones. Also during project planning, the project manager communicates with the customer to establish and document all quality activities to be implemented during the course of the project to ensure the defined quality standards will be met. This is called quality assurance. Sometimes quality assurance for specific types of deliverables is performed by a separate quality assurance department. If an organisation does not have the luxury of a quality assurance department, the required activities will need to be performed by designated project team members or customers. Examples of quality assurance activities include:

- Collecting project documentation
- Conducting audits
- Verifying business requirements
- Performing testing.

A description of all quality activities to be implemented during the course of the project should be included in the quality management plan. Work with an experienced project manager, if you can, to learn tips and techniques for breaking work down, estimating time required to complete certain pieces of work, and refining the project schedule. Someone familiar with the process and the scheduling tools can save a more inexperienced project manager a lot of time and frustration! If experienced project managers are not available, consider getting effort estimates from multiple sources, comparing results and estimating the duration based on the multiple inputs. Involving the project team in the planning process will not only help ensure estimates reflect reality, but will also help gain team buy-in and acceptance. And remember . . . always document any and all assumptions made when deriving estimates or updating the project schedule. This 'audit trail' will prove invaluable if you need to retrace your steps down the road or must explain why schedule revisions are necessary!

Refining Project Budget

Based on the information now known about the project as a result of project planning activities, the project manager recalculates the budget required to complete project activities and tasks. As in the previous phase of the project, all costs must be considered including the cost of human resources, equipment, travel, materials and supplies. In addition, the following project components must be taken into account:

(1) *Project schedule*—the schedule created during project initiation has been revised during project planning to include more detail and greater accuracy regarding project activities, tasks, and durations. This information will be used as direct input to the refined cost budget.

(2) *Staff acquisition*—the project manager must identify additional staffing requirements. Strategies defined in project initiation need to be changed accordingly. Note that if the reporting relationships among different organisations, technical disciplines, and/or individuals have changed in any way, the strategy used to acquire human resources may need to be changed. Also, if the skills required to staff the project are different from those known during project initiation, the means by which staff members are acquired could be different. The project manager must update the project schedule to include all tasks needed to acquire project team members.

(3) *Resource requirements and costs*—at this point in the project, a more detailed understanding of the resources

required to perform the work and their associated costs is most likely known and can be used in refining the budget.

(4) *Materials acquisition*—the project manager must verify whether product requirements have changed since project initiation. If changes have occurred, the product acquisition strategies need to be changed accordingly. The project manager must update the project schedule to include all tasks needed to acquire equipment, materials, and other non-human resources.

(5) *Preliminary budget estimate*—also produced during project initiation, this spreadsheet should be the place to start to refine information pertaining to the budget. The project manager should add to this spreadsheet the more detailed cost estimates for the project defined in the project schedule, and revise the hours and cost columns based upon the revised project schedule, resource rates and requirements, and cost estimates. The project manager can use cost estimating checklists to ensure all preliminary budgeting information is known and all bases are covered.

It is also recommended that you take the time to document a preliminary disbursement schedule. This will help you and the project sponsor understand how the total budget will be expended over the course of the project. Again, for historical purposes, and to enable the budget to be further refined during project execution and control, the project manager should maintain notes on how the budget was revised.

Categories of Deliverables

(1) *Project scope*—the document that describes in detail the project boundaries, including defining the deliverables: how they will be produced, who will produce them during the course of the project, and the means by which changes to the deliverables will be identified and managed.

(2) *Project schedule*—a revised, definitive representation of activities, durations, dependencies and resources to the level understood at this point in the project lifecycle. The schedule has multiple uses. It is both a task list for further planning, if necessary, and a structure for reporting status during project execution and control. As individual tasks are completed, project progress can be assessed. It also serves as a useful management communication tool by which results can be compared with expectations. Because it is critical to the success of the project going forward, the schedule must be reviewed and accepted by both the customer and the project team during project planning.

(3) *Refined quality management plan*—the quality standards defined during project initiation and refined during project planning become part of the quality management plan. The quality management plan will be expanded during project execution and control and is included as part of the project plan.

(4) *Project budget*—a revised, more accurate estimate of the dollars required to complete the project. It includes the cost of all required human resources, equipment, travel, and supplies, and the anticipated timing of expenditures. Consult with past managers of similar projects to gain their perspectives on the actual time/costs to produce their projects' outcomes. Solicit input from past project team members to gain insight into the actual effort required to perform similar project tasks.

Perform Risk Assessment

The goals of risk assessment are to predict the likelihood that a risk will occur, to quantify its potential impact on the project, and to develop plans for risk management. Risks documented during project initiation should be reassessed during project planning. Next, an approach for risk management is developed. Actions can be taken to avoid, mitigate or accept each risk, depending upon the probability of its occurrence and the magnitude of its impact on the project. If a risk event can be anticipated, there should be sufficient opportunity to weigh consequences and develop actions to minimise its negative impacts or maximise its positive ones. The list of risks created during project initiation is entered into a risk management worksheet and supplemented by any additional risks identified in project planning. Within the worksheet, information is added to describe the risk probability, impact, and the timeframe in which the impact may occur. Based on these factors, the priority level of the risk event can be derived. Last, and most important, risk management plans must specify the individuals responsible for the mitigation actions, the timing of the actions to be implemented, and the expected results of the actions. In addition to quantifying risk probability and impact and formulating risk responses, the risk assessment process facilitates establishment of an agreement for the project team, project sponsor and customer representatives to collaborate in managing risks as they arise during the project.

Role Performers

- Project manager
- Project sponsor
- Project team members
- Customer representatives.

Tasks to be Performed

Identifying New Risks, Update Existing Risks

The project manager must review the list of risks initially identified for the project to determine if all risks remain applicable. As a result of project initiation and planning, the project manager and team members should be considerably more knowledgeable about the project and, therefore, better able to recognise and predict risk events. Through other activities taking place in project planning specific to cost, scope, schedule and quality (CSSQ), additional risk variables may be introduced to the project. Further refinement of the project scope may uncover areas of concern that were previously unknown. A more detailed schedule may introduce a new level of complexity and interdependencies to the project, possibly producing more risk. More accurately defined staffing requirements may call for resources with unique skills whose availability may be diminishing. These are only a few examples of how risks in a project evolve over time, with the focus shifting from one risk source to another.

The project manager verifies the updated list of risks with the project team and project sponsor. As in project initiation, the project manager must consider both internal and external risks, internal risks being those events the project manager can directly control (e.g., staffing), and external risks, those that happen outside the direct influence of the manager (e.g., legislative action). Once again, data and experiences from previous projects may provide excellent insight into potential risk areas and ways to avoid or mitigate them. If the organisation has a list of common project risks, it can be useful to ensure that the project manager has considered all potential risk elements in the current list. The project manager should update the organisation's list as necessary based on the results of the current project.

Quantifying Risks

The project manager and project team members evaluate each risk in terms of the likelihood of its occurrence and the magnitude of its impact. Both criteria should be quantified using a five-point scale: very high, high, medium, low and very low. These measurements are used as input into the risk management worksheet for further analysis when determining how the risk threatens the project. There are many tools available to quantify risks. The risk management worksheet presented here has been selected for its simplicity and ease of use. More sophisticated tools may be necessary for large-scale high-risk projects. A factor to be considered when quantifying risks is stakeholder risk tolerance, the threshold to which the performing organisation will assume risk, which is dependent on its attitude toward and motivation for the project. For example, an agency may view a 15% chance of a project overrun as acceptable since the cost benefit for the organisation to do the project far outweighs this factor. The project manager's understanding of the organisation's strategic direction and the motivation of both the project sponsor and the customer will help determine the level of risk tolerance for the project.

Developing Risk Management Plan

The project manager evaluates the results of the previous task to determine an appropriate response for each risk: avoidance, mitigation or acceptance. Each case will require a decision by the project team. The project manager is then responsible for communicating the steps necessary to manage the risk and following up with team members to ensure those steps are taken. Solicit input from experienced project team members and/or the project sponsor to uncover potential areas of risk and to help you identify what types of risks the project sponsor views as relevant. Jointly identifying and updating the risk variables for a project results in the sharing of risk awareness by all parties involved.

Since each risk may have more than one impact, the risk management plan must describe the actions to be taken to avoid, mitigate or accept each risk impact, including contingency plans. It should also specify the individuals responsible for the mitigation actions or contingency plan execution. Attention should be directed to those risks most likely to occur, with the greatest impact on the outcome of the project. On the other hand, a conscious decision can also be made by the project team to accept or ignore certain risks. These decisions must be documented as part of the risk management plan for subsequent re-evaluations.

Some commonly employed risk mitigation strategies may include:

(1) *Procurement*—some risks can be mitigated through procurement. For example, if the project requires staff with particular skills it may be advisable to retain resources through an outside organisation. Unfortunately, this may introduce other risk factors such as the resource's unfamiliarity with the agency.

(2) *Resource management*—it may be beneficial to leverage a lead resource that has already worked on a project with similar characteristics by assigning that resource as a mentor to more junior team members. This will mitigate delays in the schedule due to the learning curve of more junior resources.

(3) *Use of best practices/lessons learned*—some organisations already have repositories of project specific or business function best practices, which may help you to prepare for unanticipated risks. Taking advantage of other project best practices, whether they are process or tool based, will help to mitigate risk. Implementing processes that have worked successfully on other projects will save time. Identifying the risk is good; but planning a wise course of action around it is infinitely better. Be aware that by addressing one risk, you may be introducing another. For example: you identified a risk that your cost estimates may be off by as much as 15%. Your mitigation plan is to request a 20% increase in funds to cover the increased cost. You may have introduced a new risk, because a red flag may be raised, inviting an audit. The frequency with

which the risk management plan will be monitored, reviewed and maintained, and the method of communicating progress of risk mitigation actions, must be incorporated in the project schedule and project plan. The risk management worksheet should be reviewed at every status meeting, and updated with each change to the project. At the end of this task, the risk management worksheet should be complete.

Risk Management Worksheet

An updated record of risk variables, impact, probability, date of impact, level of priority and risk response actions. The review and update cycle for risk assessment should be built into the project plan and schedule. When updating the risk management worksheet, maintain the original. Each revision should be kept to provide an audit trail demonstrating how the risks evolved throughout the project management lifecycle.

Refining Project Plan

It includes development of all required management processes and plans for team development and project execution and implementation. All updated work products and deliverables produced during project planning are compiled and included in the project plan.

Role Performs

- Project manager
- Project sponsor
- Project team members
- Customer decision-maker.

Tasks to be Performed

Defining Change Control Process

Every aspect of the project defined during project initiation and planning has the potential to change. In fact, change should be expected to occur throughout every project phase; but if an effective change control process is defined and agreed upon during project planning, any change should be able to be handled without negative effect on the project outcome. Project change is not defined simply as a change to the cost, end date, or project scope. Change should be defined as any adjustment to any aspect of the project plan or to any already approved deliverable(s). This includes anything formally documented in the project charter, project plan, or any deliverable produced during the course of the project. The project manager and customer decision-maker must agree on the change control process, which then must be formalized, documented, and included as a section in the project plan. Items that must be defined are:

(1) Identification of the individual(s) authorised to request a change.
(2) Identification of the person responsible for analysing the request to understand its impact on the project cost, scope, schedule, and quality, as well as the customer representative who has authority to approve the request. The project manager should never give the project team the go-ahead to begin work until a change request form has been signed by the customer decision-maker. It should be noted that the impact to the project schedule must take into account time spent to analyse the change request.
(3) The timeframe (number of business days) allowed for a change request to be approved or rejected by the customer. It is important to document the fact that approval or rejection by default is not permitted, so acceptance or rejection cannot be assumed if there is no response to a submitted change request.
(4) The process to follow if no timely decision on approval or rejection of a change request is made. The project manager

should follow up with the person to whom it was submitted to determine why the change request has not been processed. If its identification as a change is disputed, the situation should become an open issue in the project manager's status report. The project manager should attempt to negotiate a compromise, but, if there is no resolution, executive intervention may be required.

(5) The percentage of the overall project budget that has been reserved for project changes. It is important to predetermine a change budget to prevent project work from being interrupted while funds are secured to do the work. Should you advise your project sponsor to set up a change budget—set aside a pot of money (10 to 20% of the project total) for unforeseen eventualities? Let's see. Does your project sponsor enjoy 'going to the well' time and time again to ask for additional funds? Do you enjoy writing justifications and groveling repeatedly?

Defining Acceptance Management Process

A detailed definition of each deliverable that will be produced during the course of the project is included in the project scope. A deliverable is considered complete when it has been accepted by the customer. The project plan must be revised to include a definition of the acceptance management process to be used for the project. It is recommended that 'acceptance' be defined as an authorised customer decision-maker's written approval signifying that a deliverable meets expectations. It should be clearly stated that verbal acceptance or acceptance by default is not sufficient. To expedite the acceptance process, it is recommended that one individual per deliverable be given final decision-making authority. This person will be responsible for obtaining feedback from and representing the customer.

In order for a deliverable to be considered 'complete' and 'acceptable', it must be measured against pre-determined acceptance criteria. The project manager and Customer must agree on the required criteria and the criteria must be documented and included in the project plan. To ensure timely acceptance of deliverables, the project Manager and customer decision-makers should agree on the format, content and appearance of deliverables before they are produced. This information should be documented and included in the project plan. This helps to prepare the customer to receive deliverables, and to avoid situations where deliverables are rejected because they do not meet customer expectations. It is also important for the project manager to solicit feedback on deliverables throughout their development. Interim reviews of deliverables will streamline final acceptance. In addition to acceptance criteria, the project manager and customer decision-maker must agree on, formalise, and document the deliverable acceptance process. Items that must be defined are:

(1) The number and identity of customer representatives who may be required to review deliverables before final approval from the designated individual(s) is sought. A reviewer is usually an expert who is very knowledgeable about the details of the subject matter in the deliverable. In many organisations a customer decision-maker with approval authority will not sign an approval form until a deliverable is thoroughly reviewed by an expert.

(2) The number of business days in which deliverables must be either approved or rejected by the customer. When establishing an agreement regarding the acceptable number of business days for deliverable review, the project manager must consider that the process is iterative and may take more time than initially thought. The amount of time for deliverable acceptance must be included in the

project schedule, and should be sufficient to include the following activities:

(3) Presentation of the deliverable by the project manager to the appropriate customer representative.
(4) Independent review of the deliverable by subject matter expert(s). The more experts, the more time it will take.
(5) Independent review of the deliverable by customer representatives. Again, the more decision-makers, the more time it will take.
(6) Group review sessions, if required.
(7) Rework of portions of the deliverable, if required.
(8) Resubmission of the deliverable.
(9) Re-review by the subject matter expert and customer representatives.
(10) Pursuit of approval signature by the project manager.
(11) The number of times a deliverable can be resubmitted to the customer for approval. It is very important for the customer to include reason(s) when rejecting the deliverable so the project team can address them when resubmitting. If the number of iterations exceeds the number defined in the deliverable acceptance process, further work on the deliverable will require a change request. If the number of iterations becomes unreasonable, the project manager should recognise that a bigger problem most likely exists. Setting the maximum number of deliverable revisions and iterations will avoid the situation where a deliverable is 'never quite done'. Whatever the number of iterations that is agreed upon, the project manager must build time to accommodate them into the project schedule. Don't be afraid to list the names of several reviewers, as different experts may need to be consulted depending upon the contents of the deliverable being produced.
(12) The escalation process that will be followed if a timely

decision on approval or rejection of a deliverable is not met. Will the situation simply become an open issue in the project manager's status report? Will executive intervention be required? Or will it be a combination of both?

Defining Issue Management and Escalation Process

A process must be in place to manage issues, since they can potentially result in the need for change control and can become major problems if not addressed. Issue management involves capturing, reporting, escalating, tracking, and resolving problems that occur as a project progresses. The following items must be agreed upon between the project manager and project sponsor and must be documented and included as a section of the project plan:

(1) *How issues will be captured and tracked*—many project managers make use of some type of repository to ensure that issues are not lost. This repository may be either electronic or manual, depending upon the needs and size of the project. At a minimum, an issue repository must contain a description of the issue, its potential impact, the date it is recorded, its anticipated closure date, its priority, and the name of the person responsible for resolving it or getting it resolved. The due date for closure must be a specific date (i.e., the date cannot be 'ASAP'). The responsible party must be a specific individual, not a functional group (i.e., an issue should not be assigned to the 'IT Department'). As progress occurs on the resolution of an issue, the project manager should update the issue repository to reflect what has occurred. An issue log (whether electronic or paper-based) should be updated regularly, possibly as often as daily depending upon the needs of the project and issue resolution progress.

(2) *How issues will be prioritised*—the characteristics about the issue that will determine whether its resolution will be maintain an 'Acceptance Log' in your project status report to track the status of a deliverable as it goes through iterations of the acceptance process—a high, medium or low priority. Impact to the schedule, level of effort, or cost are usually the factors that determine the priority.

(3) *How and when issues will be escalated for resolution*—whether they will be escalated if they are not resolved in a given period of time or when a delivery date is missed or only when the project budget is severely affected. Whatever the decision, details of the escalation process need to be clearly stated. It is also vital to document to whom issues will be escalated.

Refining Communications Plan

A preliminary communications plan was developed for inclusion in the initial project plan during project initiation, and describes how communications will occur. As a project progresses, certain events may occur that alter the way information is accessed or change communication requirements. For example, a department may move to a new building, allowing project team members access to email for the first time. Or a change in personnel may dictate a change in the frequency of communications. During project planning and subsequent phases, the project manager should review the communications plan with the project team to be sure it is still viable. If it is determined that any portion of the plan is no longer applicable, the project manager must develop appropriate revisions to the plan.

Also, at this point in the project, sufficient information is most likely known to allow the project manager to describe in further detail what the distribution structure will look like. Part of the communications plan describes how communications will be managed. Depending on the project, communications management may be very informal or highly sophisticated. When deciding how to manage communications on a project, a project manager solicits information from the project team and stakeholders and together they decide:

(1) How project information will be collected and stored, and what procedures will be followed to disseminate the information. If an electronic filing structure will be used, someone must be responsible for its setup and maintenance. Information access should be defined.

(2) The distribution structure, specifically detailing what, how, and when information will flow to stakeholders. For internal stakeholders, communication channels currently established in the organisation should be used. For external stakeholders, different channels may be required for each discrete stakeholder group. The team must decide when it should occur, what information should be communicated, and how it should be delivered. The distribution structure for external stakeholders must take into account how the particular stakeholder group will be affected by this project.

(3) The method by which information will be accessed if it is needed between regularly scheduled communications. Information requiring communication comes from different sources. Sometimes it is already documented in hard copy or electronic form, but sometimes it is conveyed during formal meetings, informal gatherings, or simple conversations.

The project manager must be aware that this information exists and be prepared to convey it using the communications management system. Some sources of project information that may require communication include:

- Status meetings
- Status reports
- Memos
- Newsletters
- Executive correspondence
- Meeting notes
- Executive meetings
- Steering committee meetings.

Sometimes communications break down. To try to avoid these disconnects, you should:

(1) Be as concise and clear as possible in both written and verbal messages.
(2) Solicit feedback to determine if your messages have been received by the appropriate parties and interpreted correctly.

When there are problems, try to learn from them so that you can do better in the future.

Defining Organisational Change Management Plan

The project manager needs to define and document a plan to manage the changes to the organisation that could occur as a result of implementing the product. This organisational change management plan becomes part of the project plan. Organisational change management must be explicitly planned if it is to be effective. Items to include as part of an organisational change management plan are:

(1) *People*: The plan must consider how the individuals using the product will be affected by its implementation. The organisation may initiate reductions or expansions in the workforce, and shift rote clerical activities to automated processing; decision-making power may be distributed

further down the chain of command, or even regionally. If specific job duties are being added or removed, staff reductions or increases are anticipated, or the organisational structure itself will change, the plan must identify the steps to be taken. For example, the human resources manager in the performing organisation must be involved in planning for and performing many of these change management tasks. Labor/management committees, union representatives, the external agencies involved, may all need to be included in planning for such changes, depending on the scope of the changes.

(2) *Process*: The plan must consider how the product of the project will affect already existing business processes in the performing organisation. Business processes may take advantage of streamlined workflows to reduce the flow of conducting a status meeting regularly with your customer is a great habit to adopt. If you plan to discuss a certain subject area during the meeting, don't be afraid to invite members of the project team with expertise in that area. It's also not a bad idea to invite other stakeholders who have something constructive to contribute. Use the status report to drive the meeting discussion points. Remember, there can never be Too much communication! paper, or technology advances may enable electronic communications to more quickly deliver information. Procedures will need to be redesigned to align with the change. The new procedures may effect changes in the way the performing organisation develops, documents, and trains staff, and must be addressed in the organisational change management plan.

(3) *Culture*: The plan must consider how severe the project's 'culture shock' will be. The project manager must determine how much the project will affect the performing

organisation's business strategy, established norms for performance, leadership approach, management style, approach to customers, use of power, approach to decision making, and the role of the employee. Plans might include performing an assessment of the performing organisation's 'readiness for change', and include development of action plans to increase the organisation's readiness and ability to adapt to change through education and training. In cases where implementing a project will result in a significant change to the way an organisation will conduct business, the project manager, customer, and project sponsor must be able to anticipate when and how the major impacts will occur, and plan for the specific activities that will adequately prepare the performing organisation.

Establishing Time and Cost Baseline

A time and cost baseline is a project 'snapshot in time', taken at the conclusion of project planning, against which performance on the project is measured. It is one way the project manager can determine if the project is on track. Using the electronic project schedule revised during refine CSSQ, a baseline is captured. Once the baseline version is approved, the project manager should revise it only if a change control is approved that results in a change to the schedule. The time and cost baseline becomes part of the project plan. As the project progresses, subsequent schedules may be compared to the baseline version to track project performance.

Developing Project Team

To effectively perform the activities required to produce project deliverables, project team members must have appropriate levels of skill and knowledge. It is the job of the project manager to evaluate the skills of team members and determine whether or not they meet the current and future needs of the project. It is important to remember that there are many kindsof skills. Some are technical and others are 'soft skills', such as management, presentation, and negotiation skills. If it is determined that the team needs training, the project manager must include training in the project schedule and project budget. Some skills can be learned on the job, some can belearned through informal mentoring, some can be learned using computer-based courses, and others may require formal classroom training. When the training needs and the method of training for each team member have been determined and documented, the project manager or team leader documents the training plan, including a training schedule. Subsequently the project schedule If you revise the baseline as a result of change control, be sure to save the original baseline for historical purposes must be updated to reflect all added training tasks: when and where training will take place and who will do it. The target date for completion of each team member's training program should be determined. As training takes place, the project manager should update the training plan with the names of the trainees and actual training completion dates. Not only will this help the project manager measure the success of the training plan, but it will also help him/ her evaluate team members and prepare staff performance appraisals.

Developing Project Implementation and Transition Plan

The project manager must formulate and document a plan for implementing or deploying the product of the project and for transitioning the responsibility for the outcome of the project from the project team to the performing organisation. The transition plan must include all the necessary activities to perform and procedures to follow to ensure a smooth and satisfactory hand-off. When planning the implementation and transition, the project team must consider the impact the resulting product will have on the performing organisation and consumers. The consumers must be prepared to use the product and the performing organisation must be prepared to support it. The project manager needs to define and document a plan to implement the product, and should consider:

(1) What needs to be done to ensure the organisation will be ready to receive the product? These steps may include acquiring the necessary physical space, installing appropriate software, obtaining the appropriate building permits, etc.
(2) How and when the customer will test and accept the product and confirm and authorise its implementation.
(3) The steps to be taken to ensure consumers will be ready to use the product once it is transitioned. These steps must be coordinated with the organisational change management plan, and will include training and orientation on the use of the product. They also may include plans for training customers or consumers as trainers for the future. The plan must define which of the customer(s) require training, the level of training necessary, who will provide the training, and when it will occur.
(4) The appropriate strategy for implementing the product into the performing organisation, given the specific consumers and customers. For example—phased by location, phased by specific product functionality, 'big bang', etc.

The project manager should define and document a plan to transition the ongoing support of the product to the performing organisation and should consider:

(1) The people from both the project team and the performing organisation who need to be involved in the transition, and their associated roles and responsibilities. Examples include customers, consumers, and members of other specific support units within the performing organisation.

(2) The steps that should be taken to ensure that the appropriate individuals are ready to support the product once it has been implemented and is in use. This may include negotiating with various internal organisations to determine the appropriate timing of the transition of responsibility, assigning specific organisations and individuals to support the specific products, and providing necessary training.

(3) The relationship between the implementation plan and the transition plan. The project team and the performing organisation must agree on the point in implementation at which the performing organisation takes responsibility for production problems, 'help' or trouble calls, and for resolving the problems.

(4) The performing organisation's expectations regarding any documentation that is required as part of transition.

Project Plan

The revised project plan is the main deliverable of the project planning phase, incorporating the revised outputs of all other project planning components. The document should now be thorough and accurate enough to be used as the main guide to follow during project execution and control. It is important to remember that the plan will continue to be revised throughout the course of the project. Many otherwise successful projects fail due to a lack of transition planning. Don't let this happen to you! At the end of project planning, the project plan should contain the following:

- Project charter
- CSSQ (cost, scope, schedule, quality)
- Risk management worksheet
- Description of stakeholder involvement
- Communications plan
- Change control process
- Acceptance management process

- Issue esçalation and management process
- Organisational change management plan
- Time and cost baseline
- Project team training plan
- Project implementation and transition plan.

Confirming Approval to Proceed to Next Phase

The purpose of this step is to formally acknowledge that planning activities have been completed and that all deliverables produced during project planning have been completed, reviewed, accepted, and approved by the project sponsor. Formal acceptance and approval also signify that the project can continue into the next phase, project execution and control. The acceptance and approval process is ongoing. As changes are made during project planning, the project manager should be in constant communication with the project sponsor. keeping the lines of communication open will avoid a situation where a project sponsor is surprised by a deliverable or receives something he/she does not anticipate. In addition, the project manager should review the interim deliverables or work products for each process with the appropriate customer decision-maker upon their completion and gain approval before moving on to the next process. These interim acceptances should streamline the final acceptance process.

Role Performers

- Project manager
- Project sponsor
- Project team members
- Customer decision-maker.

Tasks to be Performed

Reviewing/Refining Business Case

At the end of project planning, the project manager and project sponsor should review the business case that was developed during project origination and revised during project initiation. Because more information is now known about the project, the business case may need to be refined. Any refinements should be made before proceeding to project execution and control.

At this time, the project manager should schedule a meeting to discuss and gain agreement to secure project execution and control resources. Meeting attendees should always include the project sponsor and the members of performing organisation management whose resources will be affected. Attendees may also include members of other agencies who are able to provide resources that will add value during project execution and control. During the meeting, resources are formally secured by gaining the signatures of the appropriate performing organisation managers on the project deliverable approval form. In addition to reviewing the business case, all deliverables produced during project planning should first be reviewed by the project manager to verify that customer decision-maker approval has been obtained; these are the refined CSSQ, risk management worksheet, and refined project plan. If approval is not clear and explicit, the project manager must pursue it again. When the review has been completed, the project manager should organise the deliverables into a cohesive deliverable package and prepare a formal approval form.

Gaining Approval Signature from Project Sponsor

Before gaining an approval signature, the project manager must review the revised business case with the project sponsor. Based upon changes to the business case and policies within the performing organisation, the project sponsor must decide if a project re-approval cycle is warranted. If project re-approval is necessary, the project manager should ensure the appropriate project origination processes are followed. At this point in time, the project sponsor may decide to terminate the project. This decision may be based upon factors outside the control of the project manager (i.e., the organisation may have new priorities that are in direct conflict with the project or increased risk may have been introduced to the project). Or it is possible that, having done more detailed planning, the costs of doing the work are greater than initially estimated and outweigh any project benefits. Realistically, termination of a project could happen at any point during the project. The project manager must be comfortable and confident enough to approach the project sponsor at any time during the course of the project if he/she feels the project has reached a point where termination is the best possible solution. At the end of this task, the project manager must present the acceptance package to the project sponsor and obtain his/her signature, indicating approval to proceed to project execution and control. If the project sponsor does not approve the package, he/she should indicate the reason for rejection. The project manager is then responsible for resolving issues with the deliverables and presenting the updated package to the project sponsor.

Sometimes a project manager needs to gain approval of a large number of deliverables at the same time. The project plan is a good example, as it comprises several very important (and sometimes very complex) documents. Should the project sponsor become overwhelmed by the number or volume of documents requiring his/her attention, the project manager should take steps to work with the sponsor to streamline the acceptance management process.

Key Elements of Project Planning

Project planning may afford the project manager the last opportunity to plan for the successes—and prepare for the disasters—that may follow. Once the project plan has been accepted the events will unfold in their own due course: following the plan (more or less), or arising spontaneously, haphazardly and perniciously to jeopardise it. Your mission for this phase, should you choose to accept it, is to position the project so as to enable the former and impede the latter, or your plan will self-destruct in no time flat. What are some of the key elements of project planning that require the most attention? The following processes and tasks are identified as key elements:

You Have the Wrong Team

As a project manager appointed to a project, you probably think that you have very little latitude in selecting your team. Most likely, you are right—but it never hurts to try! And considering that these are the people who will define your success (flashback: what is the definition of 'management?'—answer, getting work done through others) you should certainly make every effort to surround yourself with folks who not only have the right alphabet soup on their resumes, but also have the 'right stuff' to form a high-performing team. It is a hard, and maybe even a counter-intuitive lesson to learn, that the right combination of character and intelligence—or, in other terms, of attitude and ability to learn—is far more important than a particular type or even length of experience. Here are some pointers for selecting—and weeding out—team member candidates.

(1) When selecting new team members, the first attribute to determine is aptitude. Whatever the technology or tools they will have to use, do they have a 'knack', a natural inclination for it? Do they take to it, do they do it on their own time, do they innately like it? Have they chosen—and succeeded at it—in the past? No degree, no level of erudition or IQ, guarantees that a person has an aptitude for a given job. And if they don't—beware. No matter how hard they work, or how much they study—they will still not produce the same results as someone with an aptitude who seems to knock off tasks left and right with nary an effort.

(2) The second desirable attribute is work ethic. Whatever your expectations are of the level of effort required on the project, you must be able to answer an emphatic 'Yes!' to these two questions about each new team member: (a) in the normal course of events, will the person put in an honest day's work? and (b) when the circumstances require it, will the person do whatever it takes to get the job done? Both questions are equally important, and both demand an affirmative answer.

(3) The third requisite attribute is versatility. Despite what you forecast on your schedule, and what you outline in roles and responsibilities, your team members will have to either substitute for one another, or perform some tasks you cannot currently anticipate. The team will need to be able to adapt to different circumstances and to learn new skills. Consequently, people who have a track record of performing well in disparate environments are certainly preferable over fragile personalities who are thrown off their pace for a week when a time sheet format changes, or who cannot function unless they have the right view out their window. Likewise, folks who have a track record of learning new skills and techniques, especially on their own, are vastly preferable over the types who must attend weeklong vendor seminars (preferably in tropical locales) before they can be persuaded to learn anything new.

(4) The fourth, and final, attribute to look for—and look out for!—is temperament. Or disposition, or attitude, or character—whatever you want to call it. It makes a difference between enjoying camaraderie and synergism of a closeknit team and dreading coming to work in the morning. Another way to 'stack your deck' is to make sure you have the right combination of 'types' for your

team. Every team can benefit from one or more of the following:

- *An 'Eager Beaver'*: This is a person who typically has little experience with whatever technology your project is employing, but more than makes up for it in sheer persistence. You need these folks to carry the load.
- *A 'Guru'*: This is someone who knows everything there is to know about the subject, and is willing to teach anyone everything he or she knows; hopefully, the subject is what your team will actually need the most of. You need these folks to provide expertise and to solve real problems.
- *A 'Mother Hen'*: Male or female, this is a person who will remember everyone's birthday, take up collections for baby showers, and organise extracurricular team activities. Hopefully, they will have time left to do some actual work. You need these folks to maintain morale, provide team cohesion and balance the professional with the personal.
- *A 'Gadfly'*: Only in the sense of "acting as a constructively provocative stimulus", this person is indispensable in providing creative new ideas and challenging the *status quo*—when improvement is warranted. You need these folks to help the team come up with creative solutions, and to continuously improve the process.
- *A 'Leader'*: Finally, in addition to yourself, you need senior people on your team to inspire the other team members to accomplish their goals, as well as to hold them accountable when they don't.

You Plan for Success Only

Let's say you are going on vacation, driving through an unfamiliar area. As you are tuning the radio to a local station, you hear that there's a huge tie-up by Exit 11 of the route you're travelling on. You look up and see that you just passed Exit 10. What good is knowing about the obstacle at that point? Would hearing the news at Exit 9 or earlier make a difference? Only if you had a local map and could plot your way around the obstruction. But what if you knew, when you were first planning your trip, that Exit 11 on this highway was under construction? Would you not lay your course differently to avoid the delay? So it is with risk mitigation. Identifying the risk is good; but planning a wise course of action around it is infinitely better. Planning mitigation actions ahead of time also removes the pressure of the moment, and allows you to clearly see the forest without bumping into the trees. However, planning ahead for an eventuality that may or may not happen does not quite sharpen the mind with the same clarity that an immediate crisis does. It is not easy to be honest and tough, to avoid pat answers and rosy scenarios. That's why it is useful to prioritise the risks first (using the risk management worksheet) and start working on the ones that have the greatest chance of sinking the project. The anticipation of a disaster ought to concentrate your mind on a realistic solution, and allow you to plot the best course of action around major obstacles.

You are Overcome by Change

Some projects resemble the Blob from the eponymous 50's movie (and its unnecessary 80's remake): they absorb any obstacle in their paths, growing larger and less well defined all the time until someone finally puts them out of their misery (usually, by freezing the funds). Unfortunately, a lot of people get hurt in the debacle. One way to avoid this fate is to know what the project is—and is not—and keep it that way. A good project plan is certainly a good start. But either according to the risk mitigation planning you did, or in totally new and unpredictable ways, one thing you can definitely count on during the course of the project:

And whether you are prepared for it or not, you will have to take actions that deviate from your project plan. However, by the very nature of the dutiful signoffs you so diligently pursued, you have no authority to undertake actions that deviate from your project plan! That's where the change control process comes in handy. You will need to know:

- What constitutes a change
- How to respond when a change occurs
- Who can approve the new plan of action.

What constitutes a change? Simply put—Anything that in any way deviates from the totality of your project plan as the project sponsor accepted it. If your project approach is not working—for whatever reason—and you need to modify it—it's a change. If your project scope changes (beware the scope creep!)—it's a change. If your project schedule needs to be modified—either up or down!—it's a change. If the quality standards in the agency change—it's a change. If the budget gets cut—it's a change. If you adapt a different communications mechanism because it works better—it's a change. If your project team composition changes—it's a change. Of course, not all changes require the same level of response. It would be ludicrous to initiate a formal change control process and demand a sign-off when all you are asked to do is to change the date format on your status report. However, if you get fifty contradictory requests for formatting changes that effectively prevent you from getting your status report out on time—you may well need to wake the change control cerberus. All changes need to be documented, but it is useful to separate changes into two categories: those that affect the project's CSSQ (cost, scope, schedule and quality) and those that don't. Just remember that an accumulation of tiny, seemingly insignificant changes can affect CSSQ just as much as one big obstacle: if you remain still long enough, piranhas can get you just as surely as sharks. So your change control process needs to explicitly state that you will consider any variation to the Project Plan as a change, and will respond to it in one of two ways:

(1) Changes that do not affect CSSQ will be documented in your status report.
(2) Changes that affect CSSQ will trigger a change control process.

Finally, the change control process needs to explicitly define who has authority to approve a change. Usually, different people have the prerogative to approve changes of a different magnitude or kind. Having it clearly spelled out up front will save you many headaches later.

Why can't We All Just Get Along?

Your schedule is as tight as a drum; you've defined deliverables until no ambiguities remain; everyone knows what to expect and when. You think you are done? Only for as long as it takes one of the decision-makers to disagree with you. And disagree they will! The customers will disagree that what you are delivering is what they had in mind 'all along', The stakeholders will disagree that they are not being adversely affected by the new product or service. Your own project sponsor—your purported guardian and protector—will disagree that the budget commitments were actually made for next year's budget. When something like that happens, you need to be able to appeal to a 'higher authority'. Unfortunately, if you have not obtained the higher authority's OK, and others' concurrence, to appeal to them well ahead of time, you don't stand a chance. You have to define, right up front, who will arbitrate when you and your customer, you and your stakeholder, and you and your project sponsor, have a difference of opinion and cannot negotiate a compromise. And the time to plan for it is early on, when you are still their best friend and you have no active issues at stake.

We don't Really Need to Follow All These Steps, do We?

In most PM-immature organisations, as soon as the project enters a phase when some real work needs to get done and real resources applied, the questions start:

(1) "Do we really need all this methodology junk?"
(2) "We should just concentrate on what really needs to get done."
(3) "It's crazy to expect us to create all these deliverables!"
(4) "We don't have the luxury of making the plans look pretty."
(5) "Why do we need to do . . . (fill in any deliverable/process)."
(6) "We need to produce results—not waste time on 'methodology'."
(7) "If we produce all this make-work we will not have time to do anything."

Of course, what these comments betray is a fundamental lack of understanding of what project management is all about. Project management (as well as just basic management) methodologies were developed, all over the world, in response to crises and disasters that resulted precisely from the kind of seat-of-the-pants approach that the doubters actually advocate. To cure the root cause of this attitude would take massive organisational re-education and PM 'conscientiousness raising'. Unfortunately, you (the 'enlightened' project manager) don't have either time or authority for that. What you can do, though, is to say 'No' clearly, articulately and resolutely. No, you will not substitute a vague verbal statement of intent for a thoroughly written scope statement. No, you will not take a promise to "let you have our best people when you need them" instead of a signature on the project plan. But let's be realistic—the pressure may get intense, and you may not have a choice. Your own manager, the project sponsor, or an influential customer, may force your hand into short-changing your deliverables or skipping on your tasks. Your only recourse at that point is documentation. Document the specific risks to the project. Document the fact that a business decision was made to accept those risks. Just don't become a willing accomplice in jeopardising your own project. Don't "go along to get along". Resist organisational inertia and stick to your principles.

4

Some Important Aspects in Project Management

Certain people have an innate ability to do project management well, and others do not. Whenever this myth came up in conversation with other project managers, we always asked for an explanation of that ability—how to recognize it, categorise it, and, if possible, develop it in others. After discussion and debate, the only thing we usually identified—after considering many of the other topics and skills—is the ability to make things happen. Some people are able to apply their skills and talents in whatever combination necessary to move projects forward, and others cannot, even if they have the same or superior individual skills. The ability to make things happen is a combination of knowing how to be a catalyst or driver in a variety of different situations, and having the courage to do so.

This ability to drive is so important to some that it's used as a litmus test in hiring project managers. Even if PMs can't precisely define what the ability is without making at least some references to other skills, they do feel that they can sense or measure it in others. For example, an interviewer needs to ask herself the following question about the candidate: "If things were not going well on some important part of the project, would I feel confident sending this person into that room, into that discussion or debate, and believe he'd help find a way to make it better, whatever the problem was?" If after a round of interviews the answer is no, the candidate is sent home. The belief is that if he isn't agile or flexible enough to adapt his skills and knowledge to the situations at hand, and find ways to drive things forward, then he won't survive, much less thrive, on a typical project. This chapter is about that ability and the skills and tactics involved.

Setting Priorities

A large percentage of time as a PM was spent making ordered lists. An ordered list is just a column of things, put in order of importance. Convinced that despite all of the knowledge and skills we were expected to have and use, in total, all we really did was make ordered lists. We collected things that had to be done—requirements, features, bugs, whatever—and put them in an order of importance to the project. We spent hours and days refining and revising these lists, integrating new ideas and information, debating and discussing them with others, always making sure they were rock solid. Then, once we had that list in place, we'd drive and lead the team as hard as possible to follow things in the defined order. Sometimes, these lists involved how my own time should be spent on a given day; other times, the lists involved what entire teams of people would do over weeks or months. But the process and the effect were the same.

Making things happen is dependent on having a clear sense of which things are more important than others and applying that sense to every single interaction that takes place on the team. These priorities have to be reflected in every email you send, question you ask, and meeting you hold. Every programmer and tester should invest energy in the things that will most likely bring about success.

Someone has to be dedicated to both figuring out what those things are and driving the team to deliver on them. What slows progress and wastes the most time on projects is confusion about what the goals are or which things should come before which other things. Many miscommunications and missteps happen because person A assumed one priority (make it faster), and person B assumed another (make it more stable). This is true for programmers, testers, marketers, and entire teams of people.

If these conflicts can be avoided, more time can be spent actually progressing toward the project goals. This isn't to say those debates about priorities shouldn't happen—they should. But they should happen early as part of whatever planning process you're using. If the same arguments keep resurfacing during development, it means people were not effectively convinced of the decision, or they have forgotten the logic and need to be reminded of why those decisions were made. Entertain debates, but start by asking if anything has changed since the plans were made to justify reconsidering the priorities. If nothing has changed (competitor behavior, new group mission, more/less resources, new major problems), stick to the decision.

Ordered lists provide everyone with a shared framework of logic to inherit their decisions from. If there is an ordered list posted up on the wall clarifying for everyone which things have been agreed to be more important than which other things, these arguments end quickly or never even start. If the goals are clear and understood, there is less need for interpretation and fewer chances for wasted effort. So, if ever things on the team were not going well and people were having trouble focusing on the important things, "I knew it was my fault: either I hadn't ordered things properly, hadn't effectively communicated those priorities, or had failed to execute and deliver on the order that we had". In such a case, working with prioritisation and ordered lists meant everything.

Preparing Set Order of Priorities

By always working with a set order of priorities, adjustments and changes are easy to make. If, by some miracle, more time or resources are found in the schedule, it's clear what the next most important item is to work on. By the same token, if the schedule needs to be cut, everyone knows what the next least important item is and can stop working on it. This is incredibly important because it guarantees that no matter what happens, you will have done the most important work possible and can make quick adjustments without much effort or negative morale. Also, any prioritisation mistakes you make will be relative: if work item 10 turns out to have been more important than work item 9, big deal. Because the whole list was in order, you won't have made a horrible mistake. And besides, by having such clear priorities and keeping the team focused on them, you may very well have bought the time needed to get work item 10 done after all. For most projects, the three most important and most formal ordered lists are used to prioritise project goals, features, and work items.

The project goals are typically part of the vision document or are derived from it. The lists of features and work items are the output of the design process. Because each of these lists inherits

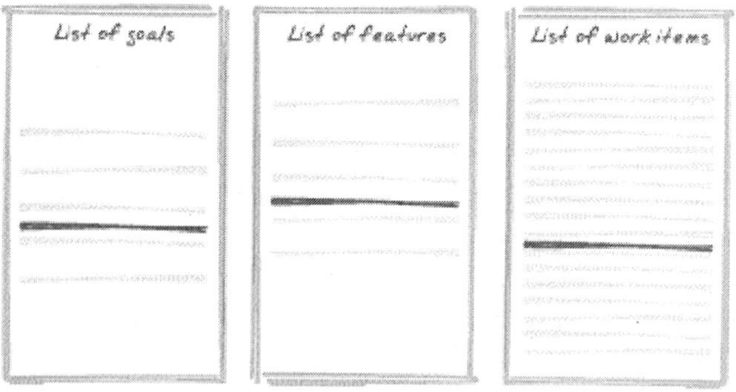

Figure 1: The Ordered Lists

priorities from the preceding list, by stepping up a level to reach a point of clarity and then reapplying those priorities back down to the level in question, any disputes can begin to be resolved. Although this may not always resolve debates, it will make sure that every decision was made in the context of what's truly important.

Other important things that might need ordered lists include bugs, customer suggestions, employee bonuses, and team budgets. They can all be managed in a similar way: put things in the order most likely to make the project or organisation successful. No matter how complex the tools you use are (say, for bug tracking), never forget that all you're doing is ordering things. If the tools or processes you use don't help you put things in order and carry out that order, find a different tool or process. Bug triage, for example, where people get in a room and decide when a bug should be fixed (if at all), is really just a group process for making an ordered list of bugs. The bugs might be classified by group rather than on an individual bug-by-bug basis, but the purpose and effect are the same. If you do use the three most common ordered lists, make sure that they always map to each other.

Every engineering work item should map to a feature, and every feature should map to a goal. If a new work item is added, it must be matched against features and goals. This is a forcing function to prevent random features. If a VP or programmer wants to slip something extra in, she should be forced to justify it against what the project is trying to achieve: "That's a great feature, boss, but which goal will it help us satisfy? Either we should adjust the goals and deal with the consequences, or we shouldn't be investing energy here." If you teach the team that it's a rule to keep these three levels of decision making in sync, you will focus the team and prevent them from wasting time.

Top Priority Versus Everything Else

Typically, these ordered lists have one important line dividing them into two pieces. The top part is priority 1: things we must do and cannot possibly succeed without. The second part is everything else. Priorities 2 and 3 exist but are understood to be entirely different kinds of things from priority 1. It is very difficult to promote priority 2 items into priority 1. This priority 1 line must be taken very seriously. You should fight hard to make that list as small and tight as possible (this applies to any goal lists in the vision document as well). An item in the priority 1 list means 'We will die without this'. It does not mean things that are nice to have or that we really want to have: it gives the tightest, leanest way to meet the project goals. For, example, if we were building an automobile, the only priority 1 things would be the engine, tires, transmission, brakes, steering wheel, and pedals. Priority 2 items would be the doors, windshield, air conditioning, and radio because you can get around without those things.

The core functionality of the automobile exists without them; you could ship it and still call it a car. Putting this line in place was always very difficult; there was lots of arguing and debating about which things customers could live without or which things were more important than others. This was fine. We wanted all of the debating and arguing to take place early, but then move on. As painful as it would be, when we were finished, we'd have a list that had survived the opinions and perspectives of the team. We could then go forward and execute, having refutations and supporting arguments for the list we'd made. Having sharpened it through debate and argument, we were ready for 90% of the common questions or challenges people might have later on (i.e., why we were building brakes but not air conditioning) and could quickly dispatch them: we'd heard the arguments before, and we knew why they didn't hold up.

The challenge of prioritisation is always more emotional/ psychological than intellectual, despite what people say. Just like dieting to lose weight or budgeting to save money, eliminating things you want (but don't need) requires being disciplined, committed, and focused on the important goals. Saying 'stability is important' is one thing, but stack ranking it against other important things is entirely different. Many managers chicken out of this process. They hedge, delay, and deny the tough choices, and the result is that they set their projects up to fail. No tough choices means no progress.

In the abstract, the word important means nothing. So, ordered lists and the declaration of a high priority 1 bar forces leaders and the entire team to make tough decisions and think clearly. Clarity is how you make things happen on projects. Everyone shows up to work each day with a strong sense of what he is doing, why he's doing it, and how it relates to what the others are doing. When the team asks questions about why one thing is more important than another, there are clear and logical reasons for it. Even when things change and priorities are adjusted, it's all within the same fundamental system of ordered lists and priority designations.

Power of Priorities

Have you ever been in a tough argument that you thought would never end? Perhaps half the engineers felt strongly for A, and the other half felt strongly for B. But then the smart team leader walks in, asks some questions, divides the discussion in a new way, and quickly gets everyone to agree. "It's happened to me many times. When I was younger, I chalked this up to brilliance: somehow that manager or lead programmer was just smarter than the rest of the people in the room, and saw things that we didn't. But as I paid more attention, and on occasion even asked them afterward how they did it, I realised it was about having rock-solid priorities. They had an ordered list in their heads and were able to get other people to frame the discussion around it". Good priorities are power.

They eliminate secondary variables from the discussion, making it possible to focus and resolve issues. If you have priorities in place, you can always ask questions in any discussion that reframe the argument around a more useful primary consideration. This refreshes everyone's sense of what success is, visibly dividing the universe into two piles: things that are important and things that are nice, but not important. Here are some sample questions:

(1) What problem are we trying to solve?
(2) If there are multiple problems, which one is most important?
(3) How does this problem relate to or impact our goals?
(4) What is the simplest way to fix this that will allow us to meet our goals?

If nothing else, you will reset the conversation to focus on the project goals, which everyone can agree with. If a debate has gone on for hours, finding common ground is your best opportunity to moving the discussion toward a positive conclusion.

Priorities and Saying No

One side effect of having priorities is how often you have to say no. It's one of the smallest words in the English language, yet many people have trouble saying it. The problem is that if you can't say no, you can't have priorities. The universe is a large place, but your priority 1 list should be very small. Therefore, most of what people in the world (or on your team) might think are great ideas will end up not matching the goals of the project. It doesn't mean their ideas are bad; it just means their ideas won't contribute to this particular project.

So, a fundamental law of the PM universe is this: if you can't say no, you can't manage a project. Saying no starts at the top of an organization. The most senior people on a project will determine whether people can actually say no to requests. No matter what the priorities say, if the lead developer or manager continually says yes to things that don't jive with the priorities, others will follow. Programmers will work on pet features. PMs will add (hidden) requirements. Even if these individual choices are good, because the team is no longer following the same rules, nor working toward the same priorities, conflicts will occur. Sometimes, it will be disagreements between programmers, but more often, the result will be disjointed final designs. Stability, performance, and usability will all suffer. Without the focus of priorities, it's hard to get a team to coordinate on making the same thing.

The best leaders and team managers know that they have to lead the way in saying no to things that are out of scope, setting the bar for the entire team. When you do say no, and make it stick, the project gains momentum. Eliminating tasks from people's plates gives them more energy and motivation to focus and work hard on what they need to do. The number of meetings and random discussions will drop and efficiency will climb. Momentum will build around saying no: others will start doing it in their own spheres of influence. In fact, we've asked team members to do this: "If you ever feel you're being asked to do something that doesn't jive with our priorities, say no. Or tell them that I said no, and they need to talk to me. And don't waste your time arguing with them if they complain—point them my way." We didn't want them wasting their time debating priorities with people because it was my expertise, not theirs. Even if they never faced these situations, we succeeded in expressing how serious the priorities were.

Many Ways to Say No

Sometimes, you will need to say no in direct response to a feature request. Other times, you'll need to interject yourself into a conversation or meeting, identify the conflict with priorities you've overheard, and effectively say no to whatever was being discussed. To prepare yourself for this, you need to know all of the different flavors that the word *no* comes in:

(1) *No, this doesn't fit our priorities*—If it is early in the project, you should make the argument for why the current

priorities are good, but hear people out on why other priorities might make more sense. They might have good ideas or need clarity on the goals. But do force the discussion to be relative to the project priorities, and not the abstract value of a feature or bug fix request. If it is late in the project, you can tell them they missed the boat. Even if the priorities suck, they're not going to change on the basis of one feature idea. The later you are, the more severe the strategy failure needs to be to justify goal adjustments.

(2) *No, only if we have time*—If you keep your priorities lean, there will always be many very good ideas that didn't make the cut. Express this as a relative decision: the idea in question might be good, but not good enough relative to the other work and the project priorities. If the item is on the priority 2 list, convey that it's possible it will be done, but that no one should bet the farm assuming it will happen.

(3) *No, only if you make <insert impossible thing here happen*—Sometimes, you can redirect a request back onto the person who made it. If your VP asks you to add support for a new feature, tell him you can do it only if he cuts one of his other current priority 1 requests. This shifts the point of contention away from you, and toward a tangible, though probably unattainable, situation. This can also be done for political or approval issues: "If you can convince Rita that this is a good idea, I'll consider it." However, this can backfire. (What if he does convince Rita? Or worse, realises you're sending him on a wild goose chase?)

(4) *No. Next release*—Assuming you are working on a web site or software project that will have more updates, offer to reconsider the request for the next release. This should probably happen anyway for all priority 2 items. This is often called postponement or punting.

(5) *No. Never. Ever. Really*—Some requests are so fundamentally out of line with the long-term goals that the hammer has to come down. Cut the cord now and save yourself the time of answering the same request again later. Sometimes it's worth the effort to explain why.

Sense of Reality in PM

Some teams have a better sense of reality than others. You can find many stories of project teams that shipped their product months or years late, or came in millions of rupees over budget. Little by little, teams believe in tiny lies or misrepresentations of the truth about what's going on, and slide into dangerous and unproductive places. As a rule, the further a team gets from reality, the harder it is to make good things happen. Team leaders must play the role of keeping their team honest (in the sense that the team can lose touch with reality, not that they deliberately lie), reminding people when they are making up answers, ignoring problematic situations, or focusing on the wrong priorities.

Calling bullshit makes things happen. If people expect you will ask them tough questions, and not hesitate to push them hard until you get answers, they will prepare for them before they meet with you. They will not waste your or your team's time. Remember that all kinds of deception, including self-deception, work against projects. The sooner the truth comes to light, the sooner you can do something about it. Because most people avoid conflict and prefer to pretend things are OK (even when there is evidence they are not), someone has to push to get the truth out. The more you can keep the truth out in the open, the more your team can stay low to the ground, moving at high speed.

The challenge with questioning others is that it can run against the culture of an individual or organisation. Some cultures see questioning as an insult or a lack of trust. They may see attempts to keep things honest as personal attacks, instead of as genuine inquiries into the truth. You may need to approach these situations more formall, make a list of questions you expect people to answer, and provide it to them before meetings. Or, create a list of questions that anyone in the organisation is free to ask anyone at any time (including VPs and PMs), and post it on the wall in a conference room. If you make it public knowledge from day one that bullshit will be called at any time, you can make it part of the culture without insulting anyone. However, leaders still have the burden of actually calling bullshit from time to time, demonstrating for the team that cutting quickly to the truth can be done.

The Critical Path of Work: Points to Know

The critical path is the shortest sequence of work that can complete the project. In critical path analysis, a diagram or flowchart is made of all work items, showing which items are dependent on which others. If done properly, this diagram shows where the bottlenecks will be. For example, if features A, B, and C can't be completed until D is done, then D is on the critical path for that part of the project. This is important because if D is delayed or done poorly, it will seriously impact the completion of work items A, B, and C. It's important then for a project manager to be able to plan and prioritise the critical path.

Sometimes, a relatively unimportant component on its own can be the critical dependency that prevents true priority 1 work from being completed. Without doing critical path analysis, you might never recognise this until it is too late. From a higher-level perspective, there is a critical path to all situations. They don't need to be diagrammed or measured to the same level of detail, but the thought processes in assessing many PM situations are similar: look at the problem as a series of links, and see where the bottlenecks or critical points are. Which decisions or actions are dependent on which other decisions or actions? Then consider if enough attention is being paid to them, or if the real issue isn't the one currently being discussed.

You dramatically accelerate a team by putting its attention directly on the elements, factors, and decisions that are central to progress. Always have a sense for the critical path of:

- The project's engineering work
- The project's high-level decision-making process (who is slowing the team down?)
- The team's processes for building code or triaging bugs (are there needless forms, meetings, or approvals?)
- The production process of propping content to the Web or intranet
- Any meeting, situation, or process that impacts project goals.

Making things happen effectively requires a strong sense of critical paths. Anytime you walk into a room, read an email, or get involved in a decision, you must think through what the critical paths are. Is this really the core issue? Will this discussion or line of thinking resolve it? Focus your energy (or the room's energy) on addressing those considerations first and evaluating what needs to be done to ensure those critical paths are made shorter, or resourced sufficiently, to prevent delays. If you can nail the critical path, less-critical issues will more easily fall into place.

For some organisations, the fastest way to improve the (non-engineering) critical path is to distribute authority across the team. Instead of requiring consensus, let individuals make decisions and use their own judgement as to when consensus is needed. Do the same thing for approvals, documentation, forms, or other possible bureaucratic overhead. Often the best way of improving critical paths in organizations is to remove processes and shift authority down and across a team, instead of creating new processes or hierarchies.

Become Action-oriented

Many smart people can recognise when there is a problem, but few are willing to expend the energy necessary to find a solution, and then summon the courage to do it. There are always easier ways: give up, accept a partial solution, procrastinate until it goes away (fingers crossed), or blame others. The harder way is to take the problem head-on and resist giving in to conclusions that don't allow for satisfaction of the goals. Successful project managers simply do not give up easily. If something is important to the project, they will act aggressively—using any means necessary—to find an answer or solve the problem. This might mean reorganising a dysfunctional team, getting a difficult room of people to agree on goals, finding answers to questions, or settling disagreements between people. Sometimes, this means asking people to do things they don't like doing, or raising questions they don't want to answer.

Without someone forcing those things to happen, the easier way out will tend to be chosen for you. Many projects consist of people with specialised roles who are unlikely to take responsibility for things that are beyond their limited scope (or that fall between the cracks of their role and someone else's). Perhaps more problematic is that most of us avoid conflict. It's often the PM who has to question people, challenge assumptions, and seek the truth, regardless of how uncomfortable it might make others (although the goal is to do this in a way that makes them as comfortable as possible). PMs have to be willing to do these things when necessary. Many times situations that initially seem untenable or intractable crumble underneath the psychological effort of a tenacious project manager.

Effective PMs simply consider more alternatives before giving up than other people do. They question the assumptions that were left unchallenged by others, because they came from either a VP people were afraid of or a source of superior expertise that no one felt the need to challenge. The question "How do you know what you know?" is the simplest way to clarify what is assumed and what is real, yet many people are afraid, or forget, to ask it. Being relentless means believing that 99% of the time there is a solution to the problem (including, in some cases, changing the definition of the problem), and that if it can't be found with the information at hand, then deeper and more probing questions need to be asked, no matter who has to be challenged. The success of the project has to come first.

If you make it clear that you are dead serious and will fight to the end about a particular issue, you force more possibilities to arise. People will question their assumptions if you hold on to yours long enough. You push people to consider things they haven't considered, and often that's where the answer lies. Even in disagreements or negotiations, if you know you're right, and keep pushing hard, people will often give in. Sometimes, they'll give in just to get you to leave them alone. Being pushy, provided you're not offensive, can be an effective technique all on its own. Being relentless is fundamental to making things happen. There are so many different ways for projects to slide into failure that unless there is at least one emotional force behind the project—pushing it forward, seeking out alternatives, believing there is always a way out of every problem and trap—the project is unlikely to succeed.

Good PMs are that force. They are compelled to keep moving forward, always on the lookout for something that can be improved in a faster or smarter way. They seek out chaos and convert it into clarity. As skeptical as project managers need to be, they are simultaneously optimistic that all problems can be solved if enough intensity and focus are applied. For reasons they themselves cannot fully explain, PMs continually hold a torch up against ambiguity and doubt, and refuse to quit until every possible alternative has been explored. They believe that good thinking wins, and that it takes work to find good thoughts.

Be Prudent and Understanding

Sheer quantity of effort can be noble and good, but always look for ways to work smart rather than just hard. But being relentless doesn't mean you have to knock on every door, chase people down the hallway, or stay at work until you pass out at your desk. Be relentless in spirit, but clever and savvy in action. Just because you refuse to give up doesn't mean you have to suffer through mindless, stupid, or frustrating activities (although sometimes they're unavoidable). Look for smart ways around a problem or faster ways to resolve them. Make effective use of the people around you instead of assuming you have to do everything yourself.

But most importantly, be perceptive of what's going on around you, with individuals and with teams. A fundamental mistake many PMs make is to forget to assess who they are working with and adjust their approach accordingly. Navy Seals and Army rangers are trained to carry out missions on many different kinds of terrain: deserts, swamps, jungles, tundra. Without this training, their effectiveness would be limited: they'd struggle to survive on unfamiliar terrain because their skills wouldn't work (imagine a solider in green and olive camouflage, trying to hide on a snow-covered field). The first lesson they learn is how to evaluate their environment and consider what tactics and strategies from their skill set will work for where they are.

The same is true for PMs. Instead of geographic environments, PMs must pay attention to the different social, political, and organisational environments they are in, and use the right approaches for where they are. Being savvy and environment-aware is most important in the following situations:

- Motivating and inspiring people
- Organising teams and planning for action

- Settling arguments or breaking deadlocks
- Negotiating with other organisations or cultures
- Making arguments for resources
- Persuading anyone of anything
- Managing reports (personnel).

Here's the savvy PM's rough guide to evaluating an environment. These questions apply to an individual you might be working with or to the larger team or group:

(1) What communication styles are being used?
(2) How broad or narrow is the group's sense of humour?
(3) Are arguments won based on data?
(4) Who is effective at doing thing you are trying to do, and what can I emulate or learn from them?
(5) In terms of actual behavior, what values are most important to this person or group?
(6) What is the organisational culture?

Depending on the answers to these questions, a PM should make adjustments to how she does her work. Every time you enter another person's office, or another meeting, there should always be some adjustments made. Like a Marine, assess the environment and then judge the best route to get to the project goals. Avoid taking the hard road if there is a smarter way to get where you need to go.

Being savvy means you are looking for, and willing to take, the smarter route. The following list contains tactics that I've used successfully. Even if you choose never to use these yourself, by being aware of them, you will be savvier about what's going on around you:

(1) Don't dillydally with people's secondhand interpretations of what someone said, and don't depend on written reports or e-mails for complex information. Find the actual person

and talk to him directly. You can't get new questions answered by reading reports or emails, and often people will tell you important things that were inappropriate for written communication. Going to the source is always more reliable and valuable than the alternatives, and it's worth the effort required. For example, if two programmers are arguing about what a third programmer said, get that third programmer in the room or on the phone. Always cut to the chase and push others to do the same.

(2) If communication isn't working, switch the mode. Instead of email, call them on the phone. Instead of a phone call, drop by their office. Everyone is more comfortable in some mediums than others. (Generally, face to face, in front of a whiteboard, trumps everything. Get people in a room with a whiteboard if the email thread on some issue gets out of control.) Don't let the limitations of a particular technology stop you. Sometimes, switching modes gets you a different response, even if your request is the same, because people are more receptive to one mode over another. For anything consequential, it's worth the money and time to get on a plane, or drive to their office, if it improves the communication dynamic between you and an important co-worker.

(3) When you talk to someone privately, her disposition toward you is different than when you talk to her in a large group. In a meeting, important people have to craft what they say to be appropriate for all of the ears in the room. Sometimes, you'll hear radically different things depending on who is in earshot. If you want a frank and honest opinion, or an in-depth intense conversation, you need to get people alone. Also, consider people of influence: if Jim trusts Beth's opinion, and you want to convince.

(4) If something is urgent and you are not getting the response time you need, carve out time on your schedule to stake out the person's office or cubicle.Don't be afraid to go after people if you need something from them. Find them in the coffee room. Look for them in the cafe at lunchtime. Ask their secretary what meetings they are in and wait outside. Be polite, but hunt and get what you need. (However, please do not cross over into their personal lives. If you hunt information well, you shouldn't ever even need to cross this particular line.)

(5) If you are behind on work and need blocks of time to get caught up, become invisible. Uninterrupted time can be hard for PMs to find, so if you can't find it, you have to make it.

(6) Don't fly solo without a map unless you have to. In a given situation, consider who involved thinks most highly of you, or who may have useful advice for how you can get what you need. Make use of any expertise or experience you have access to through others. Pull them aside and ask them for it. This can be about a person, a decision, a plan, anything. For many people, simply asking their advice will score you credibility points: it's an act of respect to ask for someone's opinion.

(7) Make use of the credibility or generosity you've developed a reputation for. If you need an engineer to do extra work for you, either because you missed something or a late requirement came in, ask her to do you a favor. Go outside the boundaries of the strict working relationship, and ask. Offer to buy her dinner (Rs. 200 is often well worth whatever the favour is), or tell her that you owe her one (and do hold yourself to this). The worst thing that can happen is that she'll say no. The more favours you've done for others, the more chips you'll have to bank on.

Also, consider working three-way trades (e.g., in the game Settlers of Cattan) if you know of something she wants that you can get from someone else. It's not unethical to offer people things that will convince them to help with work that needs to be done.

(8) This doesn't have to be evil—if you're very careful. If Shyam gives you a work estimate of 10 days, which you think is bogus, go and ask Ram. If Ram says something less than 10 days, go back to Shyam, with Ram. A conversation will immediately ensue about what the work estimate really should be. If you do this once, no engineer will ever give you bogus estimates again (you've called bullshit). However, depending on Shyam's personality, this may cost you relationship points with him, so do it as tactfully as possible, and only when necessary. Good lead programmers should be calling estimate bluffs on thseir own, but if they don't, it's up to you.

(9) This sounds stupid, but it is found that people we've argued with for days on end are somehow more receptive over a nice cup of coffee at a local coffee shop. Change the dynamic of the relationship: no matter how much you like or don't like the person, make the invitation and invest the 20 seconds of effort it requires. Even if he says "No, why can't we talk here?" you've lost nothing. Moving the conversation to a different location, perhaps one less formal, can help him open up to alternatives he wouldn't consider before. Think biologically: humans are in better moods after they've eaten a fine meal or when they are in more pleasant surroundings. Is that an act of goodwill? Yes ... but there are psychological benefits to making sure the people you are working with are well fed and associate you with good things.

(10) Everything can be represented in an ordered list. Most of

the work of project management is correctly prioritising things and leading the team in carrying them out.

(11) The three most basic ordered lists are: project goals (vision), list of features, and list of work items. They should always be in sync with each other. Each work item contributes to a feature, and each feature contributes to a goal.

(12) There is a bright yellow line between priority 1 work and everything else.

(13) Things happen when you say no. If you can't say no, you effectively have no priorities.

(14) The PM has to keep the team honest and keep them close to reality.

(15) Knowing the critical path in engineering and team processes enables efficiency.

(16) You must be both relentless and savvy to make things happen.

Creative Aspects of Project Planning

Project Specification

Before describing the role and creation of a specification, we need to introduce and explain a fairly technical term: a *numbty* is a person whose brain is totally numb. In this context, numb means "deprived of feeling or the power of unassisted activity"; in general, a numbty needs the stimulation of an electric cattle prod to even get to the right office in the morning. Communication with numbties is severely hampered by the fact that although they think they know what they mean (which they do not), they seldom actually say it, and they never write it down. And the main employment of numbties worldwide is in creating project specifications. You must know this—and protect your team accordingly. A specification is the definition of your project: a statement of the problem, not the solution.

Normally, the specification contains errors, ambiguities, misunderstandings and enough rope to hang you and your entire team. Thus before you embark upon the the next six months of activity working on the wrong project, you must assume that a numbty was the chief author of the specification you received and you must read, worry, revise and ensure that everyone concerned with the project (from originator, through the workers, to the end-customer) is working with the same understanding. The outcome of this deliberation should be a written definition of what is required, by when; and this must be agreed by all involved. There are no short-cuts to this; if you fail to spend the time initially, it will cost you far more later on.

The agreement upon a written specification has several benefits:

- The clarity will reveal misunderstandings
- The completeness will remove contradictory assumptions
- The rigour of the analysis will expose technical and practical details which numbties normally gloss over through ignorance or fear
- The agreement forces all concerned to actually read and think about the details.

The work on the specification can seen as the first stage of quality assurance since you are looking for and countering problems in the very foundation of the project—from this perspective the creation of the specification clearly merits a large investment of time. From a purely defensive point of view, the agreed specification also affords you protection against the numbties who have second thoughts, or new ideas, half way through the project. Once the project is underway, changes cost time (and money). The existence of a demonstrably-agreed specification enables you to resist or to charge for (possibly in terms of extra time) such changes.

Further, people tend to forget what they originally thought; you may need proof that you have been working as instructed. The places to look for errors in a specification are:

(1) *The global context*—numbties often focus too narrowly on the work of one team and fail to consider how it fits into the larger picture. Some of the work given to you may actually be undone or duplicated by others. Some of the proposed work may be incompatible with that of others; it might be just plain barmy in the larger context.

(2) *The interfaces*—between your team and both its customers and suppliers, there are interfaces. At these points something gets transferred. Exactly what, how and when should be discussed and agreed from the very beginning. Never assume a common understanding, because you will be wrong. All it takes for your habitual understandings to evaporate is the arrival of one new member, in either of the teams. Define and agree your interfaces and maintain a friendly contact throughout the project.

(3) *Time-scales*—numbties always underestimate the time involved for work. If there are no time-scales in the specification, you can assume that one will be imposed upon you (which will be impossible). You must add realistic dates. The detail should include a precise understanding of the extent of any intermediate stages of the task, particularly those which have to be delivered.

(4) *External dependencies*—your work may depend upon that of others. Make this very clear so that these people too will receive warning of your needs. Highlight thc effect that problems with these would have upon your project so that everyone is quite clear about their importance. To be sure, contact these people yourself and ask if they are able to fulfil the assumptions in your specification.

(5) *Resources*—the numbty tends to ignore resources. The specification should identify the materials, equipment and manpower which are needed for the project. The agreement should include a commitment by your managers to allocate or to fund them. You should check that the actual numbers are practical and/or correct. If they are omitted, add them-there is bound to be differences in their assumed values.

Each of the above could be a simple sub-heading followed by either bullet points or a table - you are not writing a brochure, you are stating the definition of the project in clear, concise and unambiguous glory. Of course, the specification may change. If circumstances, or simply your knowledge, change then the specification will be out of date. You should not regard it as cast in stone but rather as a display board where everyone involved can see the current, common understanding of the project. If you change the content everyone must know, but do not hesitate to change it as necessary.

Structure of Work

Having decide what the specification intends, your next problem is to decide what you and your team actually need to do, and how to do it. As a manager, you have to provide some form of framework both to plan and to communicate what needs doing. Without a structure, the work is a series of unrelated tasks which provides little sense of achievement and no feeling of advancement. If the team has no grasp of how individual tasks fit together towards an understood goal, then the work will seem pointless and they will feel only frustration.

To take the planning forward, therefore, you need to turn the specification into a complete set of tasks with a linking structure. Fortunately, these two requirements are met at the same time since the derivation of such a structure is the simplest method of arriving at a list of tasks.

Breakdown of Project Activities

Once you have a clear understanding of the project, and have eliminated the vagaries of the numbties, you then describe it as a set of simpler separate activities. If any of these are still too complex for you to easily organise, you break them down also into another level of simpler descriptions, and so on until you can manage everything. Thus your one complex project is organised as a set of simple tasks which together achieve the desired result. The reasoning behind this is that the human brain (even yours) can only take in and process so much information at one time.

To get a real grasp of the project, you have to think about it in pieces rather than trying to process the complexity of its entire details all at once. Thus each level of the project can be understood as the amalgamation of a few simply described smaller units. In planning any project, you follow the same simple steps: if an item is too complicated to manage, it becomes a list of simpler items. People call this producing a work breakdown structure to make it sound more formal and impressive. Without following this formal approach you are unlikely to remember all the niggling little details; with this procedure, the details are simply displayed on the final lists.

One common fault is to produce too much detail at the initial planning stage. You should be stop when you have a sufficient description of the activity to provide a clear instruction for the person who will actually do the work, and to have a reasonable estimate for the total time/effort involved. You need the former to allocate (or delegate) the task; you need the latter to finish the planning.

Allocation of Work

You now have to allocate the tasks to different people in the team and, at the same time, order these tasks so that they are performed in a sensible sequence. Task allocation is not simply a case of handing out the various tasks on your final lists to the people you have available; it is far more subtle (and powerful) than that. As a manager you have to look far beyond the single project; indeed any individual project can be seen as merely a single step in your team's development.

The allocation of tasks should thus be seen as a means of increasing the skills and experience of your team—when the project is done, the team should have gained. In simple terms, consider what each member of your team is capable of and allocate sufficient complexity of tasks to match that (and to slightly stretch). The tasks you allocate are not the ones on your finals lists, they are adapted to better suit the needs of your team's development; tasks are moulded to fit people, which is far more effective than the other way around.

Sometimes tasks can be grouped and allocated together. For instance, some tasks which are seemingly independent may benefit from being done together since they use common ideas, information, talents. One person doing them both removes the start-up time for one of them; two people (one on each) will be able to help each other. The ordering of the tasks is really quite simple, although you may find that sketching a sequence diagram helps you to think it through (and to communicate the result). Pert charts are the accepted outcome, but sketches will suffice. Getting the details exactly right, however, can be a long and painful process, and often it can be futile. The degree to which you can predict the future is limited, so too should be the detail of your planning. You must have the broad outlines by which to monitor progress, and sufficient detail to assign each task when it needs to be started, but beyond that—stop and do something useful instead.

Guessing Realistic Estimates

At the initial planning stage the main objective is to get a realistic estimate of the time involved in the project. You must establish this not only to assist higher management with their planning, but also to protect your team from being expected to do the impossible. The most important technique for achieving this is known as: guesstimation. Guesstimating schedules is notoriously difficult but it is helped by two approaches:

(1) Make your guesstimates of the simple tasks at the bottom of the work break down structure and look for the longest path through the sequence diagram.
(2) Use the experience from previous projects to improve your guesstimating skills.

The corollary to this is that you should keep records in an easily accessible form of all projects as you do them. Part of your final project review should be to update your personal data base of how long various activities take. Managing this planning phase is vital to your success as a manager.

Some people find guesstimating a difficult concept in that if you have no experience of an activity, how can you make a worthwhile estimate? The point is that from very little experience of the given problem, you can actually come up with a working estimate—and one which is far better than no estimate at all when it comes to deriving a schedule. Guesstimating does take a little practice, but it is a very useful skill to develop.

There are two practical problems in guesstimation. First, you are simply too optimistic. It is human nature at the beginning of a new project to ignore the difficulties and assume best case scenario—in producing your estimates (and using those of others) you must inject a little realism. In practice, you should also build-in a little slack to allow yourself some tolerance against mistakes. This is known as defensive scheduling. Also, if you eventually deliver ahead of the agreed schedule, you will be loved. Second, you will be under pressure from senior management to deliver quickly, especially if the project is being sold competitively. Resist the temptation to rely upon speed as the only selling point. You might, for instance, suggest the criteria of: fewer errors, history of adherence to initial schedules, previous customer satisfaction, "this is how long it takes, so how can you trust the other quotes".

Control of a Project

When the planning phase is over (and agreed), the 'doing' phase begins. Once it is in motion, a project acquires a direction and momentum which is totally independent of anything you predicted. If you come to terms with that from the start, you can then enjoy the roller-coaster which follows. To gain some hope, however, you need to establish at the start (within the plan) the means to monitor and to influence the project's progress. There are two key elements to the control of a project:

(1) Milestones (clear, unambiguous targets of what, by when)
(2) Established means of communication.

For you, the milestones are a mechanism to monitor progress; for your team, they are short-term goals which are far more tangible than the foggy, distant completion of the entire project.

The milestones maintain the momentum and encourage effort; they allow the team to judge their own progress and to celebrate achievement throughout the project rather than just at its end. The simplest way to construct milestones is to take the timing information from the work breakdown structure and sequence diagram. When you have guesstimated how long each sub-task will take and have strung them together, you can identify by when each of these tasks will actually be completed. This is simple and effective; however, it lacks creativity.

A second method is to construct more significant milestones. These can be found by identify stages in the development of a project which are recognisable as steps towards the final product. Sometimes these are simply the higher levels of your structure; for instance, the completion of a market-evaluation phase. Sometimes, they cut across many parallel activities; for instance, a prototype of the eventual product or a mock-up of the new brochure format. If you are running parallel activities, this type of milestone is particularly useful since it provides a means of pulling together the people on disparate activities, and so:

- They all have a shared goal (the common milestone)
- Their responsibility to (and dependence upon) each other is emphasised
- Each can provide a new (but informed) viewpoint on the others' work
- The problems to do with combining the different activities are highlighted and discussed early in the implementation phase
- You have something tangible which senior management (and numbties) can recognise as progress
- You have something tangible which your team can celebrate and which constitutes a short-term goal in a possibly long-term project
- It provides an excellent opportunity for quality checking and for review.

Of course, there are milestones and there are mill-stones. You will have to be sensitive to any belief that working for some specific milestone is hindering rather than helping the work forward. If this arises then either you have chosen the wrong milestone, or you have failed to communicate how it fits into the broader structure. Communication is your everything. To monitor progress, to receive early warning of danger, to promote cooperation, to motivate through team involvement, all of these rely upon communication.

Regular reports are invaluable—if you clearly define what information is needed and if teach your team how to provided it in a rapidly accessible form. Often these reports merely say 'progressing according to schedule', These you send back, for while the message is desired the evidence is missing: you need to insist that your team monitor their own progress with concrete, tangible, measurements and if this is done, the figures should be included in the report. However, the real value of this practice comes when progress is not according to schedule—then your communication system is worth all the effort you invested in its planning.

Involvement of Team

At the planning stage, you can deal with far more than the mere project at hand. You can also shape the overall pattern of your team's working using the division and type of activities you assign. They too must be involved in the planning of projects, especially in the lower levels of the work breakdown structure. Not only will they provide information and ideas, but also they will feel ownership in the final plan.

This does not mean that your projects should be planned by committee—rather that you, as manager, plan the project based upon all the available experience and creative ideas. As an initial approach, you could attempt the first level(s) of the work breakdown structure to help you communicate the project to the team and then ask for comments. Then, using these, the final levels could be refined by the people to whom the tasks will be allocated. However, since the specification is so vital, *all* the team should vet the penultimate draft.

Project Review

There are two pitfalls to avoid in project reviews:

- They can be too frequent
- They can be too drastic.

The constant trickle of new information can lead to a vicious cycle of planning and revising which shakes the team's confidence in any particular version of the plan and which destroys the very stability which the structure was designed to provide. You must decide the balance. Pick a point on the horizon and walk confidently towards it. Decide objectively, and explain beforehand, when the review phases will occur and make this a scheduled milestone in itself.

Even though the situation may have changed since the last review, it is important to recognise the work which has been accomplished during the interim. Firstly, you do not want to abandon it since the team will be demotivated feeling that they have achieved nothing. Secondly, this work itself is part of the new situation: it has been done, it should provide a foundation for the next step or at least the basis of a lesson well learnt. Always try to build upon the existing achievements of your team.

Provision for Testing and Quality

No plan is complete without explicit provision for testing and quality. As a wise manager, you will know that this should be part of each individual phase of the project. This means that no activity is completed until it has passed the (objectively) defined criteria which establishes its quality, and these are best defined (objectively) at the beginning as part of the planning.

When devising the schedule therefore you must include allocated time for this part of each activity. Thus your question is not only: "how long will it take", but also: "how long will the testing take". By asking both questions together you raise the issue of "how do we know we have done it right" at the very beginning and so the testing is more likely to be done in parallel with the implementation. You establish this philosophy for your team by include testing as a justified (required) cost.

Another reason for stating the testing criteria at the beginning is that you can avoid futile quests for perfection. If you have motivated your team well, they will each take pride in their work and want to do the best job possible. Often this means polishing their work until is shines; often this wastes time. If it clear at the onset exactly what is needed, then they are more likely to stop when that has been achieved. You need to avoid generalities and to stipulate boundaries; not easy, but essential.

The same is also true when choosing the tools or building-blocks of your project. While it might be nice to have use of the most modern versions, or to develop an exact match to your needs; often there is an old/existing version which will serve almost as well (sufficient for the purpose), and the difference is not worth the time you would need to invest in obtaining or developing the new one. Use what is available whenever possible unless the difference in the new version is worth the time, money and the initial, teething pains.

A related idea is that you should discourage too much effort on aspects of the project which are idiosyncratic to that one job. In the specification phase, you might try to eliminate these through negotiation with the customer; in the implementation phase you might leave these parts until last. The reason for this advice is that a general piece of work can be tailored to many specific instances; thus, if the work is in a general form, you will be able to rapidly re-use it for other projects. On the other hand, if you produce something which is cut to fit exactly one specific case, you may have to repeat the work entirely even though the next project is fairly similar. At the planning phase, a manager should bare in mind the future and the long-term development of the team as well as the requirements of the current project.

Managing Workload and Time

As a manager, you have to regulate the pressure and work load which is imposed upon your team; you must protect them from the unreasonable demands of the rest of the company. Once you have arrived at what you consider to be a realistic schedule, fight for it. Never let the outside world deflect you from what you know to be practical. If they impose a deadline upon you which is impossible, clearly state this and give your reasons. You will need to give some room for compromise, however, since a flat no will be seen as obstructive. Since you want to help the company, you should look for alternative positions. You could offer a prototype service or product at an earlier date. This might, in some cases, be sufficient for the customer to start the next stage of his/her own project on the understanding that your project would be completed at a later date and the final version would then replace the prototype.

The complexity of the product, or the total number of units, might be reduced. This might, in some cases, be sufficient for the customer's immediate needs. Future enhancements or more units would then be the subject of a subsequent negotiation which, you feel, would be likely to succeed since you will have already demonstrate your ability to deliver on time. You can show on an alternative schedule that the project could be delivered by the deadline if certain (specified) resources are given to you or if other projects are rescheduled. Thus, you provide a clear picture of the situation and a possible solution; it is up to your manager then how he/she proceeds.

Planning for Error in Implementation

The most common error in planning is to assume that there will be no errors in the implementation: in effect, the schedule is derived on the basis of "if nothing goes wrong, this will take ...". Of course, recognising that errors will occur is the reason for implementing a monitoring strategy on the project. Thus when the inevitable does happen, you can react and adapt the plan to compensate. However, by carefully considering errors in advance you can make changes to the original plan to enhance its tolerance.

You can try to predict where the errors will occur. By examining the activities' list you can usually pinpoint some activities which are risky (for instance, those involving new equipment) and those which are quite secure (for instance, those your team has done often before). The risky areas might then be given a less stringent time-scale—actually planning—in time for the mistakes. Another possibility is to apply a different strategy, or more resources, to such activities to minimise the disruption.

5

Project Execution and Control

Introduction

The purpose of project execution and control is to develop the product or service that the project was commissioned to deliver. Typically, this is the longest phase of the project management lifecycle, where most resources are applied. Project execution and control utilises all the plans, schedules, procedures and templates that were prepared and anticipated during prior phases. Unanticipated events and situations will inevitably be encountered, and the project manager and project team will be taxed to capacity to deal with them while minimising impact on the project's CSSQ. The conclusion of the phase arrives when the product of the project is fully developed, tested, accepted, implemented and transitioned to the performing organisation. Accurate records need to be kept throughout this phase. They serve as input to the final phase, project closeout.

Processes Involved

This phase consists of the following processes:

(1) *Conducting project execution and control kick-off*, where the project manager conducts a meeting to formally begin the project execution and control phase, orient new project team members, and review the documentation and current status of the project.
(2) *Managing CSSQ*, where the project manager must manage changes to the project scope and project schedule, implement quality assurance and quality control processes according to the quality standards, and control and manage costs as established in the project budget.
(3) *Monitoring and control risks*, where the project manager and project team utilise the risk management plan prepared in previous phases, and develop and apply new response and resolution strategies to unexpected eventualities.
(4) *Managing project execution*, where the project manager must manage every aspect of the project plan to ensure that all the work of the project is being performed correctly and on time.
(5) *Gaining project acceptance*, where the project manager, customer decision-makers and project sponsor acknowledge that all deliverables produced during project execution and control have been completed, tested, accepted and approved, and that the product or service of the project has been successfully transitioned to the performing organisation. The following chart illustrates all of the processes, tasks, and deliverables of this phase in the context of the project management lifecycle.

Role Performers

The following roles are involved in carrying out the processes of this phase:

- Project manager

- Project sponsor
- Project team member
- Customer
- Customer representative
- Consumer
- Stakeholders.

Categorisation of Deliverables

This phase differs from all other phases in that, between phase kick-off and project acceptance, all processes and tasks occur concurrently and repeatedly, and continue almost the entire duration of the phase. Thus, the earlier concept of a 'process deliverable' is not applicable to this phase, and even task deliverables are mostly activities, not products.

Of course, there is the ultimate phase deliverable—the product of the project, and it is formally recognised via the signed project approval form. The following table lists all project execution and control processes, tasks and their deliverables.

Conducting Project Execution and Control Kick-off

The purpose of this process is to formally acknowledge the beginning of project execution and control and facilitate the transition from project planning. Similar to project planning kick-off, project execution and control kick-off ensures that the project is still on track and focused on the original business need. Many new team members will be introduced to the project at this point, and must be thoroughly oriented and prepared to begin work. Most importantly, current project status is reviewed and all prior deliverables are re-examined, giving all new team members a common reference point.

Role Performers

- Project manager

- Project sponsor
- Project team members
- Stakeholders.

Tasks to be Performed

Orienting New Project Team Members

The goal of orienting new project team members is to enhance their abilities to contribute quickly and positively to the project's desired outcome. If the project manager created a team member orientation packet during project planning, the packet should already contain an orientation checklist, orientation meeting agenda, project materials, and logistical information that will again be useful. The project manager should review the contents of the existing team member orientation packet to ensure that they are current and still applicable to the project. Any changes needed to the contents of the packet should be made at this time. Once updated, packet materials can be photocopied and distributed to new team members to facilitate their orientation process. The project manager or team leader should conduct one-onone orientation sessions with new members to ensure that they read and understand the information presented to them.

If the orientation packet was not created during project planning and new team members are coming on board, the project manager must gather and present information that would be useful to new team members, including:

(1) All relevant project information from project origination, project initiation, and project planning.
(2) Organisation charts—project team, customer, performing organisation.
(3) Information on project roles and responsibilities.
(4) General information on the customer (what they do for a living!).

(5) Logistics (parking policy, work hours, building/office security requirements, user id and password, dress code, location of rest rooms, supplies, photocopier, printer, fax, refreshments, etc.).

(6) Project procedures (team member expectations, how and when to report project time and status, sick time and vacation policy).

Reviewing Outputs of Project Planning and Current Project Status

Before formally beginning project execution and control, the project team should review recent project status reports and the project plan. At this point in the project, the project plan comprises all deliverables produced during project initiation and project planning:

- Project charter
- CSSQ (scope, schedule, quality plan, budget)
- Risk management worksheet
- Description of stakeholder involvement
- Communications plan
- Time and cost baseline
- Change control process
- Acceptance management process
- Issue management and escalation process
- Project organisational management plan
- Project team training plan
- Project implementation and transition plan.

This will serve to remind the team of what has been produced so far, to clarify understanding of the work to be produced during project execution and control, and to again communicate the management processes that will be followed during the remainder of the project.

Kicking off Project Execution and Control

A meeting is conducted to kick-off project execution and control. During the meeting, the project manager should present the main components of the project plan for review. Other items to cover during the meeting include:

- Introduction of new team members
- Roles and responsibilities of each team member
- Restating the objective(s) of the project and goals for execution and control
- Latest project schedule and timeline
- Communications plan
- Project risks and mitigation plans
- Current project status, including open issues and action items.

The goal of the kick-off meeting is to verify that all parties involved have consistent levels of understanding and acceptance of the work done so far, to validate expectations pertaining to the deliverables to be produced during project execution and control, and to clarify and gain understanding of the expectations of each team member in producing the deliverables. Attendees at the project execution and control kick-off meeting include the project manager, project team, project sponsor, and any other stakeholders with a vested interest in the status of the project. This is an opportunity for the project sponsor to reinforce the importance of the project and how it supports the business need.

As at every formal project meeting, the project manager should be sure that one of the project team members in attendance is designated as the scribe for the session, to capture notes and action items. Following the session, the notes and action items should be compiled into meeting minutes to be distributed to all attendees for review and approval, and should be added to the project repository.

Managing CSSQ

As project-specific tasks are performed during project execution and control, CSSQ will need to be managed according to the processes established during project planning. The CSSQ is not static—although project planning is complete and has been approved, some components of CSSQ will continue to evolve as a result of the execution of project tasks. Throughout execution and Control, as more information about the project becomes known and the product of the project is developed, CSSQ is likely to be affected and will need to be closely managed. The purpose of Managing CSSQ is to:

- Manage changes to project scope
- Control the project schedule and manage schedule changes
- Implement quality assurance and quality control processes according to the quality standards revised during project planning
- Control and manage costs established in the project budget.

Role Performers

- Project manager
- Project sponsor
- Project team member
- Customer representative.

Tasks to be Performed

Managing Project Scope

During project planning, the project manager, through regular communication with the customer representatives and project sponsor, refined the project scope to clearly define the content of the deliverables to be produced during project execution and control.

This definition includes a clear description of what will and will not be included in each deliverable.

The process to be used to document changes to the project scope was included in the project plan. This process includes a description of the way scope will be managed and how changes to scope will be handled. It is important that the project manager enforce this process throughout the entire project, starting very early in project execution and control. Even if a scope change is perceived to be very small, exercising the change process ensures that all parties agree to the change and understand its potential impact. Following the process each and every time scope change occurs will minimise confusion as to what actually constitutes a change. Additionally, instituting the process early will test its effectiveness, get the customer and project sponsor accustomed to the way change will be managed throughout the remainder of the project, and help them understand their roles as they relate to change.

As part of managing scope change, one of the project manager's functions is to ensure that the project produces all the work but only the work required and documented in the project scope. Any deviation to what appears in the scope document is considered change and must be handled using the change control process. Sometimes, despite the best effort of the project manager to carefully document what is in and outside of scope, there is disagreement between the project manager and customer representative or project sponsor regarding whether something is a change. When conflicts occur, the project manager and appropriate customer must be willing to discuss their differences of opinion and reach a compromise. If a compromise cannot be reached, it may be necessary to escalate the issue to a higher level of management. Once the project manager, the project sponsor, and the appropriate customer representative agree that scope change is occurring, they all must take the time to thoroughly evaluate the change. In order to effectively evaluate change, the project manager must forecast the impact of the change on the remaining three 'quadruple constraints': cost, schedule and quality. Equipped with this information, the project manager and project sponsor will be able to determine if implementing the proposed change would be beneficial. If it is determined, for example, that the cost of implementing a change outweighs the benefit, the change should most likely be rejected or put aside for future consideration.

When a scope change is determined to be beneficial to the outcome of the project, approval and funding for the change is secured. At this point, the project manager must follow the procedures defined in the project plan to implement the change. The project manager must incorporate any agreed-upon changes or addenda into the deliverables produced during project initiation and project planning. This ensures that all project deliverables are in line with the revised project scope. Any lessons learned from scope change control should be documented and included in the project repository for later use by the current project and any other projects to be performed by the organisation.

Throughout project execution and control, continuous communication between the project manager, project sponsor, and customer representative is crucial in managing scope.

Managing Project Schedule

During project planning, an agreed-upon baseline was established for the project schedule. This baseline will be used as a starting point against which performance on the project will be measured. It is one of many tools the project manager can use during project execution and control to determine if the project is on track. Project team members must use the communications mechanisms documented in the communications plan to provide feedback to the project manager on their progress. It is recommended that each team member prepare a progress report. This report documents effort spent on tasks and provides estimates of the effort required to complete them. Progress reports are used by the project manager to update the project schedule. The project manager must emphasise to the team the importance of accurate reporting, and must be vigilant in collecting information at a detailed level. Using the information contained in the progress reports, the project manager tracks work done against the tasks in the project schedule. If the time remaining to complete a task in the schedule differs from the estimated time, the schedule should be updated accordingly. It is recommended that the project manager update the project schedule on a regular basis. Frequent updates to the schedule not only save time in the long run, they also allow the project manager to quickly spot potential problem areas. Small slippages on individual tasks may combine to create significant issues with other, dependent tasks. After updating the project schedule, the project manager must take the time to review the status of the project.

Some questions that the project manager should be able to answer by examining the project schedule include:

(1) Is the project on track?
(2) Are there any issues that are becoming evident that need to be addressed now?
(3) Which tasks are taking more time than estimated? Less time?
(4) If a task is late, what is the effect on subsequent tasks?
(5) What is the next deliverable to be produced and when is it scheduled to be complete?
(6) What is the amount of effort expended so far and how much is remaining?
(7) Are any project team members over-allocated or under-allocated?
(8) How much of the time allocated has been expended to date and what is the time required to complete the project?

Most project scheduling tools provide the ability to produce reports to display a variety of useful information. It is recommended that the project manager experiment with all available reports to find those that are most useful for reporting information to the project team, customer, and project sponsor. When updating the project schedule, it is very important that the project manager maintain the integrity of the current schedule. Each version of the schedule should be archived. By creating a new copy of the schedule whenever it is updated, the project manager will never lose the running history of the project and will also have a copy of every schedule for audit purposes. The project manager should begin tracking actual work in the project schedule as soon as the work commences, which is usually as soon as the project is initiated and project planning begins. Work done in parallel with planning, before the project schedule is completed and approved, must be recorded. Remember that updates to the project schedule are not limited to tracking hours worked—any changc resulting from the execution of the change control process will usually require future tasks to be re-planned and the schedule to be updated! If the project schedule is updated to reflect approved change control, a new baseline schedule must also be created. Updates must then be made against the new baseline. The previous baseline should be saved for historical purposes.

Implementing Quality Control

Quality control involves monitoring the project and its progress to determine if the quality assurance activities defined during project planning are being implemented and whether the results meet the quality standards defined during project initiation. The entire organisation has responsibilities relating to quality, but the primary responsibility for ensuring that the project follows its defined quality procedures ultimately belongs to the project manager. Quality control should be performed throughout the course of the project. Some of the activities and processes that can be used to monitor the quality of deliverables, determine if project results comply with quality standards, and identify ways to improve unsatisfactory performance, are described below. The project manager and project sponsor should decide which are best to implement in their specific project environment.

Conducting Peer Reviews

The goal of a peer review is to identify and remove quality issues from a deliverable as early and as efficiently as possible. A peer review is a thorough review of a specific deliverable, conducted by members of the project team who are the day-to-day peers of the individuals who produced the work. The peer review process adds time to the overall project schedule, but in many project situations the benefits of conducting a review far outweigh the time considerations. The project manager must evaluate the needs of his/her project, determine and document which, if any, deliverables should follow this process, and build the required time and resources into the project schedule.

Prior to conducting a peer review, a project team member should be identified as the facilitator or person responsible for keeping the review on track. The facilitator should distribute all relevant information pertaining to the deliverable to all participants in advance of the meeting to prepare them to participate effectively.

During the meeting, the facilitator should record information including:

- Peer review date
- Names and roles of participants
- The name of the deliverable being reviewed
- Number of quality issues found
- Description of each quality issue found
- Actions to follow to correct the quality issues prior to presenting the deliverable to the approver

- Names of the individuals responsible for correcting the quality issues
- The date by which quality issues must be corrected.

This information should be distributed to the project manager, all meeting participants, and those individuals not involved in the meeting who will be responsible for correcting any problems discovered or for producing similar deliverables. The facilitator should also solicit input from the meeting participants to determine if another peer review is necessary. Once the quality issues have been corrected and the project manager is confident the deliverable meets expectations, it may be presented to the approver.

Using Quality Checklists

Both the project manager and project team members can create and make use of various checklists to be sure items are not overlooked while a product is being developed. Checklists may be simple hardcopy lists of 'things to do', or may be generated using more formal, electronic-based tools. In either case, a checklist should be comprehensive and detailed enough to ensure that the resulting product or deliverable has been built to the level required to meet quality standards. An example of a quality checklist is the End-of-Phase Checklist found at the end of each project management lifecycle phase.

Maintaining and Analyse the Project Schedule

This activity should never be taken lightly, regardless of the size of the project. Updating the project schedule on a regular basis while keeping a close watch on the timeline and budget is the primary mechanism to measure quality of the schedule. If the project timeline or budget are not on track, the project manager can determine why and take immediate action to remedy the problem.

Conducting Project Audits

The goal of a project audit is to ensure that the quality assurance activities defined in project planning are being implemented and to determine whether quality standards are being met. It is a process to note what is being done well, to identify real or potential issues, and to suggest ways for improvement. Audits should be performed on a regular basis, depending upon the size and length of the project. At a minimum, it is recommended that an audit be performed at the end of each phase, at lease once during project execution and control, and at the end of the project. The individual(s) performing the audit can be a member of a quality assurance department or team, if one exists, or any stakeholder determined by the project sponsor to be unbiased toward the project. The individual should also be very familiar with the quality standards and procedures in place in the performing organisation, but should have no involvement in day-to-day project activities. An auditor will most likely use a checklist questionnaire to interview the project manager, selected project team members, the project sponsor, and selected customer representatives to gain insight into how the project is progressing. One of the most important measurements the auditor will look for during these interviews is project team and customer satisfaction. Poor satisfaction is an indicator of an underlying problem that should be uncovered as the auditor delves into the specifics of the project. In addition, the project repository will be examined to determine if it Checklists can be refined and expanded over the course of several projects. This is a great way to reuse best practices and maintain historical information. contains sufficient documentation. An auditor will look for and review the components of the current project plan—including the project scope, project schedule, and risk management worksheet. The questions listed below are examples of what an auditor may be asking when reviewing the project plan.

Upon completion of the audit and repository review, the auditor writes a summary report documenting his/her findings and recommendations. This report is reviewed with the project manager, who should immediately implement recommendations and corrective actions identified. Every member of the project team must be committed to producing a quality product. Quality control cannot rely on 'adding' quality at the end of a process; quality must be built into the work of each individual on the team. It is far more cost effective to have project team members add quality into their day-to-day jobs than to have an auditor find a problem after a process has been completed. As a result of implementing quality control, the project manager should be able to determine and take the appropriate actions to increase the project's effectiveness and provide better service to the customer. Successful quality control processes always strive to see quality through the eyes of the customer. The customer is the ultimate judge of the quality of the product.

Managing Project Budget

The project manager must know the extent of his/her authority to make budget decisions. For example, is the project manager allowed to authorize work that requires additional hours of salaried personnel time, or must employee time extensions go through the same approval process as contract personnel or equipment purchases? Often, the project manager must work closely with fiscal and contract personnel in other divisions to track and control costs. These relationships must be established early in the project management lifecycle. Part of the project manager's job is to ensure that the project is completed within the allocated and approved budget. Budget management is concerned with all costs associated with the project, including the cost of human resources, equipment, travel, materials and supplies. Increased costs of materials, supplies, and human resources, therefore, have a direct impact on the budget. Just as task duration estimates are tracked carefully against actuals, the actual costs must be tracked against estimates. The same analysis should be conducted and the same questions asked: What other aspects of the budget were constructed based upon these estimates?

Changes to the scope of the project will most often have a direct impact on the budget. Just as scope changes need to be controlled and managed, so do changes to the project budget. It is the responsibility of the project manager to closely monitor the financial performance of the project and take responsibility for addressing cost-related issues as they arise. In addition, the project manager should always be aware of the effect his/her decisions may have on the total cost of the project, both before and after the product or service is implemented. Monitoring the financial performance of your project on a regular basis is the only way you can keep a handle on the project budget. Don't let the project budget get away from you—get into the habit of updating the schedule and analysing the financial impact on a regular basis.

Taking the time to do these administrative tasks will save you countless hours of reconciliation and balancing down the road, and warn you of impending cost issues! There are several financial characteristics the project manager should monitor to determine if a project is performing satisfactorily against its budget. Most often, these values are entered into the scheduling tool by the project manager and calculated and displayed using its corresponding capabilities. Some budget-related characteristics the project manager should examine each time the schedule is updated include:

(1) *Original contract value*: the original estimated budget (cost) that was approved by the project sponsor.
(2) *Total approved changes*: the total cost of approved changes as a result of change control.
(3) *Total current budget*: the sum of the original contract

value and the total approved changes. This is the most current approved project budget.

(4) *Cost to date*: the actual dollars (cost) expended to date on all tasks and materials in the project. The labor costs can be calculated by the scheduling tool based upon the time the project manager tracks against the tasks in the project schedule.

(5) *Estimate to complete*: The dollars (cost) estimated to be expended to complete remaining project tasks. The project manager must verify and assess the impact of team members' revised effort estimates to complete tasks. The project manager must also validate that the remaining material costs are in line with the budget. These have a direct effect on the project budget.

(6) *Forecast total*: The sum of the cost to date and the estimate to complete.

(7) *Project variance*: The difference between all estimated and all actual dollars. It is calculated by subtracting the Forecast Total from the total current budget. A positive variance means that the actual cost of the product is less than the budgeted cost. A negative variance means that the actual cost of the product is greater than the budgeted cost.

It is of utmost importance for the project manager to take the time to analyse, understand, and document the reason for variance every time the project schedule is updated. Whether positive or negative, the project manager needs to understand what is causing variance and take proactive steps to keep it under control. The project manager must be able to explain the cause of variance to others and determine if corrective actions need to be taken to maintain the project's budget. For example, if a negative effort variance develops while a task is being executed, then more money may be needed than originally planned for, potentially impacting the success of the project. On the other hand, some tasks may finish ahead of schedule, freeing up money and offsetting the negative impact of those that finish late. The project manager must remain aware of such situations, working with the project team members and customers to determine the causes of variance and to mitigate any associated risks. It is the responsibility of the project manager to ensure the currency, accuracy, and viability of the project schedule as the primary mechanism for managing the budget. He/she must know and be able to communicate exact project status relative to budget, impact of changes, estimates to complete, and variance. This information must be known by task, process, phase, resource, and deliverable and be communicated to the project sponsor as part of the status meeting.

Monitoring and Controlling Risks

In prior phases, the project manager defined these events as accurately as possible, determined when they would impact the project, and developed a risk management plan. As the impact dates draw closer, it is important to continue re-evaluating probability, impact, and timing of risks, as well as to identify additional risk factors and events. When the risk event actually occurs, the risk (which is by definition a future, potential event) becomes an issue (which is by definition a current, definite condition) and issue monitoring and control takes over. The purpose of this process is to deploy the risk management plans prepared in prior phases to anticipate project challenges, and to develop and apply new response and resolution strategies to unexpected eventualities.

Role Performers

- Project manager
- Project sponsor
- Project team member
- Customer.

Tasks to be Performed

Monitoring Risks

During project initiation and planning, risks were remote events with uncertain probabilities of coming true. In execution and control, however, impact dates draw closer, and risks become much more tangible. The project manager must continually look for new risks, reassess old ones, and re-evaluate risk mitigation plans. The project manager should involve the whole project team in this endeavor, as various team members have their particular expertise and can bring a unique perspective to risk identification. As the risk management worksheet is integrated into the status reporting process, this review and re-evaluation should take place automatically, with the preparation of each new status report.

Because the risk management worksheet places risks in order according to their priority level, it is important to update all quantifiable fields to portray an accurate risk landscape. The risk probabilities may have changed; the expected level of impact may be different, or the date of impact may be sooner or later than originally anticipated—all of these variables determine which risks the project team will concentrate on first. Likewise, the risk management plan needs to be constantly re-evaluated. Make sure the right people are still assigned to mitigation actions and that the actions still make sense in the context of the latest project developments. Another consideration is whether a specific risk's probability level is high enough to warrant incorporating the risk management plan in the project schedule via the change control process. If so, the risk should be removed from the worksheet. Finally, the project manager must be constantly on the lookout for additional risks. Reviewing the risks as part of regular status reporting should involve the whole project team via bidirectional communications.

Controlling Risks

Sooner or later, one of the events on the risk management worksheet—or an entirely new and unexpected risk—will actually occur. The project manager and project team members must evaluate the risk event and invoke the risk management plan. There are generally three possible response scenarios:

(1) If the risk occurred as expected, the existing risk management plan may be adequate for dealing with it.

(2) If the risk occurred in a different manner, or other circumstances have come to bear, the risk management plan may have to be modified.

(3) If the risk event was unexpected and unanticipated, a whole new risk management plan must be created to address it.

Monitoring Impact on CSSQ

During the entire risk management process, the project manager should be especially vigilant regarding the effect on the project's cost, scope, schedule and quality (CSSQ). With the proper risk management processes in place, many risk events may come to pass without affecting (either positively or negatively) the project's defining parameters. However, when a risk event occurs that threatens the project's scope, quality standards, schedule or budget, the project manager must determine the proper course of action to protect the integrity of the project. Until CSSQ impact is certain, the project manager must, at a minimum, introduce the event to the list of current project issues. The issue's action plan must reflect all the tasks required to accurately determine what impact (if any) the event will have on CSSQ. Once the impact is certain and quantifiable, the project manager should transition the issue to the change control process.

Managing Project Execution

Project execution is typically the part of the lifecycle of a project when the majority of the actual work to produce the product is performed and the majority of the project budget is expended. The purpose of manage project execution is to manage every aspect of the project plan as work is being done to make certain the project is a success. This process is performed concurrently with the managing CSSQ and monitor and control risks processes. The tasks in this process are performed concurrently and repeatedly as various aspects of the product of the project are constructed, tested, and accepted.

Role Performers

- Project manager
- Project sponsor
- Project team
- Customer.

Tasks to be Performed

Managing Change Control Process

During project planning, the project manager, project sponsor, and customer agreed on a formal change control process that was documented and included in the project plan. The change control process describes:

(1) The definition of change and how to identify it.
(2) How requests for change will be initiated?
(3) How requests for change will be analysed to determine if they are beneficial to the project?
(4) The process to approve or reject change requests.
(5) How funding will be secured to implement approved changes?

Although changes can be expected to occur throughout every project phase, any negative effect on the project outcome should be avoidable if the change control process is executed and managed effectively. The need for change is usually discovered during project execution, as actual task work is being performed. It is during execution that the project team may discover their original effort estimates were not accurate and will result in more or less effort being required to complete their work. It is also during execution that the project sponsor or customer may realise that, despite their best efforts to thoroughly document the project scope, the product being produced is not exactly what they need. It is the responsibility of the project manager to keep a close watch on factors that could introduce potential 'scope creep' and take proactive steps to prevent it from occurring, or to manage it as it occurs. Sometimes change control is required if a project team member is not able to complete what was documented in the project scope, because of lack of skill, time constraints, or other factors outside his/her control. In most cases, these difficult to manage situations often result in lost time in the project schedule and can have a major impact on the project. Sometimes change is simply informational and will most likely not affect the project scope or schedule (e.g., the name of a project team member or the physical location of the project team offices may change).

Changes that do not affect the project's CSSQ do not need to follow the formal change control process, but should be documented in the project status report or any other appropriate communication mechanism. However, for all changes that affect the project's CSSQ, it is vitally important for the project manager to implement and manage the change control process in every situation. Not doing so will cause confusion on the part of the customer as to what constitutes a change. The change control process also helps maintain balance between the requirements of the project and the timeline and cost. During project planning, individuals authorised to be requestors, reviewers, and approvers of change requests were identified and information about them was documented in the change control process. Change control begins when a requestor completes a change request form and submits it to the appropriate reviewer(s). When someone does not do something he or she was supposed to do as documented in the project plan, the resulting change is called a 'Non-Compliance' change.

The role of the reviewer(s) in the change control process is to analyse the request in terms of the level of effort and skill required to implement it. The reviewer, typically an expert in the subject area, will also make a recommendation to accept or reject the change request based upon its feasibility from a technical or implementation standpoint. He/she will communicate this information to the project manager and document it on the project change request. One of the roles of the project manager in the change control process is to analyse the reviewer's recommendation, and determine the overall effect of the requested change on the project schedule in terms of effort, cost, and resource requirements and availability. This information will be documented on the project change request and presented to the approver(s). The approver(s) review the information and make a determination whether to approve the change request based upon the potential benefit of its implementation to the organisation. If, for example, the implementation costs far outweigh the business benefit, the change request will most likely be rejected. A signature is required of all approvers, whether they are accepting or rejecting the request. If the request is being rejected, the approver must provide a reason. A signature of approval on the project change request indicates that the approver accepts the consequences (impact) of the request on the project's cost, scope, schedule or quality.

Once a change request has been approved, the project manager must incorporate the effect of the change into the project schedule. All affected tasks, estimated durations, dependencies, and resources must be modified. A new baseline should then be created for the amended schedule and budget. These become the new tools against which hours will be booked and project performance measured going forward. Never execute a change request without first obtaining all required approval signatures! In addition, if new deliverables will be produced as a result of the change, their exact description must be included in the project plan, either as appendices to the project scope, or as separate attachments. In addition, any changes that affect the remaining components of CSSQ must be documented. All correspondence, supporting documentation and other information pertaining to the change should be saved in the appropriate location in the project repository.

Managing Acceptance of Deliverables

The goal of this task is to manage the acceptance of deliverables according to the acceptance management process developed during project planning. The acceptance management process is part of the project plan, and documents:

(1) The definition of 'acceptance'.

(2) The criteria that must be met for each deliverable to be considered 'acceptable'.

(3) The number and identity of customers designated to be reviewers of each deliverable—typically reviewers are experts in the subject matter the deliverable covers.

(4) The number and identity of customers designated to be approvers—approvers have the authority to sign the approval form, indicating acceptance

(5) The number of business days in which deliverables must be either approved or rejected by the reviewers and approvers.

(6) The number of times a deliverable can be resubmitted.

(7) The escalation process that will be followed if a timely

decision on approval or rejection of a deliverable is not met.

The acceptance management process must be followed throughout the project. As with the change control process, the earlier in the life of the project the process begins, the sooner everyone will understand how it works and what to expect. Using input and recommendations provided by the reviewer, the approver reviews the deliverable and decides if it meets the acceptance criteria documented in the acceptance management process. He/she will indicate acceptance or rejection of the deliverable on the project deliverable approval form. Once again, this must be done within the turnaround time documented in the acceptance management process. If the approver recommends the deliverable be rejected, he/she must provide the reason and forward the package to the project manager. It is then the responsibility of the project manager to have the deliverable adjusted as necessary and then resubmit it to the approver. This process should be followed for each person designated as an approver in the acceptance management process. The project manager must ensure that for rejected deliverables, specific corrective actions are defined.

It is the responsibility of the project manager to be cognisant of the time elapsing during the review and approval process, in an attempt to complete the process within the maximum number of business days agreed upon and documented. Significant delays in the process should trigger the project manager to escalate the situation, following the documented escalation procedure. Similarly, the project manager should be aware of the number of times the acceptance process is being repeated. How many times is the project team making changes to a deliverable based upon its rejection? The number of times a deliverable can be resubmitted to the approver was also documented in the acceptance management process. If a deliverable is rejected more than once, the project manager should take immediate action to analyse the situation, resolve the conflict, or exercise the appropriate escalation procedure to get it resolved. A serious delay in the acceptance of a deliverable will almost always result in project delays. The project manager should maintain a log of the activity that transpires while a deliverable is going through the acceptance management process. The deliverable acceptance log can be If the number of iterations becomes unreasonable, the project manager should recognise that a bigger problem may exist, and should take the appropriate action to find out what it is and fix it! included as part of the status report that is reviewed with the project sponsor. Once a deliverable is considered acceptable, the project manager should gain the appropriate signatures on the project deliverable approval form. Signatures on the form indicate formal acceptance of the deliverable.

Managing Issues

Managing issues involves documenting, reporting, escalating, tracking, and resolving problems that occur as a project progresses. During project planning, the project manager and project sponsor agreed upon and documented the process for managing issues and included the process in the project plan. The issue escalation and management process addresses the following:

- How issues will be captured and tracked
- How issues will be prioritised
- How and when issues will be escalated for resolution?

Issues are usually questions, suggestions, or problems raised by project team members, including the project manager and customer. They are different from changes in that they do not usually have an immediate impact on the project scope or schedule. If issues remain unresolved, however, they are likely to affect the project schedule or budget, resulting in the need for change control. It is, therefore, very important to have an issue escalation and management process in place, and to execute the process before change control procedures become necessary. Anyone involved in a project in any way can and should inform the project manager of issues. It is the responsibility of the project manager and project sponsor to foster an environment where communicating issues is not only acceptable but strongly encouraged.

Individuals should feel a responsibility to the organisation to voice their concerns. If individuals are fearful of communicating issues, the resulting effect on the project can be devastating. The project manager is responsible for capturing and tracking issues as soon as they arise, using the issues log section in the project status report. Every issue, whether technical or business related, should be documented in the report. Below are some examples of project issues:

- Computer system will be down for routine maintenance
- Project sponsor is taking another job
- Project team member start date may be sooner (or later) than expected
- There is a delay in approving or rejecting a change request or deliverable
- Severe weather is predicted in the area of the building site.

Once the description of a new issue has been logged, the project manager should estimate the potential impact the issue could have on the project. Based upon potential impact, the project manager prioritizes the issue in relation to all other open issues. The goal of issue management is to resolve all concerns completely and promptly, but in reality the issues with the highest priority should be addressed first. The issues log should also include the date the issue is recorded, its anticipated closure date, and the name of the individual responsible for resolving it or seeing that it is resolved. The due date for closure must be a specific date (i.e., the date cannot be 'ASAP'). The responsible party must be a specific individual, not a functional group (i.e., an issue should not be assigned to the 'IT Department' or the 'DBA group'). While the issue remains open, its continuing impact and the status of its action plan should be discussed at every status meeting. If appropriate resources or materials are not available to complete the action items, or if there is disagreement about any the project manager should be cautious about reacting to an issue that is communicated by 'shooting the messenger'. This sends the wrong message to the project team.

No matter how devastating the news or the issue, the project manager should thank the person who raised the issue and solicit ideas from that individual and other team members for its mitigation. Of the elements on the issues log, the project manager should invoke previously-defined escalation procedures. Unresolved issues are one of the leading causes of project failure, and the project manager must pursue issue resolution relentlessly. As progress occurs on the resolution of an issue, the project manager should update the issues log to reflect what has occurred. As issues are closed, they should be moved to a different section of the issues log. Along with a description of how the issue was resolved, the project manager should document who resolved the issue and the closure date.

Executing Communications Plans

As a project progresses from planning to execution, events may occur to alter the way information is accessed or change communications requirements. During project execution, the project manager and project team must again review whether the communications plan is still current and applicable to the project. If it is determined that any portion of the plan is no longer applicable, the project manager should update the document. During project execution the communications plan is carried out so that required information is made available to the appropriate individuals at the appropriate times, and new or unexpected requests receive a prompt response. Communications must continue to be bi-directional during project execution. The project manager must provide required information to the project team and appropriate stakeholders on a timely basis, and the project team and stakeholders must provide required information to the project manager. When managing issues, document everything that happens as issues are resolved. Be sure to note what happened, when it happened and who was involved. Don't skimp on the details. Keep an issues 'diary'. When issues are closed, don't delete them from your issues log—instead maintain the 'diary' of closed issues in a separate file or folder or section of the log. This 'diary' will ensure that you cover your bases, and the information included in it may become invaluable to you or another project manager as lessons learned when resolving similar issues down the road!

In addition to having a solid communications plan in place, it is the responsibility of members of the project team to exercise good communication skills. When composing correspondence, progress reports, meeting minutes, etc., and when speaking with individuals face to face, the team members are responsible for clear, unambiguous, and complete communication of information. The receiver, in turn, must be sure information is not only received correctly and completely, but that it is understood. During project execution, the project manager, project team, and stakeholders will share information using a variety of communication mechanisms. These were defined during project planning and may include:

- Status reports
- Memos
- Newsletters
- Executive correspondence
- Meeting notes

- Executive meetings
- Steering committee meetings.

This information is collected, stored and disseminated based upon procedures established and documented in the communications plan.

Using the progress reports prepared by the project team, the project manager should complete a status report to be presented to the project sponsor. In this report, the project manager measures the 'health and progress' of the project against the project plan. It is the primary communication vehicle between the project manager and the project sponsor, and should contain the following information:

(1) *Summary of progress to project schedule*—a high-level glance at the major project deliverables, with their intended and actual start and end dates.
(2) *Issues and action items*—a running list of open and closed issues, including the name of the person responsible for taking action to resolve them.
(3) *Significant accomplishments*—a list of the most important completed tasks, or a description of work done toward their completion.

- *Significant planned accomplishments for the following weeks*—a description of the most important tasks scheduled for completion during the following weeks.
- *Deliverable acceptance log*—a running diary of actions taken toward acceptance of deliverables.
- *Change control log*—a running diary of actions taken toward acceptance of change control.
- *Lost time*—a description of any situation that occurred that resulted in the project team being unable to perform work.

Other project documents that should be attached to the status report include any change control requests, deliverable acceptance forms, meetings notes, and the risk management worksheet. The status report becomes the point of discussion for the status meeting, the regularly scheduled forum where the project manager presents the project status and discusses issues with the project sponsor.

Detailed information can be included as an appendix to your status report, or maintained in a separate document. Regardless of its location, detailed information should always be made available to the project team, and will be invaluable to you if your project sponsor requests clarification or more information. Reports, to verify estimates to complete tasks and to discuss issues that may impact estimates. The project manager can then use information communicated during the project team meetings as input to the status report. The regularly-scheduled project team meeting is also a good forum to recognise individual accomplishments, and to reward team members for outstanding work. As documents are gathered and generated during project execution, the project manager is responsible for filing them in the appropriate location in the project repository. The repository must be maintained on a continuous basis, as it represents a history of the project, from its inception through closure. It will be used as a reference manual throughout the project and should, therefore, be made available to every member of the project team.

On large projects where gathering the entire team is prohibitive, team leaders can assemble the appropriate project team members for meetings. It will then be necessary for team leaders to meet regularly with the project manager to ensure all communication lines remain open.

Managing Organisational Change

During project execution, as the product is being produced, the project manager and customer must evaluate the organisational change management plan documented during project planning to be sure it is still current. Because more information about the specific changes to the organisation in terms of people, process and culture is known, it is quite likely that the plan will need to be adjusted and more details developed. It is extremely important for the project manager and project sponsor to be actively involved in the change effort, and to proactively manage communications with the performing organisation and consumers. As specific changes are implemented in advance of and in preparation for the final product of the project, all involved parties must be made aware of the anticipated timing of events to give them ample time to prepare and participate as required. Managing organisational change should include:

(1) *People*—Planned workforce changes must be executed in careful coordination with, and usually at the direction of, the human resource department of the performing organisation, and in conjunction with appropriate labor/management practices. Specific changes in job duties, staff reductions or increases, and any changes in the organisational structure itself should be performed in accordance with the plan, and should include appropriate coordination and communication with union representatives and the external agencies involved. It ensures project continuity even if the project manager gets promoted or reassigned execute the changes as planned and scheduled, being sensitive to minimise any impact to them.

(2) *Process*—The redesign of existing business processes affected by the implementation of the product of the project, and the development of corresponding procedures, must be managed in coordination with product development. The redesigned processes and procedures must align with the product and associated changes. The implementation of the new processes, and any associated training or announcements regarding their introduction into the performing organisation, must be integrated with the product

implementation (to coincide with or precede the product, as appropriate). The project manager must manage these particular aspects of the schedule with diplomacy and tact. The active involvement of the project sponsor may be required as changes are implemented.

(3) *Culture*—Specific plans were developed based on the extent of the 'culture shock' the product of the project was expected to introduce into the performing organisation and its business strategy, established norms for performance, leadership approach, management style, approach to customers, use of power, approach to decision making, and employee roles. Using the results of the assessment of the performing organisation's 'readiness for change', the project manager can develop more specific action plans to increase the organisation's readiness and ability to adapt to the changes of the project. Most likely, these will include education and training events that can be targeted to specific audiences affected by the changes. The plans should provide information about the changes well in advance of implementation, so that affected stakeholders have ample opportunity to express their concerns. To the greatest extent possible, the stakeholders should be given a 'preview' of how the product will actually work. They should also be given adequate training on how to adjust to change, how to work in the new environment, or similar 'soft skills'. The project manager, with the active participation and support of the customer and project sponsor, must be able to manage the specific activities that will adequately prepare the performing organisation for the anticipated changes.

Managing the Project Team

In order to successfully meet the needs of a project, it is important to have a high-performing project team made up of individuals who are both technically skilled and motivated to contribute to the project's outcome. One of the many responsibilities of a project manager is to enhance the ability of each project team member to contribute to the project, while also fostering individual growth and accomplishment. At the same time, each individual must be encouraged to share ideas and work with others toward a common goal. The project manager, then, must be a leader, communicator, negotiator, influencer, and problem solver! The level of skills and competencies to successfully fill these roles helps distinguish good project managers from great ones.

To maximize the successful performance of the project team, the project manager must do the following: Execute the training plan to evaluated the skills of each team member to determine whether he/she met the current and future needs of the project. For each team member requiring training, the project manager established a training plan. The training plan includes the method by which each team member will be trained, and the corresponding training schedule. During project execution, the project manager must review the contents of the training plan to be sure they are still applicable to the project. If additional training is necessary, it should be added to the plan. If it is determined that planned training is no longer necessary, it must be removed from the plan. If new team members have joined the project since the training plan was established, the project manager must evaluate the skill level of the new members to determine if additional training is needed. In all cases, training tasks must be added to or removed from both the training plan and the project schedule, since they will affect the end date of the project.

As training takes place during project execution, the project manager should update the training plan with the names of the trainees and actual training completion dates. This information will be used to measure the success of the training plan, and enable the project manager to provide input for evaluating team members and preparing staff performance appraisals. In addition, the project manager should mark the corresponding project schedule tasks as complete. Allocate work properly and ensure accountability. A basic responsibility of the project manager is to assign work to the project team and ensure that the work is completed according to the project schedule. The project manager (or team leaders if the project is large) is responsible for allocating tasks to appropriate team members at the appropriate times. A good project manager establishes and maintains a project schedule that minimises team member down time. Along with the team leaders, the project manager must continuously communicate to each member of the team what is required and by when, and then manage the performance of each team member in meeting the requirements.

Since the project manager is ultimately responsible for the success or failure of a project, he/she must direct project team endeavors and encourage team members to be accountable for their work. Accountability should be formally documented and measured through the use of team member progress reports. But the project manager must also be willing to communicate face-toface with the project team. Regular personal communication is one of the most effective ways to gather input on the status of project activities, discuss issues and concerns, recognise good work, encourage and provide support to team members who are struggling, and build relationships. It is also one of the primary ways to discover and take action to resolve team member performance issues.

Project managers must develop sufficient management competencies to be able to create an environment that encourages team members to excel. The project manager may consider implementing some of the following:

(1) *Team-building activities*—these are actions taken specifically to improve the performance of the entire team.

Activities can range from short items on a meeting agenda to extended, off-site professionally facilitated sessions. However implemented, team-building activities provide opportunities for team members to improve their interpersonal and working relationships.

(2) *Team recognition and rewards*—these are actions intended to promote, encourage, and reinforce desired behavior or exceptional performance. Frequently they are initiated by individuals at management level, but they are also very effective when initiated by an individual's peer. In all cases, recognition programs must be documented clearly enough so team members understand what level of performance warrants an award. The primary objective for establishing an appropriate team environment is to improve overall project performance. When team members are encouraged to do their best and are motivated about a project, they are more likely to do whatever is necessary to improve their individual skills so they are more efficient and effective in performing their assigned activities. And when team members understand the importance of interacting with each other, they are more willing to identify and proactively deal with conflict. Resolving issues early leaves team members more time for producing actual project work.

Managing Project Implementation and Transition

During project execution and control, this implementation and transition plan will be more fully developed as the product of the project is developed, and as specific activities in the plan are executed. During project execution and control, the project team will gain a better understanding of the impact the resulting product will have on the performing organisation and consumers. Activities begin that are required to prepare the consumers to use the product, along with the tasks to prepare the performing organisation to support it. Managing implementation and transition includes:

(1) Monitoring and ensuring timely completion of all facilities issues, such as acquiring the necessary physical space, installing appropriate software, obtaining the appropriate building permits, etc.

(2) Coordinating customer acceptance testing, including logistics of when and how customers will test the product to confirm that it meets requirements before it is formally implemented and transitioned. Customer testing is one of the last opportunities for necessary changes to be identified and made to the product before rollout. Time for sufficient customer testing and any resulting rework that will affect the project team must be incorporated in the project schedule.

(3) Managing the steps that need to be taken to ensure consumers will be ready to use the product once it is implemented. These steps must be coordinated with the organisational change management plan, and will include training and orientation on the use of the product. Any training for customers or consumers must be provided according to the plan and coordinated with other aspects of the implementation of the product.

(4) Managing the detailed implementation. The project manager must monitor implementation activities and make any necessary adjustments. The implementation will vary depending upon the needs of the performing organisation and the product of the project. Some implementations are 'done' at the flip of the final switch, such as opening a new highway, or publishing a book. Others are phased into implementation, like installing an inventory management system module-by-module, moving to a new building

floor-by-floor, or implementing a new business process location-by-location.

(5) Managing the steps that need to be taken to ensure the appropriate individuals are ready to support the product once it has been implemented and is in use. This may include negotiating with various internal organisations to determine the appropriate timing of the transition of responsibility, assigning specific organisations and individuals to support the specific products, and providing necessary training. The project manager must carefully manage the point in implementation that the performing organisation takes responsibility for production problems, 'help' or trouble calls, and for resolving the problems, and ensure that all pre-requisites for transition have been met—for example, performance standards, quality standards, etc.

(6) Managing production of all necessary documentation. The project manager must ensure that all documents or records that will be provided with the product are produced.

Overall, the project manager must be sure each required activity is carried out according to the implementation and transition plan and schedule, and to immediately communicate any discrepancies to the project sponsor.

Gaining Project Acceptance

This process acknowledges that all deliverables produced during project execution and control have been completed, tested, accepted, and approved by the project's customers and the project sponsor, and that the product or service the project developed was successfully transitioned from the project team to the performing organisation. Formal acceptance and approval also signify that the project is essentially over, and is ready for project closeout.

Role Performers

- Project manager
- Project sponsor
- Project team members
- Customer representatives
- Customer decision-maker.

Tasks to be Performed

Conducting Final Status Meeting

Once the product of the project has been successfully transitioned to the performing organisation, the project manager should prepare the final status report and conduct the final status meeting. The project schedule must be up to date for all completed project and project management lifecycle phases. This is the final opportunity for all participants to confirm that the product of the project has been successfully developed and transitioned. Any outstanding issues or action items must be transitioned from the project team to the performing organisation.

Gaining Acceptance Signature from Project Sponsor

As the deliverables of the project are produced and accepted, approval signatures are gained from the project sponsor and customer decision-makers. Following the final status meeting, the project manager must obtain the project sponsor's signature one final time, indicating acceptance of the project to date, and indicating approval to proceed to project closeout. If the project sponsor does not accept the project, he/she must indicate the specific reason(s) for rejection. The project manager is then responsible for resolving the issues and seeking the project sponsor's acceptance again.

Key Elements in Execution and Control

Project execution and control is where the rubber meets the road.

In the immortal words of Yoda, it's "Do! Or do not! There is no try." What are some of the key elements of Project Execution and Control that require the most attention? Not surprisingly, this phase has the most pitfalls and the most areas for consideration.

Your Slip is Showing

OK, the unthinkable has happened. Your project is actually behind schedule. Every week, something seems to happen, something quite outside everyone's control. You analyse, advise, reason, plead—and yet here you are, adjusting your deliverable dates once again. And the worst part of it is, deep down you really don't know why or, more importantly, what you can do about it. Well, there is no need to panic. After all, you can always turn to the wise old project manager in the office across the hall who is ready and willing to help you, right? No? Oh well, then, you can always panic. But before you do, let's figure out what's wrong. There may be myriad reasons why the schedule slips, but some of them are much more likely to occur than others. Broadly speaking, the fault may lie not in our stars, but in:

(1) Our customers. They love to change their minds—all the time!
(2) Our teammates. They may not be prepared, or may not have 'the right stuff'.
(3) Our environment. We may be camouflaged for desert warfare, but find ourselves fighting through the swamp.
(4) Ourselves. In the final analysis, the buck always stops with the project manager. So whatever is going wrong—it's probably your fault (at least for not managing it properly!).

You Drop the Issue Ball

In the course of the project, many issues come up. By definition, issues have a potentially adverse impact on the project's CSSQ. Most of them are solved internally, within the project team, but some require actions or decisions on the part of other players with whom you may have little influence. The important fact to remember is that project issues are the project manager's responsibility. No matter how clear you are in communicating the issue, no matter how little say you have in its resolution—it remains your responsibility. Identifying another person as a party who can resolve the issue does not abdicate your responsibility to follow it through. Even obtaining consensus that another agency unit should, or a promise that they would, resolve it does not remove your obligation to track the issue to a successful conclusion. One of the most natural pitfalls is to assume that once you have successfully convinced everyone that someone else has to solve the issue, you are done. On the contrary! Because it is now out of your control, you must be all the more dogged in the pursuit of its resolution. Tell the responsible parties that you're not going away. Keep asking them what you can do to help get the issue resolved, but keep tracking their progress—or lack therefore—on your status reports. Use all the tools in the project communications plan to continuously shine light on the issue.

You Fall into the Project Black Box

(1) *Scene 1*—You employ the latest facilitation techniques to extract all possible requirements from your customers, even requirements they did not know they had.

(2) *Scene 2*—Your team performs wonders to design the perfect product, exactly as the customers requested, and works like the dickens to develop it exactly as envisioned.

(3) *Scene 3*—You beam with pride as you deliver your masterpiece to an eager customer.

(4) *Scene 4*—You slink away in shame as the customer continues to rant and rave about all the features that the

product does not have even though they told you about them all along.

What happened? You 'black-boxed' your project. The customers saw you when you were gathering the requirements. Then you and your team went away into the project black box, and only came out in time to show the customer the finished product. The problem is, things changed in the interim! The customer cast of characters may have changed. The business conditions may have changed. The expectations may have changed. And you did not keep in synch. Worse, you did not keep your customers in synch with your project. You just assumed that because you are giving your customers exactly what they originally asked for, they would like it. But you know what happens when you assume.

The simple remedy for the black box phenomenon is keeping the customers involved every step of the way. You should constantly show select customers project deliverables as they are being developed. Not so they can change their minds but so they know what to expect on delivery. You certainly want to minimise the number of decision-makers who will accept and sign off on your deliverables (chasing signatures of more than a couple of people is a pain) but you want to maximise the number of people who review, or even preview your stuff.

You Remain Incommunicado

Once the project really gets going in project execution, it is very easy to focus internally—on project team dynamics, on technical challenges, on deliverables and schedules—to the exclusion of everything else; yet it is also important to pay attention to the externals.

Executing all aspects of your communications plan is your responsibility, and nothing is more important than accurate and frequent status reporting. A project status report is the most effective way for all stakeholders to remain closely connected to and aware of the project's progress—and potential problems. The two most important questions the project status report must answer are:

(1) What is the latest, best available estimate for the remaining work, and how does it compare with the schedule?
(2) What issues have come up that may affect the project cost, scope, schedule, or quality, and what is being done about them?

These questions are far more important to the eventual success of the project, and to minimising surprises along the way, than the usual dissertations on project status and enumerations of immediate tasks at various levels—not that the status report should not include them. But after collecting, analysing and evaluating the status information, the project manager's job is to make decisions or suggestions regarding changes to be made—if necessary—to keep the project on track. Of course, the best status report in the world will make no impact if there is no one there to hear it. A regularly scheduled status meeting, attended by as many members of the project team as practical, dedicated to a thorough review of the status report, is irreplaceable.

You Confuse Desire with Ability

Your customers sincerely want what your project is developing. They demonstrated their desire for it by committing funds to the project; by allocating resources to the project team; and by devoting time to meetings, reviews, and other project-related activities. And yet they may be totally unprepared to actually make use of it, or even to implement it at all. But whose fault do you think it will be when they realise their inability to utilise it? That's right, yours. So it is up to you to make sure that someone determines organisational readiness for the product or service, and that someone prepares for a smooth transition of the product from the project team to the performing organisation. Notice that it does not say you have to do it—just that you have to make sure it gets done. And that requires including in the project plan that organisational readiness assessment and transition planning need to be done.

They Blinded You with Science (or Technology)

There is no law that says that a project manager must be a master of whatever technology the project employs. Nevertheless, you will be called upon to manage numerous technical decisions on the project. A frequent pitfall in those circumstances is over-delegating those decisions to the more technical members of the team, or accepting the recommendations of your technical experts on blind faith, both of which result in unacceptable loss of control. Instead, make the team explain the issue and alternative solutions to you. As a reasonably intelligent person, you should be able to understand the concepts by listening and asking questions. If, however, the technical folks can't explain to your satisfaction why they are advocating a certain position—watch out! It is indicative of a position dictated more by desire than by reason, or of poor understanding on the part of the supposed experts. Get a second opinion, and trust your own instincts.

6

Teamwork and Leadership in Project Management

The moment you start doing anything at all with another person, you've established a team. Begin a conversation, pick up the phone, brainstorm an idea and you're in teamwork. Every possibility, from landing the contract to the romantic evening hinges on your ability to relate. But neither profit nor pleasure are the primary motivation for teamwork. Productive teamwork moves you toward challenge, through change, with more confidence. Working well on any team generates energy and enthusiasm for life.

Fundamental Principles

This ability is learned. You do not need complex interaction formulas. You don't have to be easy-going, well-educated, hard-nosed, or even especially intelligent to build a team. You don't have to be anything other than yourself. You can be effective with people using common sense and a few fundamental principles.

Vision

Vision means being able to excite the team with large, desired outcomes. Large outcomes mean devising goals that attract missionaries. The first step in vision is to project such a goal. This goal must be bigger than a pay check. It must contain challenge, appeal to personal pride, and provide an opportunity to make a difference and know it. Then the goal can become a powerful vision.

Next, team leaders position the goal by picturing success. Initial questions might be, "What will it look like when we get there?", "What will success be like, feel like?," "How will others know?" When a large, missionary-friendly goal has been pictured and clearly communicated, the vision is complete.

Commitment

Commitment can be a dangerous concept because of its attendant assumptions. Some may assume, for example, that commitment means long hours, while to others it may mean productivity. When expectations are defined, success rates soar. When leaders assume that everyone 'should' be committed, as a matter of course, we overlook the difficulties many have with certain commitments. If people cannot initially commit, it doesn't mean they don't care. More often, it means they do care, and they are caught up in a process of doubt. This process precedes every meaningful commitment.

Effective leaders catalyze this process, so that the critical mass of people can pass through this stage efficiently on their way to genuine commitment and innovative strategies. This pre-commitment process is the same for team leaders and members. When we ponder a new commitment, we climb up to a kind of mental diving board. Commitments contain unknowns, and some warn of possible failure. It is common for people to neither jump nor climb back down the 'ladder', but rather to stay stuck at the end of the board, immobilized in pros, cons, obstacles, and worries.

In this state of mind, the obstacles begin to rule, obscuring the vision, blunting motivation. When leaders do not understand the commitment process they tend to seek accountability without providing support. Without a means to process doubts and fears, people often feel pressured to commit, but can't. One option, often unconscious, is to pretend to commit, to say 'yes' and mean 'maybe' at best. The pretended commitment is a form of wholly unnecessary corporate madness. The solution to this set of problems is two fold: establish an atmosphere of trust, and within that atmosphere encourage inclusion.

Trust

Trust is the antidote to the fears and risks attendant to meaningful commitment. Trust means confidence in team leadership and vision. When trust prevails, team members are more willing to go through a difficult process, supported through ups, downs, risk and potential loss. Trust is most efficiently established when leadership commits to vision first, and everyone knows those commitments are genuine. The process for leaders to commit is the same as for everyone else: assess pre-commitment doubts, questions, unknowns and fears. This involves three simple steps:

- List the unknowns
- Assess worst case scenarios and their survivability
- Research the unknowns.

The list of unknowns reveals some answers and further questions. Some of these questions lend themselves to research (others' experience, a small pilot plan), and some have no apparent answers from our pre-commitment position. These latter comprise the bottom line or irreducible risk. We learn the outcome only after commitment. Every major commitment contains some irreducible risk, some lingering unknowns. We therefore make every major commitment in at least partial ignorance.

Leadership now understands the potential loss and gain involved in the new vision. At this point, leadership can commit itself, and prepare to include other team members. That preparation must include a plan for leadership to share visibly both risk and reward with the other team members who will be coming on board. With leadership's commitment to a clear vision, and a genuine plan to share risks and rewards, the atmosphere for trust is in place. We are now ready to include others in our team effort.

Inclusion

Inclusion means getting others to commit to the team effort, helping others through their 'diving board doubts' to genuine commitment. Since leaders now understand this process first hand, we need only communicate with the potential team members to complete inclusion. The best setting to obtain buy-in and build trust is in small groups that facilitate thorough give and take. The basic tasks are to communicate the vision, make sure it is understood, communicate leadership's commitment (including sharing risk and reward, and how), and elicit and address peoples' doubts.

Leaders will need three communication skills to achieve inclusion. These are the non-assumptive question, good listening, and directed response.

(1) *Non-assumptive questions* ("What do you think?", "Can you tell me what is happening with this report?")—invite real answers because they are inclusive, not intrusive. Questions containing assumptions ("Why are you skeptical?", "Why is this report so incomplete?") invite defensiveness. When converting an atmosphere of change and possibly skepticism to trust, added defensiveness is counter-productive.

(2) Listening means separating the process of taking in information from the process of judging it. Kept separate, both processes are valuable. Mixed, especially when the

receiver is a designated leader, the sender is invited to stop communicating or to change the message midstream.

(3) *Directed response*—Effective team leaders demonstrate responsiveness. Since leaders have already processed their own pre-commitment doubts, many questions can be answered on the spot. Some require research and a time line for response. And some, which relate to the bottom line, irreducible risk, require a truthful "I don't know. I'm in the same soup as you."

Help Information Exchange

The final step in creating the team is to establish a corroborative, balanced strategy for reaching the committed vision. This plan will consist of all of the tasks and help exchange necessary to realise the overall vision. Your teammates themselves are in the best position to supply this information. Since by this time you have laid the groundwork for trust, and established good buy-in, your teammates are likely to be enthusiastically cooperative.

At this point, the leadership role is to catalyze consensus, not to issue orders. Consensus means that team members agree to, whether they necessarily agree with, a particular approach. Consensus occurs easily when most feel their ideas were heard and considered, whether or not the team ultimately chooses those ideas. Obtaining consensus again requires use of leadership communication skills: non-assumptive questions, good listening, and directed response.

Effective teams often produce lively discussions of divergent viewpoints before reaching consensus. Diverse views can mean unresolved argument, or they can mean increased team intelligence and ultimate consensus. The difference is a well built team. To improve the effectiveness of your team, Learning Center offers customised teamwork training

Making the Effective Team

"Everyone wants to feel that they are on a winning team, that the company is moving ahead, and that they are an integral part of the group". Building the winning team requires more than just hiring a bunch of talented people.

(1) It means hiring people who will work well together.
(2) It means developing a shared vision and commitment.
(3) It means physically bringing people together in formal group meetings for open discussion of broad-based issues.
(4) It means encouraging positive, informal interactions between group members.
(5) It means instilling a 'winning' attitude throughout the organisation.
(6) It means watching for and quickly trying to reverse team-building problems such as jealousy, cynicism, and defensive behavior.

To build the winning team, you not only need to show people what direction the company is headed in, but you need to get them to 'buy into' this direction. Otherwise, you can't expect people to support a group if they don't agree with where it's headed or, worse, don't even know where it's headed. Specifically, you need to show people:

(1) Your vision for the future.
(2) Your strategy for getting there.
(3) Why this is the best strategy.
(4) Every achievement that indicates this team is winning.

This is not a one-time discussion or announcement. You need to constantly remind people what the organisation stands for and that it does indeed hold a bright future for them!

Solidarity through Meetings

Part of building the winning team is having some group meetings. Meetings, or even parties or celebrations, with as many people as possible from the entire organisation, help build a feeling of solidarity throughout the organisation. But it is also important to have everyone participate in smaller group meetings where some work is done or some decisions are made. This makes people feel that they aren't just part of some big group, but that they are an active, important part of a team.

For key managers, or people in your work group, you should have an interactive meeting once per week-not a meeting where you just make announcements and summarise the work that's been done and needs to be done, but a meeting where everyone has an opportunity to give feedback on substantive issues.

Encourging People to Work Together

Perhaps the most difficult part of building a winning team is encouraging positive, informal interaction between team members when you are not present. Here are some thoughts on this:

(1) Have team members take part in the hiring process of new team members.

(2) Assign specific projects for two team members to work on together.

(3) Try to arrange for close proximity of offices.

(4) Create an incentive-pay plan based on common goals such as profitability.

(5) Have a specific part of the salary review dependent upon 'interaction with others'.

(6) Take your team off-site for formal meetings as well as casual get-togethers to build a sense of bonding.

Avoid Problems

Here are some of the problems that can rip the team-building process apart.

(1) *Jealousy*: Be on guard for jealousy whenever a new member is hired into the group. Go out of your way to tell other team members how much their work is appreciated.

(2) *Cynicism*: Some people are just negative by nature. Others might feel your company can't possibly prosper or they just don't like small companies, big companies, or whatever. . . . Be sure you are emphasising the company's positive achievements to the group as a whole. And don't hesitate to confront any openly cynical individual and demand their behavior change at once.

(3) *Lack of confidence*: Some people lack confidence in themselves and view attacks on their opinions as attacks on themselves, responding with statements like "Are you telling me my fifteen years of experience don't matter?" Stop any discussion like this immediately and, in a private one-on-one meeting, patiently point out the defensive behaviour.

Characteristics of a Team

(1) There must be an awareness of unity on the part of all its members.

(2) There must be interpersonal relationship. Members must have a chance to contribute, learn from and work with others.

(3) The member must have the ability to act together toward a common goal.

Ten characteristics of Well-functioning Teams

(1) *Purpose*: Members proudly share a sense of why the

team exists and are invested in accomplishing its mission and goals.

(2) *Priorities*: Members know what needs to be done next, by whom, and by when to achieve team goals.

(3) *Roles*: Members know their roles in getting tasks done and when to allow a more skilful member to do a certain task.

(4) *Decisions*: Authority and decision-making lines are clearly understood.

(5) *Conflict*: Conflict is dealt with openly and is considered important to decision-making and personal growth.

(6) *Personal traits*: members feel their unique personalities are appreciated and well utilized.

(7) *Norms*: Group norms for working together are set and seen as standards for every one in the groups.

(8) *Effectiveness*: Members find team meetings efficient and productive and look forward to this time together.

Team Building Must be:	**Team Building Must not be:**
• a way of life • the responsibility of every team member • a continuous process • about developing a clear and unique identity • focused on a clear and consistent set of goals • concerned with the needs and ambitions of each team member recognizing the unique contribution that each individual can make • an awareness of the potential of the team as a unit • results oriented • enjoyable	• a short term, flavor of the month • imposed without regard to peoples' feelings • spasmodic • reserved for only some members of the team • an excuse for not meeting personal responsibilities • a process where actions clearly contradict intentions • seen as a chore

(9) *Success*: Members know clearly when the team has met with success and share in this equally and proudly.

(10) *Training*: Opportunities for feedback and updating skills are provided and taken advantage of by team members.

Guidelines for Effective Team Membership: Some Guidelines

- Contribute ideas and solutions
- Recognise and respect differences in others
- Value the ideas and contributions of others
- Listen and share information
- Ask questions and get clarification
- Participate fully and keep your commitments
- Be flexible and respect the partnership created by a team—strive for the 'win-win'
- Have fun and care about the team and the outcomes.

Characteristics of a High-performance Team

(1) *Participative leadership*: Creating an interdependence by empowering, freeing up and serving others.

(2) *Shared responsibility*: Establishing an environment in which all team members feel responsibility as the manager for the performance team.

(3) *Aligned on purpose*: Having a sense of common purpose about why the team exists and the function it serves.

(4) *High communication*: Creating a climate of trust and open, honest communication.

(5) *Future focused*: Seeing change as an opportunity for growth.

(6) *Focused on task*: Keeping meetings and interactions focused on results.

(7) *Creative talents*: Applying individual talents and creativity.

(8) *Rapid response:* Identifying and acting on opportunities.

Cross-Functional Teams

Some of the factors that lead to poor communication among cross-functional team members include the following:

(1) *Lack of appreciation of the contributions of other functions*. For example, in telecommunications projects, some engineers do not value the input provided by human factors psychologists.

(2) *Plain old-fashioned turf battles*. Some departments play out their competitive games on the field provided by the cross-functional team.

(3) *Different jargon*. For example, line department users often do not understand the terminology and technology employed by computer programmers.

(4) *Different work orientations*. For example, researchers tend to take a long-term view and have an informal work climate; operation people are more short term and formal; salespeople are usually informal and have a short-term focus. While one may argue with these generalisations, it is clear that each department or function develops it own work style, which may clash with other styles from other functions.

(5) *Different degrees of interest in the team's outcome*. Some cross-functional team members are simply more interested in the team's purpose and may have more to gain from a successful outcome. In one government agency, team embers from one bureau have more interest in the outcome of the team because it affects their client group more than it does the other bureaus represented on the team.

(6) *Mistaken goals*. Some team members mistakenly see harmony as the goal of cross-functional teamwork. As a result, they are afraid to express a contrary point of view

for fear that it will destroy the positive feelings among team members. The new result is a false consensus and a less than satisfactory outcome.

While these factors explain lack of trust and communication on cross-functional teams, they do not excuse it. Members of cross-functional teams are there because they have something to contribute. They must be allowed and even encouraged to share their ideas, information, and opinions without restrictions. Open communication is an absolute requirement for successful cross-functional teamwork. The concept of the cross-functional team is that the outcome—the product, the system, the service—will be better because it has been created by the combined expertise of people from a variety of functions. Viewing a problem or an issue from many vantage point is the strength of the cross-functional team. However, the value of divergent views can only be realised when there is a free flow of information.

Leadership Paradigms

A leader is a person you will follow to a place you wouldn't go by yourself. You manage within a paradigm (Paradigm enhancement). Give a good manager the system (the rules, the guiding principles, the system, the standards, the protocols.) and he/she will optimise it. We spend 90% of our lives doing just this—evolution.

You lead between paradigms (Paradigm shift). Leaders, with their intuitive judgment, assess the seeming risk, determine that shifting paradigms is the correct thing to do, and instill the courage in others to follow them. This kind of change occurs during less than 10% of our lives.

Paradigm shifting without the follow-on skills of paradigm enhancing leaves you vulnerable to the paradigm pioneers who practice Total Quality. Paradigm enhancement without the skills of paradigm shifting will lead you to continually improve obsolete products and services. Nobody will buy obsolete excellence.

The manager administers	The leader innovates
The manager has a short-range view	The leader has a long-range perspective
The manager asks how and when	The leader asks what and why
The manager has his eye on the bottom line	The leader has his eye on the horizon
The manager accepts the status quo	The leader challenges it

(Warren Bennis,May,1990)

Developing Team Effectiveness

Meaning of Team

Teams are an important element in the new high performance forms of organisation. It is important to understand what teams are and what they aren't, if they are to be used effectively. Teams differ from committees, groups of co-workers, and other groups. Teams have performance goals to achieve and member of the teams feel mutually accountable for achieving them.

What is the definition of a team? A team is defined as a reasonably small group of people, who bring to the table a set of complementary and appropriate skills, and who hold themselves mutually accountable for achieving a clear and identifiable set of goals.

Effectiveness of Team

It is almost imposable to open a business magazine today without some guru exhorting the benefits of working in teams. In many situations teams can achieve more than individuals working on their own.

This is because teams can bring to bear a wider range of skills and experience to solve a problem. Teams also produce better quality decisions. When a team has been working on a problem, and they have a sense of commitment to the common solution.

They are not always effective. They can be highly dysfunctional. They can develop a 'group think' mentality that can produce bad decisions. They can be disruptive, leading to arguments and discord in the organisation. They can be enormously wasteful of people's time and energy.

In short, teams can be good, but they can also be bad. In the new organisation teams have a critical role to play. Work teams are used as the basic unit of organisation. Problem solving teams are used to improve the way the organisation performs, and management teams are used to develop strategy and to drive the changes. If the role of teams is to be positive, people must learn how to make them work effectively. What do we mean by team effectiveness?

A team can be considered to be effective if their output is judged to meet or exceed the expectations of the people who receive the output. This is a question of the customer being right. If the team has been given some task to perform, the people who have given them the task are the people who will judge whether the result is satisfactory.

Producing a quality output is not enough to judge the effectiveness of the team. The second criteria is that the team should still be able function effectively after they have completed their task. It should not be torn apart by dissension. This is not just a question of the members of the team still being on speaking terms. It means that after the team has been disbanded, the people should have an enhanced working relationship that benefits the organisation.

Finally, effectiveness is judged by whether the team feels satisfied with its efforts. If the team members are pleased with their efforts, if the experience has been a good one, if time spent away from their normal work has been worth the effort, the team has likely been effective.

Factors Making Effective Team

There has been a great deal of research into the subject of team effectiveness over the last decade or so and there is a consensus on what factors must be controlled in order to set up and run effective teams. There are three areas of group behaviour that must be addressed for teams to be effective.

The team must work hard. The effort that the team puts in to get the job done is dependent on whether the nature of the task motivates the members of the team and whether the goals are challenging. The team must have the right mix of skills to bring to the table. These skills include technical, problem solving and interpersonal skills.

The team must be able to develop appropriate approaches to problem solving. This depends on developing a plan of attack and using appropriate techniques for analysis.

The following factors contribute to hard work, skill development and effective problem solving strategies:

Motivating Nature of the Task

One of the factors affecting the effort the team is likely to put into the job is the job itself. The characteristics of the job should provide motivation. The job should require a variety of high level skills to make it interesting. The task itself should be seen as being worthwhile. It needs to be a whole piece of work with a clear and visible outcome so that people can feel a sense of ownership.

The outcome of the task should be perceived as being important to other people's lives. It should affect others in the organisation or impact on the external customer. The job should provide the team with an opportunity for self regulation. They should decide how the work is to be done. Meaningful feedback should be provided on the how well the team is performing. The job characteristics are particularly important for work teams who are part of the day to day running of the organisation.

Well-defined Challenging Goals

For problem solving teams the most important factor that fosters the hard work and effort necessary for success is having meaningful goals. During the eighties quality circles were the latest fad. They generally failed to achieve any worthwhile results because they were not focused on results. They were aimless.

If goals are foggy or too easy to achieve the team will not be motivated to make the extra effort that separates a high performance team from an ineffective group. Goals are needed to spur a team. When challenging goals are set the team will mobilise its efforts to find innovative ways to achieve feats that may have been considered impossible.

Providing a challenging job is the most important motivator to sustain group effort. Goals provide a sense of direction to the team so that when conflict occurs it is possible to channel the conflict more constructively by returning to the goals for direction. The team needs to buy in to the goals. In most cases a team has been set up to achieve a set of prescribed goals. They should spend some time discussing the goals and if necessary they should have the opportunity to negotiate them with their management. They must have the opportunity to buy in and commit to achieving the goals. Goals need to be challenging, but not impossible to achieve. They also need to be measurable so that progress towards achieving them can be monitored and results confirmed.

Rewards

Rewards reinforce the motivational aspects of having a well designed task and challenging goals. People tend to engage in those behaviours that are rewarded, so the rewards need to suit the personal characteristics of the people on the team. These rewards do not need to be financial rewards although they may be. Simply providing recognition for a job well done can be all that is required. Whatever form the reward takes, it is important that group effort be recognised. One should avoid the destructive effect of trying to single out individuals from the group, when there has been a group effort.

The impact of rewards will be heightened if the team understands that the provision of the reward is contingent on meeting the agreed goals. On the whole, hard work and effort are best sustained by having a worthwhile task to perform and having clear challenging goals to meet. Rewards merely reinforce these conditions for fostering group effort.

The Right Mix of Skills

The right mix of skills should be brought to the task at hand. This is partly a matter of assigning talented individuals and avoiding the temptation to assign people to a team for political reasons. It is also a question of carefully reviewing the job to determine what relevant skills are required and selecting staff so that the team has the right balance.

Any shortfall in skills is then made up by providing relevant training. Technical skills are required. For teams who are trying to improve a process that cuts across department boundaries, each function should be represented. One should achieve a balance of skills. This means avoiding having a preponderance of skills and experience in one specialised area. Sheer numbers may weigh the solution towards the dominant group.

In the case of permanent work teams it is likely that team members will not have all the task relevant skills at the onset. When the group is new, it is likely that members will bring narrow skills learned in their old roles. They will need to develop broader skills for the new job.

To ensure that this is done, training and coaching should be provided. The members of the team need to have problem solving and decision making skills as well as technical skills. When a business is making its first venture into team based work, it is likely that people will not have a good grasp of the techniques related to problem analysis and solution.

These relevant skills must be acquired, so it will be necessary to provide training. Over a period of time staff will become experienced in problem solving techniques and the organisation will develop a repertoire of skills among the staff so this training will not always be necessary.

Interpersonal skills are also important. This is not as obvious as it may sound. Most people do not listen well. Listening is much more than being quiet when some else is talking. Active listening is required. Many people do not speak to the point but ramble on or go off at a tangent. Most people do not take criticism well and tend to be defensive about their own opinions.

Agreed on a Code of Conduct

At the beginning of the team project it is important to develop a code of conduct for meetings. The team needs to agree on a set of rules to ensure that their efforts are purposeful and that all members contribute to the work.

The most critical rules pertain to attendance, open discussion, using an analytical approach, not pulling rank over other members, planning the work and sharing work assignments. This will ensure that the work is done well and done on time. In summary, to ensure that the best possible set of skills and experience is brought to the task, able people should be selected on the basis of their relevant skills, and training or coaching should be provided to make up any skill deficiencies.

Team activities are in fact a powerful vehicle for building skills. People learn skills from each other. They learn how other parts of the organisation function. Teams serve to build up a repertoire of skills in the organisation and this enhances the organisation in the long term.

Effective Problem Solving Strategies

Behaviour in some groups can be chaotic. Early on, the team must develop a consensus about the general strategy for approaching problems. Failure to do so will seriously inhibit the ability of the team to tackle its tasks. For the team to be able to develop an appropriate strategy, it must have a clear definition of the problem, know what resources it has available and the limits, and understand the expectations.

It must then develop a problem solving plan, based on the approach suggested in the section on continuous improvement. An effective team must develop good synergy. When a group finally clicks and become a team, it will find creative ways to solve problems and come up with innovative solutions. Synergy comes about when gains from the team setting exceed the losses. When this does not happen, people are passive. Their skills and knowledge are not utilised and they waste their time.

Synergy is effected by group interaction. It is also dependent upon the group size. A larger group has the potential to be able to provide a greater variety of skills. However, when the group is too large the individual contribution of each person decreases.

Some people feel intimidated by large group and don't contribute. Also when the group is large members become inactive. Small size is better, it generates team spirit. The team should have just enough hands to do the work and no more.

Special Teams Have Special Issues

From the perspective of organisational improvement we are interested in three types of teams. One is the problem solving team, another is the work team and then there is the senior management team. Problem solving teams are set up with a clearly defined task to investigate a problem and recommend a solution. Sometimes the same team will go on to implement the solution.

When their task is completed the team is disbanded and members go back to their normal organisational duties. There are two important issues facing these teams. One is getting started and the other is handing over the recommendations for implementation.

The key to getting started is to ensure that the team is committed to achieving an agreed set of goals. Goals serve to focus the team's effort. Implementation is important. It will not just happen; it must be planned. The implementors must be brought into the solution stage so that they develop a sense of ownership towards the solution and buy into it. The best way to do this is to have the problem solving team do the implementation.

Another approach is to phase the implementors into the team so that the membership changes prior to the implementation. Whatever approach is used one should remember that the idea is to implement a solution and not to produce a report. Work teams are different in that they are a fixed part of the organisation. They have an ongoing function which is to control a set of activities that make up a discrete operation in the overall business process. They need to focus on the critical factors in their process and to control these factors to ensure a quality product.

Their work is ongoing. There are no completion dates. They must think in terms of how they can constantly improve their work to cut cost, cycle time, or improve quality. One of the management issues is how to keep track of the performance of a large number of work teams to ensure that effort is focused on improving the performance of the key processes. Management teams are another thing altogether. At the senior level in an organisation there should be a team approach taken towards the effective implementation of business strategy. This implementation should include the achievement of a range of performance improvement goals. It is important to identify specific measurable business objectives and monitor the progress towards meeting them.

For the management team to behave as a real team they should be prepared to roll up their sleeves and help with the change effort. They should perform the higher level activities that support people at the lower level. These include communications, resolving road blocks and providing support and encouragement to those affected by the changes.

Building Quality in Team

Meaning of Quality

Quality is primarily viewed in terms of corporate culture, multi-departmental ad-hoc task forces and the salvation of entire companies. This article, instead, will view these ideas as they might be applied by a team leader with a small permanent staff (Gerard M. Blair). Quality has become the philosophers' stone of management practice with consultants and gurus vying to charm lead-laden corporations into gold-winning champions. Stories abound of base companies with morose workers and mounting debts being transformed into happy teams and healthy profits; never a day goes by without a significant improvement, a pounds-saving suggestion or a quantum leap in efficiency. With this professed success of 'Quality' programmes, there has evolved a proscriptive mythology of correct practise which has several draw backs:

- The edicts call for nothing less than a company wide, senior-management led programme
- The adherence to a single formula has a limited effect, precludes innovation outside these boundaries, and reduces the differentiation which such programmes profess to engender
- The emphasis on single-task, specially formed groups shifts the focus away from the ordinary, daily bread-and-butter.

Of course, these criticisms do not invalidate the ideas of quality but are simply to suggest that the principles might well be viewed from a new angle—and applied at a different level. This article attempts to provide a new perspective by re-examining some of the tenets of quality in the context of a small, established team: simply, what could a team leader do with his/her staff.

In current management writings "Quality" has come to refer to a whole gambit of practices which themselves have resulted in beneficial side-effects; as a team leader, you will want to take advantage of these benefits also.

Quality and the Customer

In simple terms, attaining quality has something to do with satisfying the expectations of the customer. Concern for the wishes and needs of customers becomes the focus for every decision. What the customer wants, the company provides. This is not philanthropy, this is basic survival. Through careful education by competitors, the customer has begun to exercise spending power in favour of quality goods and services; and while quality is not the sole criterion in selecting a particular supplier, it has become an important differentiator.

If one ten-rupees ball-point runs dry in one month and another ten-rupees ball-point lasts for three then the second ball-point is the make which the customer will buy again and which he/she recommends to others—even if it costs a little more. The makers of the first ball-point may have higher profit margins, but eventually no sales; without quality in the product, a company sacrifices customers, revenue and ultimately its own existence. In practical terms, quality is that something extra which will be perceived by the customer as a valid reason for either paying more or for buying again.

In the case where the product is a service, quality is equated with how well the job is done and especially with whether the customer is made to feel good about the whole operation. In this respect quality often does cost more, but the loss is recouped in the price customers are prepared to pay and in the increase of business.

Quality and Reliability

The clearest manifestation of quality is in a product's reliability: that the product simply works. To prevent problems from arising after the product is shipped, the quality must be checked beforehand—and the best time to check quality is throughout the whole design and manufacturing cycle. The old method of quality control was to test the completed product and then to rework to remove the problems. Thus while the original production time was short, the rework time was long. The new approach to quality simply asserts that if testing becomes an integral part of each stage of production, the production time may increase but the rework time will disappear. Further, you will catch and solve many problems which the final 'big-bang' quality-check would miss but which the customer will find on the first day.

To achieve this requires an environment where the identification of errors is considered to be 'a good thing', where the only bad bugs are the ones which got away. One of the most hallowed doctrines of quality is that of zero defects. 'Zero defects' is a focus, it a glorious objective, it is the assertion that nothing less will suffice and that no matter how high the quality of a product, it can still be improved. It is a paradox in that it is an aim which is contrary to reason, and like the paradoxes of many other religions it holds an inner truth. This is why the advocates of quality often seem a little crazy: they are zealots.

Workforce as Resource for Quality

While quality has its own reward in terms of increased long-term sales, the methods used to achieve this quality also have other benefits. In seeking to improve the quality of the product, manufacturers have found that the people best placed to make substantial contributions are the workforce: people are the most valuable resource. It is this shift in perspective from the management to the workforce which is the most significant consequence of the search for quality.

From it has arisen a new managerial philosophy aimed at the empowerment of the workforce, decision-making by the front line, active worker involvement in the company's advancement; and from this new perspective, new organisational structures have evolved, exemplified in 'Quality Circles'. Without digressing too much, it is important to examine the benefits of this approach. For such delegation to be safely and effectively undertaken, the management has to train the workforce; not necessarily directly, and not all at once, but often within the Quality Circles themselves using a single 'facilitator' or simply peer-coaching. The workforce had to learn how to hold meetings, how to analyse problems, how to take decisions, how to present solutions, how to implement and evaluate change.

These traditionally high-level managerial prerogatives are devolved to the whole staff. Not only does this develop talent, it also stimulates interest. Staff begin to look not only for problems but also for solutions. Simple ideas become simply implemented: the secretary finally gets the filing cabinet moved closer to the desk, the sales meetings follow an agenda, the software division creates a new bulletin board for the sports club. The environment is created where people see problems and fix them. Larger problems have more complex solutions. One outcome of the search for quality in Japan is the system of just-in-time flow control. In this system, goods arrive at each stage of the manufacturing process just before they are needed and are not made until they are needed by the next stage. This reduces storage requirements and inventory costs of surplus stock.

Another outcome has been the increased flexibility of the production line. Time to change from one product run to the next was identified as a major obstacle in providing the customer with the desired range of products and quantities, and so the whole workforce became engaged in changing existant practices and even in redesigning the machinery.

Team Quality

While the salvation of an entire corporation may rest primarily with senior management, the fate of a team rests with the team leader. The team leader has the authority, the power to define the micro-culture of the work team. It is by the deliberate application of the principles of quality that the team leader can gain for the team the same benefits which quality can provide for a corporation.

The best ideas for any particular team are likely to come from them—the aim of the team leader must be to act as a catalyst through prompts and by example; the following are possible suggestions.

Beginning

There will be no overnight success. To be lasting, quality must become a habit and a habit is accustomed practise. This takes time and training—although not necessarily formal training but possibly the sort of reinforcement you might give to any aspect of good practise. To habituate your staff to quality, you must first make it an issue. Here are two suggestions. The first idea is to become enthusiastic about one aspect at a time, and initially look for a quick kill. Find a problem and start to talk about it with the whole team; do not delegate it to an individual but make it an issue for everybody.

Choose some work-related problem like 'how to get the right information in time' and solicit everybody's views and suggestions—and get the problem solved. Demand urgency against a clear target. There is no need to allocate large amounts of resource or time to this, simply raise the problem and make a fuss. When a solution comes, praise it by rewarding the whole team, and ensure that the aspects of increased efficiency/productivity/calm are highlighted since this will establish the criteria for 'success'. Next, find another problem and repeat.

The second idea is the regular weekly meeting to discuss Quality. Of course meetings can be complete time wasters, so this strategy requires care. The benefits are that regularity will lead to habit, the formality will provide a simple opportunity for the expression of ideas, and the inclusion of the whole group at the meeting will emphasize the collective responsibility. By using the regular meeting, you can establish the 'ground rules' of accepted behaviour and at the same time train the team in effective techniques.

One problem is that the focus on any one particular issue may quickly loose its efficacy. A solution is to have frequent shifts in focus so that you maintain the freshness and enthusiasm (and the scope for innovative solutions). Further benefits are that continual shifts in emphasis will train your team to be flexible, and provide the opportunity for them to raise new issues. The sooner the team takes over the definition of the 'next problem', the better.

Initial Phases

The initial phases are delicate. The team will be feeling greater responsibility without extra confidence. Thus you must concentrate on supporting their development. Essentially you will be their trainer in management skills. You could get outside help with this but by undertaking the job yourself, you retain control: you mould the team so that they will reflect your own approach and use your own criteria. Later they will develop themselves, but even then they will understand your thinking and so your decisions.

One trap to avoid is that the team may focus upon the wrong type of problem. You must make it clear any problem which they tackle should be:

- related to their own work or environment
- something which they can change.

This precludes gripe sessions about wages and holidays. As with all group work, the main problem is clarity. You should provide the team with a notice board and flip-charts specifically for Quality problems. These can then be left on display as a permanent record of what was agreed.

If you can, steer the group first to some problem which has a simple solution and with obvious (measurable) benefits. A quick, sharp success will motivate.

Team Building

To succeed, a quality push must engage the enthusiasm of the entire team; as team leader, you must create the right atmosphere for this to happen. Many aspects of team building can be addressed while quality remains the focus. You must create the environment where each team member feels totally free to express an idea or concern and this can only be done if there is no stigma attached to being incorrect.

No idea is wrong—merely non-optimal. In each suggestion there is at least a thread of gold and someone should point it out and, if possible, build upon it. Any behaviour which seeks laughter at the expense of others must be swiftly reprimanded. One crude but effective method is to write down agreed ground rules and to display them as a constant reminder for everyone, something like:

- All criticism must be kind and constructive
- All our-problems are all-our problems
- Bugs wanted: dead or alive (but not for long)
- If it saves time later, do it now.

Another method is to constantly talk about the group as the plural pronoun: 'we decided', 'we can do this', 'we'll get back to you'. This is especially effective if it is used in conversation with outsiders (especially management) within ear-shot of the team. Praise and reward the whole team; get the team wider fame by a success story in an internal newspaper.

Most importantly, you must enable failure. If the team is unable to try out ideas without rebuke for errors, then the scope of their solutions will be severely limited. Instead, a failure should be an opportunity to gain knowledge and to praise any safe-guards which were included in the plan.

Role of Mutual Support

An important aspect of team interaction is the idea of mutual support. If you can instill the idea that all problems are owned by the entire team then each member will be able to seek help and advice when needed from every other team member. One promoter of this is to encourage mutual coaching. If one team member knows techniques or information which would be useful to the rest, then encourage him/her to share it. Specifically this will raise the profile, confidence and self-esteem of the instructor at the same time as benefiting the entire group. And if there is one member who might never have anything useful to impart— send him/her to a conference or training session to find something.

Statistical Quality Control

One of the central tenets of quality programmes is the idea of monitoring the problem being addressed: Statistical Quality Control. Quite simply, if you can't measure an improvement, it probably isn't there. Gathering statistics has several benefits in applying quality:

- It identifies (the extent of) the problem
- It allows progress to be monitored
- It provides an objective criterion for the abandonment of an idea
- It can justify perceived expense in terms of observed savings/improvements
- It motivates staff by providing a display of achievement

and, of course, some problems simply disappear when you try to watch them.

The statistics must be gathered in an objective and empirical manner, the outcome should be a simple table or graph regularly updated to indicate progress, and these results must be displayed where all the team can watch. For example, if your team provides product support, then you might monitor and graph the number of repeat enquiries or the average response time. Or if you are in product development, you might want to monitor the number of bugs discovered (i.e., improvement opportunities).

In the long term, it may be suitable to implement the automatic gathering of statistics on a wide range of issues such as complaints, bug reports, machine down-time, etc. Eventually these may either provide early warning of unexpected problems, or comparative data for new quality improvement projects. It is vital, however, that they focus upon an agreed problem and not upon an individual's performance or else all the positive motivation of staff involvement will be lost.

Any plan to improve the quality or effectiveness of the group must contain:

- The objective
- The method
- The statistical display for monitoring the outcome
- The agreed criteria for completion or curtailment.

By insisting on this format, you provide the plan-owners with a simple mechanism for peer recognition (through the displayed notice board) and yet enable them to manage their own failure with grace.

For a small established team, the 'customer' includes any other part of the company with which the team interacts. Thus any themes regarding customer satisfaction can be developed with respect to these so called internal customers. In the end, the effectiveness of your team will be judged by the reports of how well they provide products for others.

A simple innovation might be for a member of your team to actually talk to someone from each of these internal customer groups and to ask about problems. The interfaces are usually the best place to look for simply solved problems. The immediate benefit may be to the customer, but in the long run better communications will lead to fewer misunderstandings and so less rework.

Building Quality

Quality costs less than its lack; look after the pennies and the profits will take care of themselves. To build a quality product, you must do two things:

- Worry the design and the procedures
- Include features to aid quality checking.

It is a question of attitude. If one of the team spots a modification in the design or the procedures which will have a long term benefit, then that must be given priority over the immediate schedule. The design is never quite right; you should allocate time specifically to discussing improvement. In this you should not aim at actual enhancements in the sense of added features or faster performance, but towards simplicity or predicting problem areas. This is an adjunct to the normal design or production operations—the extra mile which lesser teams would not go.

Many products and services do not lend themselves to quality monitoring. These should be enhanced so that the quality becomes easily tracked. This may be a simple invitation for the 'customer' to comment, or it could be a full design modification to provide self-checking or an easy testing routine. Any product whose quality can not be tracked should naturally become a source of deep anxiety to the whole team—until a mechanism is devised.

One of the least-used sources of quality in design and production in the engineering world is documentation. This is frequently seen as the final inconvenience at product release, sometimes even delegated to another (non-technical) group—yet the writing of such documentation can be used as an important vehicle for the clarification of ideas.

In devising a mechanism for monitoring quality, many teams will produce a set of test procedures. As bugs emerge, new procedures should be added which specifically identify this problem and so check the solution.

Leadership in Organisations

Many people today are seeking to understand—and many people are writing about—the concept and practices of leadership. There are a great many reasons for the popularity of the topic, including that organisations are faced with changes like never before. The concept of leadership is relevant to any aspect of ensuring effectiveness in organisations and in managing change. This topic in the Library helps you to fully understand the concept and practices of leadership.

There has been an explosion of literature about leadership lately. Leading is a very human activity—we're all human—so there are many people who consider themselves experts on leadership. Unfortunately, many people make strong assertions about leadership without ever really understanding a great deal about leadership. Understanding the concept of leadership requires more than reading a few articles or fantasising about what great leaders should be.

What is Leadership?

Many people believe that leadership is simply being the first, biggest or most powerful. Leadership in organisations has a different and more meaningful definition. Very simply put, a leader is interpreted as someone who sets direction in an effort and influences people to follow that dircction. How they set that direction and influence people depends on a variety of factors that we'll consider later on below. To really comprehend the 'territory' of leadership, you should briefly scan some of the major theories, notice various styles of leadership and review some of the suggested traits and characteristics that leaders should have.

'Leading' and "Managing"

Another view is that to be a very effective member of an organisation (whether executive, middle manager, or entry-level worker), you need skills in the functions of planning, organizing, leading and coordinating activities—the key is you need to be able to emphasise different skills at different times.

Yes, leading is different than planning, organizing and coordinating because leading is focused on influencing people, while the other functions are focused on 'resources' in addition to people. But that difference is not enough to claim that 'leading is different than managing' any more than one can claim that 'planning is different than managing' or 'organising is different than managing'.

The assertion that 'leading is different than managing'—and the ways that these assertions are made—can cultivate the view that the activities of planning, organising and coordinating are somehow less important than leading. The assertion can also convince others that they are grand and gifted leaders who can ignore the mere activities of planning, organising and coordinating—they can leave these lesser activities to others with less important things to do in the organisation. This view can leave carnage in organisations.

Factors Affecting Competencies in Leadership

The particular competencies (knowledge, skills and abilities) that a person needs in order to lead at a particular time in an organisation depend on a variety of factors, including:

- Whether that person is leading one other individual, a group or a large organisation
- The extent of leadership skills that person already has
- That person's basic nature and values (competencies should be chosen that are in accordance with that nature and those values)
- Whether the group or organisation is for-profit or non-profit, new or long-established, and large or small
- The particular culture (or values and associated behaviours) of whomever is being led.

The above considerations can make it very challenging when trying to determine what competencies someone should have in order to be a better leader. Perhaps that's why leadership training programmes in institutions typically assert a set of standard competencies, for example, decision making, problem solving, managing power and influence, and building trust.

7

Role of Meetings in Project Management

Introduction

Great meetings don't just happen—they're designed. Producing a great meeting is a lot like producing a great product. You don't just build it. You think about it, plan it, and design it: What people and processes do you need to make it successful? But first you have to create agreement among people that meetings are work—they are not an empty ritual to be suffered through before getting 'back to the office', Meetings are events in which real work takes place.

That's a big mind flip. All primates—monkeys, apes, humans—are social creatures. When you're out in the wild, studying nonhuman primates, one of the things you appreciate is just how social they are. They hang out together, they play together, they groom each other. You very rarely see solitary behavior. But if you walk into a typical company, what you see are rows and rows of cubicles. We've taken these wonderfully social creatures— human primates—and we've isolated them. And then we've asked them to be productive in that environment.

Now, as more and more of what people do takes place in teams, meetings become the setting in which most of the really important work gets done. We see this everyday in our own work and life. We do almost all of our work with a team of people.

So many people complain, "I wish I didn't spend so much time in meetings." The simple fact is, some of our peak experiences as people take place in work groups. Most people have attended at least a few meetings in which there's been a real breakthrough: People are facing a problem, banging heads, not making very much headway—and then a kind of magic overtakes them. A wind comes along, it blows away the clouds, and you can just feel the energy in the room. It's possible to have more experiences like that—if you design your meetings with the same care that you use to design your products.

Organisations call meetings for lots of different reasons. And it turns out that different kinds of meetings require different kinds of conversations. If you're not clear about the kind of conversation that you should be having, then your meeting probably won't achieve a clear outcome.

For example, some meetings are built around a 'conversation for possibility'. The group acknowledges that it has come together to generate ideas, not to make decisions. The goal is to maximize creativity. Other meetings are built around a 'conversation for opportunity'. The goal is not to reach a final decision but to narrow down a field of ideas or options. You gather lots of information; you do some analysis; people take positions. Finally, there are meetings that are built around a 'conversation for action'. The goal is to decide, to commit: "We want to leave this room with our three investment priorities for 2008."

Unless everyone understands these distinctions, you run into certain familiar problems. You convene a brainstorming session (a 'conversation for possibility'), and people are afraid to speak up because someone might shoot down their idea—or worse, someone might say, 'Let's do it'. Or you convene a budgeting session (a 'conversation for action'), and someone loops back to an idea that was rejected earlier—which drives everyone else crazy. If you call a meeting, make it clear to people what kind of conversation they're going to have, and then impose a certain amount of discipline on them.

Most participants come to a meeting with clear expectations about how other people should act. And if the meeting lives up to such expectations, the participants will feel like they've had a really good experience. If the meeting violates those expectations, then people will become upset or withdrawn. So the key is to translate implicit expectations into explicit agreements—Do people feel strongly about starting and ending on time? Then make an explicit commitment to doing that. Are people concerned that a meeting doesn't have a clear enough objective? Then make an explicit promise: "If we can't agree on a clear objective within the first 10 minutes, then the meeting is over. We'll schedule another meeting when the objective becomes clear."

You can even create rules of engagement about individual behavior. For example: Before anyone makes a point, that person has to find merit in the point made by the previous speaker. Or, the senior people in the meeting can speak only after the junior people have had a chance to express themselves. It's a pretty simple idea, really. All you are trying to do is to make the invisible visible, to make the automatic deliberate. These rules of engagement take the bad behaviours that groups stumble into, shine a light on those behaviors, and then address basic questions: How can we change all of this? How do we want to act? Such rules of engagement give people a chance to design how they treat one another in meetings.

One last point about rules of engagement: You should be clear that not all successful meetings end with a decision. Decisions are the Valium of meetings. They offer relief from the tension of what lies ahead, from the uncertainty of the world. They tend to create an illusion of progress: “We’ve finally made a decision. Now we don’t have to worry about that issue anymore.” Often it takes courage for a group to end a meeting without making a decision.

There is a legitimate social component to meetings. Sure, we’d all rather be efficient than sloppy in our work. Sure, we’d all rather spend our time on ‘real work’ than on ‘idle chitchat’. But you should never overlook the social side of work rituals—even in meetings that are ‘all business’.

Remember, just because people walk into a conference room doesn’t mean that their mind is on your meeting. They may be thinking about an argument that they just had with a colleague, or about a computer glitch that they’ve been struggling with all day. If you let people express their frustrations before you get down to business, you allow them to clear their mind and to focus on your meeting.

There is much more to people—even serious businesspeople—than what’s above the neck. We are not just intellects that come together to interact with other intellects. The more you involve the whole person in your meetings, the more people will learn, and the more of that learning they will retain. If you want people to work together effectively, let them play together.

If you’re serious about improving the quality of your meetings, then you should borrow an idea from the quality people: continuous improvement. Set aside five minutes at the end of every meeting you hold—make it a discipline for your team or your company—and ask some simple questions: What did we do in this meeting that really worked well? What happened that we never want to repeat? Are there bad habits that we seem to keep falling into?

Write down people’s answers, keep a running record of their comments, and then see how well the entire group improves over time. A written record can also be a great source of ideas for future rules of engagement. It can tell you not just how to behave, but why people believe it’s important to behave that way.

But don't overdo this. The best medicine in the world can make you sick if you take too much of it. If you become too intent on improving meetings, you're likely to become the most dreaded person in your department:

One classic meeting dilemma is deciding how much to record. Michael Begeman's proposal: Don't worry too much about taking detailed minutes—that is, exhaustive notes about who said what. Focus instead on three categories of information: decisions reached, action items that people need to follow up on, and open issues. "The record of all this becomes input for future meetings," says Begeman. "Plus, encouraging people to use these categories will sharpen the quality of their participation."

Actions speak louder than rules. Leaders send nonverbal as well as verbal messages. So it's quite possible, says Michael Begeman, for your words to abide by the 'rules of engagement', for a meeting, while your informal actions don't. If you're leading a meeting and people expect you to move the group toward a decision, then act accordingly. Sit at the head of the table to signal, 'I'm in charge', Stand while others are sitting to signal, 'I have the floor'. If participants expect a collaborative meeting, ask one of your team members to run the meeting—to signal, 'I want to share leadership'. Or to signal, 'I'm with you', sit on one side of the table. All of this may sound obvious, but it's amasing how small, nonverbal behaviours can undermine—or promote—what you are trying to accomplish.

Meetings Management: Suggestions

Meeting management tends to be a set of skills often overlooked by leaders and managers. The following information is a rather 'Cadillac' version of meeting management suggestions. The reader might pick which suggestions best fits the particular culture of their own organisation. Keep in mind that meetings are very expensive activities when one considers the cost of labor for the meeting and how much can or cannot get done in them. So take meeting management very seriously.

The process used in a meeting depends on the kind of meeting you plan to have, e.g., staff meeting, planning meeting, problem solving meeting, etc. However, there are certain basics that are common to various types of meetings. These basics are described below. (Note that there may seem to be a lot of suggestions listed below for something as apparently simple as having a meeting. However, any important activity would include a long list of suggestions. The list seems to become much smaller once you master how to conduct the activity.)

Selecting Participants

(1) The decision about who is to attend depends on what you want to accomplish in the meeting. This may seem too obvious to state, but it's surprising how many meetings occur without the right people there.

(2) Don't depend on your own judgment about who should come. Ask several other people for their opinion as well.

(3) If possible, call each person to tell them about the meeting, it's overall purpose and why their attendance is important.

(4) Follow-up your call with a meeting notice, including the purpose of the meeting, where it will be held and when, the list of participants and whom to contact if they have questions.

(5) Send out a copy of the proposed agenda along with the meeting notice.

(6) Have someone designated to record important actions, assignments and due dates during the meeting. This person should ensure that this information is distributed to all participants shortly after the meeting.

Developing Agendas

(1) Develop the agenda together with key participants in the meeting. Think of what overall outcome you want from the meeting and what activities need to occur to reach that outcome. The agenda should be organized so that these activities are conducted during the meeting. In the agenda, state the overall outcome that you want from the meeting

(2) Design the agenda so that participants get involved early by having something for them to do right away and so they come on time.

(3) Next to each major topic, include the type of action needed, the type of output expected (decision, vote, action assigned to someone), and time estimates for addressing each topic.

(4) Ask participants if they'll commit to the agenda.

(5) Keep the agenda posted at all times.

(6) Don't overly design meetings; be willing to adapt the meeting agenda if members are making progress in the planning process.

(7) Think about how you label an event, so people come in with that mindset; it may pay to have a short dialogue around the label to develop a common mindset among attendees, particularly if they include representatives from various cultures.

Opening Meetings

(1) Always start on time; this respects those who showed up on time and reminds late-comers that the scheduling is serious.

(2) Welcome attendees and thank them for their time.

(3) Review the agenda at the beginning of each meeting, giving participants a chance to understand all proposed major topics, change them and accept them.

(4) Note that a meeting recorder if used will take minutes and provide them back to each participant shortly after the meeting.
(5) Model the kind of energy and participant needed by meeting participants.
(6) Clarify your role(s) in the meeting.

Establishing Ground Rules for Meetings

(1) You don't need to develop new ground rules each time you have a meeting, surely. However, it pays to have a few basic ground rules that can be used for most of your meetings. These ground rules cultivate the basic ingredients needed for a successful meeting.
(2) Four powerful ground rules are: participate, get focus, maintain momentum and reach closure. (You may want a ground rule about confidentiality.)
(3) List your primary ground rules on the agenda.
(4) If you have new attendees who are not used to your meetings, you might review *each* ground rule.
(5) Keep the ground rules posted at all times.

Time Management

(1) One of the most difficult facilitation tasks is time management—time seems to run out before tasks are completed. Therefore, the biggest challenge is keeping momentum to keep the process moving.
(2) You might ask attendees to help you keep track of the time.
(3) If the planned time on the agenda is getting out of hand, present it to the group and ask for their input as to a resolution.

Evaluations of Meeting Process

(1) It's amazing how often people will complain about a meeting

being a complete waste of time—but they only say so after the meeting. Get their feedback during the meeting when you can improve the meeting process right away. Evaluating a meeting only at the end of the meeting is usually too late to do anything about participants' feedback.

(2) Every couple of hours, conduct 5-10 minutes 'satisfaction checks'.

(3) In a round-table approach, quickly have each participant indicate how they think the meeting is going.

Evaluating the Overall Meeting

(1) Leave 5-10 minutes at the end of the meeting to evaluate the meeting; don't skip this portion of the meeting.

(2) Have each member rank the meeting from 1-5, with 5 as the highest, and have each member explain their ranking.

(3) Have the chief executive rank the meeting last.

Closing Meetings

(1) Always end meetings on time and attempt to end on a positive note.

(2) At the end of a meeting, review actions and assignments, and set the time for the next meeting and ask each person if they can make it or not (to get their commitment).

(3) Clarify that meeting minutes and/or actions will be reported back to members in at most a week (this helps to keep momentum going).

Confrontations

When you have a difficult encounter, be professional, do not lose your self-control because, simply, it is of no use. Some managers believe that it is useful for 'discipline' to keep staff a little nervous. Thus, these managers are slightly volatile and will be willing 'to let them have it' when the situation demands. If you do this, you must be consistent *and fair* so that you staff know where they stand. If you deliberately lose your temper for effect, then that is your decision—however, you must never lose control.

Insults are ineffective. If you call people names, then they are unlikely to actually listen to what you have to say; in the short term you may feel some relief at "getting it off your chest", but in the long run you are merely perpetuating the problem since you are not addressing it. This is common sense. There are two implications. Firstly, even under pressure, you have to remember this. Secondly, what you consider fair comment may be insulting to another—and the same problem emerges. Before you say anything, stop, establish what you want as the outcome, plan how to achieve this, and then speak.

Finally, if you are going to criticise or discipline someone, always assume that you have misunderstood the situation and ask questions first which check the facts. This simple courtesy will save you from much embarrassment.

Seeking Information

There are two ways of phrasing any question: one way (the closed question) is likely to lead to a simple grunt in reply (yes, no, maybe), the second way (the open question) will hand over the speaking role to someone else and force them to say something a little more informative.

Suppose you conduct a review of a recently finished (?) project with Mr. X and it goes something like this:

(1) "Have you finished project Mr. X?"
(2) "Yes".
(3) "If everything written up?"
(4) "Nearly".
(5) "So there is documentation left to do?"
(6) "Some".

(7) "Will it take you long?"
(8) "No, not long".

Before your fingers start twitching to place themselves around Mr. X neck, consider that your questions are not actually helping the flow of information. The same flow of questions in an *open* format would be: what is left to do of project, what about the documentation, when will that be completely finished? Try answering Yes or No to those questions. Open questions are extremely easy to formulate. You establish in your own mind the topic/aim of the question and then you start the sentence with the words:

Let Others Speak and Finish

Of course, there is more to a conversation (managed or otherwise) than the flow of information. You may also have to win that information by winning the attention and confidence of the other person. There are many forms of flattery—the most effective is to give people your interest. To get Mr. X to give you all knowledge, you must give him all your attention; talk to her about him view on the subject. Ask questions: what do you think about that idea, have you ever met this problem before, how would you tackle this situation?

Silence is effective—and much under-used. People are nervous of silence and try to fill it. You can use this if you are seeking information. You ask the question, you lean back, the person answers, you nod and smile, you keep quiet, and the person continues with more detail simply to fill your silence.

At the end of a conversation, you have to give people a clear understanding of the outcome. For instance, if there has been a decision, restate it clearly (just to be sure) in terms of what should happen and by when; if you have been asking questions, summarise the significant (for you) aspects of what you have learnt.

Preparation for Meeting Management

In any organisation, 'meetings' are a vital part of the organisation of work and the flow of information. They act as a mechanism for gathering together resources from many sources and pooling then towards a common objective. They are disliked and mocked because they are usually futile, boring, time-wasting, dull, and inconvenient with nothing for most people to do except doodle while some opinionated has-been extols the virtues of his/her last great (misunderstood) idea. Your challenge is to break this mould and to make your meetings effective. As with every other managed activity, meetings should be planned beforehand, monitored during for effectiveness, and reviewed afterwards for improving their management.

A meeting is the ultimate form of managed conversation; as a manager, you can organise the information and structure of the meeting to support the effective communication of the participants. Some of the ideas below may seem a little too precise for an easy going, relaxed, semi-informal team atmosphere—but if you manage to gain a reputation for holding decisive, effective meetings, then people will value this efficiency and to prepare professionally so that their contribution will be heard.

As with all conversations, you must first ask: is it worth your time? If the meeting involves the interchange of views and the communication of the current status of related projects, then you should be generous with your time. But you should always consider cancelling a meeting which has little tangible value.

Participants

You must be strict. A meeting loses its effectiveness if too many people are involved: so if someone has no useful function, explain this and suggest that they do not come. Notice, they may disagree with your assessment, in which case they should attend (since they may know something you do not); however, most people are only too happy to be released from yet another meeting.

Duration

It may seem difficult to predict the length of a discussion - but you must. Discussions tend to fill the available time which means that if the meeting is open-ended, it will drift on forever. You should stipulate a time for the end of the meeting so that everyone knows, and everyone can plan the rest of their day with confidence.

It is wise to make this expectation known to everyone involved well in advance and to remind them at the beginning of the meeting. There is often a tendency to view meetings as a little relaxation since no one person has to be active throughout. You can redress this view by stressing the time-scale and thus forcing the pace of the discussion: "this is what we have to achieve, this is how long we have to get it done."

If some unexpected point arises during the meeting then realise that since it is unexpected: (1) you might not have the right people present, (2) those there may not have the necessary information, and (3) a little thought might save a lot of discussion. If the new discussion looks likely to be more than a few moments, stop it and deal with the agreed agenda. The new topic should then be dealt with at another 'planned' meeting.

Subject/Agenda

The purpose of an agenda is to inform participants of the subject of the meeting in advance, and to structure the discussion at the meeting itself. To inform people beforehand, and to solicit ideas, you should circulate a draft agenda and ask for notice of any other business. Still before the meeting, you should then send the revised agenda with enough time for people to prepare their contributions. If you know in advance that a particular participant either needs information or will be providing information, then make this explicitly clear so that there is no confusion.

The agenda states the purpose of each section of the meeting. There will be an outcome from each section. If that outcome is so complex that it can not be summarised in a few points, then it was probably too complex to be assimilated by the participants. The understanding of the meeting should be sufficiently precise that it can be summarised in short form—so display that summary for all other interested parties to see. This form of display will emphasize to all that meetings are about achieving defined goals—this will help you to continue running efficient meetings in the future.

Conduction of Metting

Whether you actually sit as the Chair or simply lead from the side-lines, as the manager you must provide the necessary support to coordinate the contributions of the participants. The degree of control which you exercise over the meeting will vary throughout; if you get the structure right at the beginning, a meeting can effectively run itself especially if the participants know each other well. In a team, your role may be partially undertaken by others; but if not, you must manage.

Maintaining Communication

Your most important tools are:

(1) *Clarification*—always clarify: the purpose of the meeting, the time allowed, the rules to be observed (if agreed) by everyone.

(2) *Summary*—at each stage of the proceedings, you should summarize the current position and progress: this is what we have achieved/agreed, this is where we have reached.

(3) *Focus on stated goals*—at each divergence or pause, re-focus the proceedings on the original goals.

Code of Conduct

In any meeting, it is possible to begin the proceedings by establishing a code of conduct, often by merely stating it and asking for any objections (which will only be accepted if a demonstrably better system is proposed). Thus if the group contains opinionated wind-bags, you might all agree at the onset that all contributions should be limited to two minutes (which focuses the mind admirably). You can then impose this with the full backing of the whole group.

Matching with to Purpose

The (stated) purpose of a meeting may suggest to you a specific way of conducting the event, and each section might be conducted differently. For instance, if the purpose is:

- To convey information, the meeting might begin with a formal presentation followed by questions
- To seek information, the meeting would start with a short (clear) statement of the topic/problem and then an open discussion supported by notes on a display, or a formal brainstorming session
- To make a decision, the meeting might review the background and options, *establish the criteria* to be applied, agree who should make the decision and how, and then do it
- To ratify/explain decisions, etc.

As always, once you have paused to ask yourself the questions: what is the purpose of the meeting and how can it be most effectively achieved; your common sense will then suggest a working method to expedite the proceedings. You just have to deliberately pause. Manage the process of the meeting and the meeting will work.

Support

The success of a meeting will often depend upon the confidence with which the individuals will participate. Thus all ideas should be welcome. No one should be laughed at or dismissed ('laughed with' is good, 'laughed at' is destructive). This means that even bad ideas should be treated seriously—and at least merit a specific reason for not being pursued further. Not only is this supportive to the speaker, it could also be that a good idea has been misunderstood and would be lost if merely rejected. But basically people should be able to make naive contributions without being made to feel stupid, otherwise you may never hear the best ideas of all.

Avoid direct criticism of any person. For instance, if someone has not come prepared then that fault is obvious to all. If you leave the criticism as being simply that implicit in the peer pressure, then it is diffuse and general; if you explicitly rebuke that person, then it is personal and from you (which may raise unnecessary conflict). You should merely seek an undertaking for the missing preparation to be done: we need to know this before we can proceed, could you circulate it to us by tomorrow lunch?

Concluding Remarks

You need to communicate to coordinate your own work and that of others; without explicit effort your conversation will lack communication and so your work too will collapse though misunderstanding and error. The key is to treat a conversation as you would any other managed activity: by establishing an aim, planning what to do, and checking afterwards that you have achieved that aim. Only in this way can you work effectively with others in building through common effort.

Richard Collard, senior manager of network operations at Federal Express, is simply exasperated: "We just seem to meet and meet and meet and we never seem to do anything."

Meetings are the most universal—and universally despised—

part of business life. But bad meetings do more than ruin an otherwise pleasant day.

A variety of tools and techniques (plus a healthy dose of common sense) can make meetings less painful, more productive, may be even fun. There's also an important role for technology, although the undeniable power of computer-enabled meeting systems usually comes with astronomical price tags. Still, there's lots to learn from electronic 'meetingware' even if you never buy it.

Board Meetings, Meeting Process, Retreats, etc.

Members of the Board do their work, primarily in their Board meetings. Thus, these meetings should be carefully planned, facilitated and documented. Meetings can be highly participative with very focused deliberations that result in strong, strategic decisions—decisions that are captured in meeting minutes and then closely monitored for implementation. Or, meetings can drag on with only some members participating—participating in spotted discussions about whatever topic was first brought up in the meeting. It's often the most dedicated Board members who become frustrated with these unproductive Board meetings and soon leave the organisation, leaving the rest of the members to continue this ineffective approach to Board governance.

One of the most effective ways to accomplish productive meetings—and strong governance—is to carefully design an agenda and then closely facilitate to that agenda. Agendas should include (1) strategic topics to address in that meeting, (2) specification of how each topic is to be addressed in that meeting (for example, to make a decision, assign further research, etc.), and (3) specific times to address each topic. Without that careful design and facilitation of the agenda, Board meetings too often result in prolonged confusion and frustration of members — and overall ineffective governance of the organisation.

Effective Committees

Committees are often the working force at the heart of an organisation. Effective organisations are often directly related to effective committees.

They are used to save time at general meetings. Matters can be discussed and reviewed in detail by a committee and recommendations brought to the general meeting. The work of the organisation becomes more efficient. The specialised skills and interests of members are used to their full advantage. More members get involved in the detail work of the organisation. Responsibilities are shared according to skills and interests of members. New or inexperienced members can gain valuable insight into the organisation and develop confidence by serving on committees.

There are two basic kinds of committees:

(1) *Standing*: Committees are created by the standing orders, rules, by-laws, or regulations of an organisation. They function on a permanent basis. Examples of common standing committees would be finance, nomination, education, etc.

(2) *Ad Hoc*: Committees are appointed for a specific purpose on a short-term basis. An example is organising an educational event.

Many organisations have too many committees, often with unclear responsibilities. You should be able to answer the following before any committee is established:

(1) What's the purpose and authority of this committee?

(2) What are the responsibilities and specific tasks of this committee?

(3) What are the time limits on this committee?

(4) What type of reporting to the organisation is expected?

(5) How are members picked for this committee?
(6) What's the budget of this committee?
(7) What's the term of office for members? How do we fill vacancies?
(8) What resources does this committee have and what will it need to complete it's task?

The committee's terms of reference should be written and included in the organisation's policies or recorded in a motion. These terms of reference are available to all organisation members.

Selecting committee members is the best way to ensure that you get the people with the right skills, interests and commitment to the task. Three to seven people is a good size for most committees.

Committees are directly responsible to the organisation that created them. The committee chair usually reports to the general meeting. Reports should be concise, but should show that a full discussion was held and all options were considered. The organisation should never feel that the committee missed something. The committee should present specific recommendations. Reports that are for information only don't require a motion. If a committee wants to bring ideas, actions or recommendations to the members through their report, the committee chair should say, "By direction of the committee, I move . . . ."

8

Tools and Skills of Project Management

Introduction

This chapter discusses some of the specific skills you will need to run projects successfully. It concentrates on two main areas: scheduling skills, including use of Gantt Charts and Critical Path Analysis, and overall project planning following the planning cycle.

We look at these tools:

- Estimating time accurately
- Time planning for small and medium sized projects—Gantt Charts
- Time planning for large, complex projects
- Critical Path Analysis and PERT
- Effective planning for middle-sized projects—the planning cycle
- Planning large projects—using planning and management methodologies
- Winning support for your projects—stakeholder analysis.

Going through the chapter you whould understand how to plan and schedule small and middle-sized projects. You will know how to complete them on time and on budget. While running a project you will know which jobs are most important, and which deadlines are most important to meet. You will also be able to decide when to take remedial action to bring a project back on course. These skills are perfectly sufficient for running small and medium-sized projects. As projects become larger, however, a pragmatic general management approach can often be overwhelmed by the sheer complexity of the projects being run. Larger projects benefit from formal, methodology-based project and programme management. This is a specialism in its own right.

Estimating Time Accurately

Accurate time estimation is a skill essential to good project management. It is important to get time estimates right for two main reasons:

(1) Time estimates drive the setting of deadlines for delivery of projects, and hence peoples' assessments of your reliability.

(2) They often determine the pricing of contracts and hence their profitability.

Usually people vastly underestimate the amount of time needed to implement projects. This is true particularly when they are not familiar with the task to be carried out. They forget to take into account unexpected events or unscheduled high priority work. People also often simply fail to allow for the full complexity involved with a job.

This section discusses how to estimate time on small projects. Time estimates are important inputs into the other techniques used to organise and structure medium and large sized projects (Gantt charts and use of Critical Path Analysis). Both of these techniques reduce large projects down into a set of small projects.

The first stage in estimating time accurately is to fully understand what you need to achieve. This involves reviewing the task in detail so that there are no unknowns. Inevitably it is the difficult-to-understand, tricky problems that take the greatest amount of time to solve. The best way to review the job is to list all tasks in full detail. Simple techniques such as Drill Down are useful for this.

Breaking Problems Down into Manageable Parts

How to Use Tool

Drill Down is a simple technique for breaking complex problems down into progressively smaller parts. To use the technique, start by writing the problem down on the left-hand side of a large sheet of paper. Next, write down the points that make up the next level of detail on the problem a little to the right of this. These may be factors contributing to the problem, information relating to it, or questions raised by it. This process of breaking the problem down into its component part is called 'drilling down'. For each of these points, repeat the process.

Keep on drilling down into points until you fully understand the factors contributing to the problem. If you cannot break them down using the knowledge you have, then carry out whatever research is necessary to understand the point.

Drilling into a question helps you to get a much deeper understanding of it. The process helps you to recognise and understand the factors that contribute to it. Drill Down prompts you to link in information that you had not initially associated with a problem. It also shows exactly where you need further information.

For example, the owner of a windsurfing club is having complaints from its members about the unpleasant quality of the water close to the clubhouse. This seems like a huge problem. She carries out the analysis in Figure 1. This gives her a starting point in which to begin thinking about the problem. It highlights where she does not fully understand the problem, and shows where she needs to carry out further research.

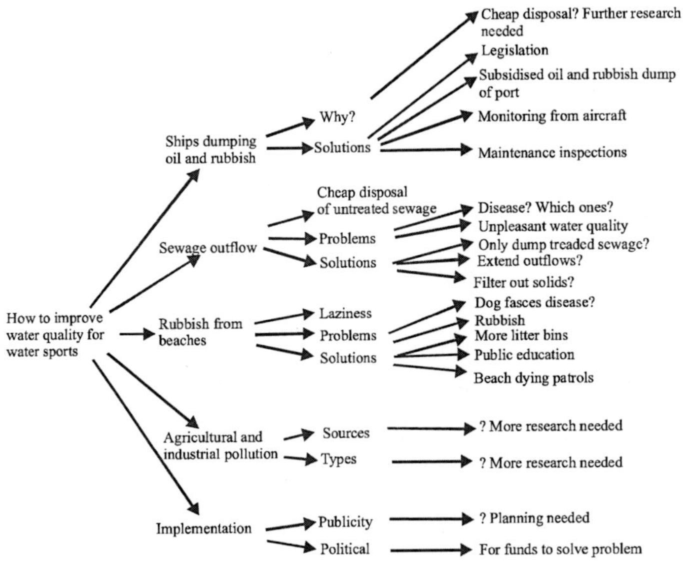

Figure 1: Drill Down into Problem of Improving Quality of Sea Water

Main Points

'Drill Down' helps you to break a large and complex problem down into its component parts, so that you can develop plans to deal with these parts. It also shows you which points you need to research in more detail.

Estimating Time

You can only start to estimate time accurately when you have a detailed list of all the tasks that you must achieve. When you have this, you can make your best guess at how long each task will take to complete. Ensure that within your estimate you also allow time for project management, detailed project planning, liaison with outside bodies, meetings, quality assurance and any supporting documentation necessary. Also make sure that you have allowed time for:

- Other high urgency tasks to be carried out which will have priority over this one
- Accidents and emergencies
- Internal meetings
- Holidays and sickness in essential staff
- Contact with other customers, perhaps to arrange the next job
- Breakdowns in equipment
- Missed deliveries by suppliers
- Interruptions
- Quality control rejections.

These factors may double (or more than double) the length of time needed to complete a project. If the accuracy of time estimates is critical, you may find it effective to develop a systematic approach to including these factors. If possible, base this on past experience.

Main Points

You can lose a great deal of credibility by underestimating the length of time needed to implement a project. If you underestimate time, not only do you miss deadlines, you also put other project workers under unnecessary stress. Projects will become seriously unprofitable, and other tasks cannot be started.

The first step towards making good time estimates is to fully understand the problem to be solved.

You can then prepare a detailed list of tasks that must be

achieved. This list should include all the administrative tasks and meetings you need to carry out as well as the work itself. Finally, allow time for all the expected and unexpected disruptions and delays to work that will inevitably happen.

How to Schedule Simple Projects

Simple projects involve only one or a few people over a short time. Typically, simple projects will have few tasks dependent on other tasks, and will be relatively simple and easy to coordinate. Examples might be coordinating delivery of resources for a workshop session, implementing a small marketing plan, or delivering a simple software enhancement.

With simple projects, tools like Gantt Charts and Critical Path Diagrams may overcomplicate project scheduling and communication. Unless project team members are trained in their use, they can often 'blind people with science', leading to poor communication and muddled projects.

Appropriate timetables and action plans are often sufficient to coordinate and implement simple projects. These should be explained and negotiated with project staff to improve the plans and get staff understanding, input and buy-in.

Small Scale Planning Action Plans

How to Use Tool

An action plan is a list of tasks that you have to carry out to achieve an objective. It differs from a To-Do List in that it focuses on the achievement of a single goal. Wherever you want to achieve something, draw up an action plan. This allows you to concentrate on the stages of that achievement, and monitor your progress towards it. To draw up an action plan, simply list the tasks that you need to carry out to achieve your goal. This is simple, but still very useful!

Main Points

An action plan is a list of things that you need to do to achieve a goal. To use it, simply carry out each task in the list! It will often be enough to create a workback schedule, starting from the date by which the project must be completed, and listing all of the tasks in reverse order with due dates for each.

How to Remember All Essential Jobs, in the Right Order

How to Use Tool

A 'To-Do List' is a list of all the tasks that you need to carry out. It consolidates all the jobs that you have to do into one place. You can then prioritise these tasks into order of importance. This allows you to tackle the most important ones first.

To-Do Lists are essential when you need to carry out a number of different tasks or different sorts of task, or when you have made a number of commitments. If you find that you are often caught out because you have forgotten to do something, then you need to keep a To-Do List.

Whilst To-Do Lists are very simple, they are also extremely powerful, both as a method of organising yourself and as a way of reducing stress. Often problems may seem overwhelming or you may have a seemingly huge number of demands on your time. This may leave you feeling out of control, and overburdened with work.

Maining a To-Do List

The solution is often simple: Write down the tasks that face you, and if they are large, break them down into their component elements. If these still seem large, break them down again. Do this until you have listed everything that you have to do. Once you have done this, run through these jobs allocating priorities from A (very important) to F (unimportant). If too many tasks have a high priority, run through the list again and demote the less important ones. Once you have done this, rewrite the list in priority order.

You will then have a precise plan that you can use to eliminate the problems you face. You will be able to tackle these in order of importance. This allows you to separate important jobs from the many time-consuming trivial ones.

How to Use To-Do Lists

Different people use To-Do Lists in different ways in different situations: if you are in a sales-type role, a good way of motivating yourself is to keep your list relatively short and aim to complete it every day. In an operational role, or if tasks are large or dependent on too many other people, then it may be better to keep one list and 'chip away' at it.

It may be that you carry unimportant jobs from one To-Do List to the next. You may not be able to complete some very low priority jobs for several months. Only worry about this if you need to—if you are running up against a deadline for them, raise their priority.

If you have not used To-Do Lists before, try them now, as they are one of the keys to being really productive and efficient.

Main Points

Prioritised To-Do Lists are fundamentally important to efficient work. If you use To-Do Lists, you will ensure that:

- You remember to carry out all necessary tasks
- You tackle the most important jobs first, and do not waste time on trivial tasks
- You do not get stressed by a large number of unimportant jobs.

To draw up a prioritised To-Do List, list all the tasks you must carry out. Mark the importance of the task next to it, with a priority from A (very important) to F (unimportant). Redraft the list into this order of importance.

Now carry out the jobs at the top of the list first. These are the most important, most beneficial tasks to complete. Simple projects are often best run using simple timetables and action plans. These should be prepared and negotiated with project staff to improve plans and get buy-in.

During the project these will contain sufficient control points and deliveries to monitor project progress and take any appropriate remedial action.

Planning and Scheduling more Complex Projects Gantt Charts

How to Use Tool

Gantt Charts (Gant Charts) are useful tools for analyzing and planning more complex projects. They:

- Help you to plan out the tasks that need to be completed
- Give you a basis for scheduling when these tasks will be carried out
- Allow you to plan the allocation of resources needed to complete the project
- Help you to work out the critical path for a project where you must complete it by a particular date.

When a project is under way, Gantt Charts help you to monitor whether the project is on schedule. If it is not, it allows you to pinpoint the remedial action necessary to put it back on schedule.

Sequential and Parallel Activities

An essential concept behind project planning (and Critical Path Analysis) is that some activities are dependent on other activities being completed first. As a shallow example, it is not a good idea to start building a bridge before you have designed it! These dependent activities need to be completed in a sequence, with each stage being more-or-less completed before the next activity can begin. We can call dependent activities 'sequential'. Other activities are not dependent on completion of any other tasks. These may be done at any time before or after a particular stage is reached. These are nondependent or 'parallel' tasks.

Drawing a Gantt Chart

To draw up a Gantt diagram (Gant diagram), follow these steps:

(1) *List all activities in the plan*: For each task, show the earliest start date, estimated length of time it will take, and whether it is parallel or sequential. If tasks are sequential, show which stages they depend on. You will end up with a task list like the one in Figure 2. This example shows the task list for a custom-written computer project. We will use this same example for both this section and the section on Critical Path Analysis and PERT. This will allow you to compare the results of the two approaches.

Figure 2: Gantt Chart Example: Planning a Custom-written Computer Project

NB: The start week shows when resources become available. Whether a task is parallel or sequential depends largely on context.

Task	*Possible Start*	*Length*	*Type*	*Dependent on...*
1. High level analysis	week 1	5 days	sequential	
2. Selection of hardware platform	week 1	1 day	sequential	1
3. Installation and commissioning of hardware	week 3	2 weeks	parallel	2
4. Detailed analysis of core modules	week 1	2 weeks	sequential	1

5. Detailed analysis of supporting utilities	week 1	2 weeks	sequential	4
6. Programming of core modules	week 4	3 weeks	sequential	4
7. Programming of supporting modules	week 4	3 weeks	sequential	5
8. Quality assurance of core modules	week 5	1 week	sequential	6
9. Quality assurance of supporting modules	week 5	1 week	sequential	7
10. Core module training	week 7	1 day	parallel	6
11. Development of accounting reporting	week 6	1 week	parallel	5
12. Development of management reporting	week 6	1 week	parallel	5
13. Development of management analysis	week 6	2 weeks	sequential	5
14. Detailed training	week 7	1 week	sequential	1-13
15. Documentation	week 4	2 weeks	parallel	13

(2) Head up graph paper with the days or weeks through to task completion.

(3) Plot the tasks onto the graph paper. Next draw up a rough draft of the Gantt Chart. Plot each task on the graph paper, showing it starting on the earliest possible date. Draw it as a bar, with the length of the bar being the length of the task. Above the task bars, mark the time taken to complete them. Do not worry about task scheduling yet. All you are doing is setting up the first draft of the analysis.

(4) *Schedule activities*: Now take the draft Gantt Chart, and use it to schedule actions. Schedule them in such a way that sequential actions are carried out in the required sequence. Ensure that dependent activities do not start until the activities they depend on have been completed. Where possible, schedule parallel tasks so that they do not interfere with sequential actions on the critical path. While

scheduling, ensure that you make best use of the resources you have available, and do not over-commit resource. Also allow some slack time in the schedule for holdups, overruns, quality rejections, failures in delivery, etc.

(5) *Presenting the analysis*: The final stage in this process is to prepare a final version of the Gantt Chart. This should combine the draft analysis (see above) with your scheduling and analysis of resources. This chart will show when you anticipate that jobs should start and finish.

By drawing this example Gantt Chart, you can see that:

(1) If all goes well, the project can be completed in 10 weeks.

(2) If you want to complete the task as rapidly as possible, you need:

- 1 analyst for the first 5 weeks
- 1 programmer for 6 weeks starting week 4
- 1 programmer for 3 weeks starting week 6
- Quality assurance resource for weeks 7 and 9
- Hardware to be installed by the end of week 7.

(3) Analysis, development and installation of supporting modules are essential activities that must be completed on time.

(4) Hardware installation is a low priority task as long as it is completed by the end of week 7.

While this section describes how to draw a Gantt Chart manually, in practice project managers tend to use software tools like Microsoft Project to create Gantt Charts. Not only do these ease the drawing of Gantt Charts, they also make modification of plans easier and provide facilities for monitoring progress against plans, as well as generating resource histograms.

Main Points

Gantt Charts are useful tools for planning and scheduling projects. They allow you to assess how long a project should take, determine the resources needed, and lay out the order in which tasks need to be carried out. They are useful in managing the dependencies between tasks.

When a project is under way, Gantt Charts are useful for monitoring its progress. You can immediately see what should have been achieved at a point in time, and can therefore take remedial action to bring the project back on course. This can be essential for the successful and profitable implementation of the project.

Most project managers use tools such as Microsoft Project to build and manage Gantt Charts. The software can also calculate resource histograms that correspond to the project activities.

Critical Path Analysis and PERT Charts

Critical Path Analysis and PERT are powerful tools that help you to schedule and manage complex projects. They were developed in the 1950s to control large defence projects, and have been used routinely since then. As with Gantt Charts, Critical Path Analysis (CPA) helps you to plan all tasks that must be completed as part of a project. They act as the basis both for preparation of a schedule, and of resource planning. During management of a project, they allow you to monitor achievement of project goals. They help you to see where remedial action needs to be taken to get a project back on course.

The benefit of using CPA over Gantt Charts is that Critical Path Analysis formally identifies tasks which must be completed on time for the whole project to be completed on time, and also identifies which tasks can be delayed for a while if resource needs to be reallocated to catch up on missed tasks. The disadvantage of CPA is that the relation of tasks to time is not as immediately obvious as with Gantt Charts. This can make them more difficult to understand for someone who is not familiar with the technique.

A further benefit of Critical Path Analysis is that it helps you to identify the minimum length of time needed to complete a project. Where you need to run an accelerated project, it helps you to identify which project steps you should accelerate to complete the project within the available time. This helps you to minimise cost while still achieving your objective.

As with Gantt Charts, the essential concept behind Critical Path Analysis is that you cannot start some activities until others are finished. These activities need to be completed in a sequence, with each stage being more-or-less completed before the next stage can begin. These are 'sequential' activities.

Other activities are not dependent on completion of any other tasks. You can do these at any time before or after a particular stage is reached. These are non-dependent or 'parallel' tasks.

Steps in Drawing a Critical Path Analysis Chart

List All Activities in the Plan

For each activity, show the earliest start date, estimated length of time it will take, and whether it is parallel or sequential. If tasks are sequential, show which stage they depend on. For the project example used here, you will end up with the same task list as explained in the article on Gantt Charts (we will use the same example as with Gantt Charts to compare the two techniques).

Plot the Activities as a Circle and Arrow Diagram

Critical Path Analyses are presented using circle and arrow diagrams. In these, circles show events within the project, such as the start and finish of tasks. Circles are normally numbered to allow you to identify them. An arrow running between two event circles shows the activity needed to complete that task. A description of the task is written underneath the arrow. The length of the task is shown above it. By convention, all arrows run left to right.

An example of a very simple diagram is shown below:

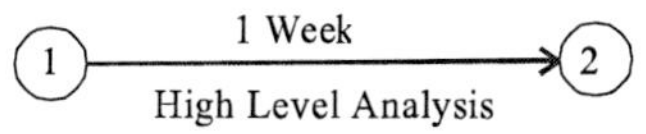

Figure 2: Simple Circle and Arrow Diagram

This shows the start event (circle 1), and the completion of the 'High Level Analysis' task (circle 2). The arrow between them shows the activity of carrying out the High Level Analysis. This activity should take 1 week.

Where one activity cannot start until another has been completed, we start the arrow for the dependent activity at the completion event circle of the previous activity. An example of this is shown below:

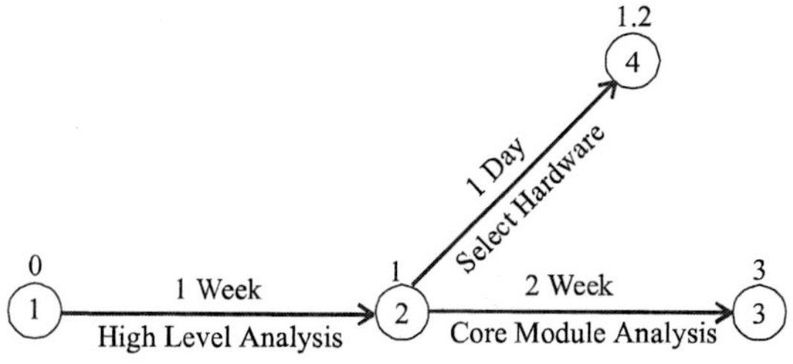

Figure 3: Circle and Arrow Diagram Showing on Activities that cannot Started until the Fist Activity has been Completed

Here the activities of 'Selecting Hardware' and 'Core Module Analysis' cannot be started until 'High Level Analysis' has been completed. This diagram also brings out a number of other important points:

(1) Within Critical Path Analysis, we refer to activities by the numbers in the circles at each end. For example, the task 'Core Module Analysis' would be called 'activity 2 to 3'. 'Select Hardware' would be 'activity 2 to 4'.

(2) Activities are not drawn to scale. In the diagram above, activities are 1 week long, 2 weeks long, and 1 day long. Arrows in this case are all the same length.

In the example above, you can see numbers above the circles. These show the earliest possible time that this stage in the project will be reached. Here units are whole weeks.

A different case is shown below:

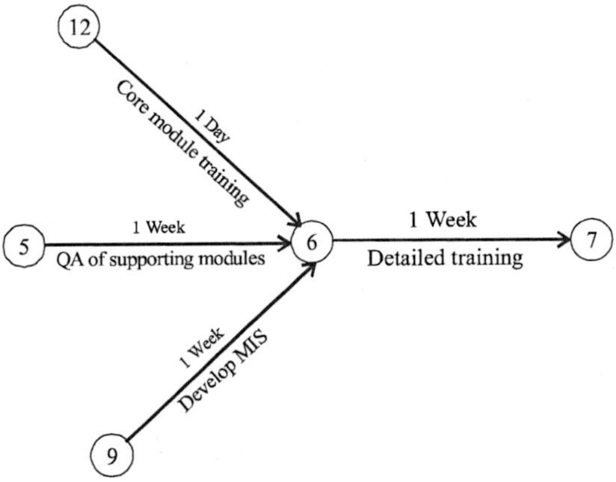

Figure 5: Circle and Arrow Diagram Showing on Activity (6 to 7) that cannot Start until other Activities (12 t 6, 5 to 6, and 9 to 6)

Here activity 6 to 7 cannot start until the other three activities (12 to 6, 5 to 6 and 9 to 6) have been completed.

See Figure 6 for the full circle and arrow diagram for the computer project we are using as an example.

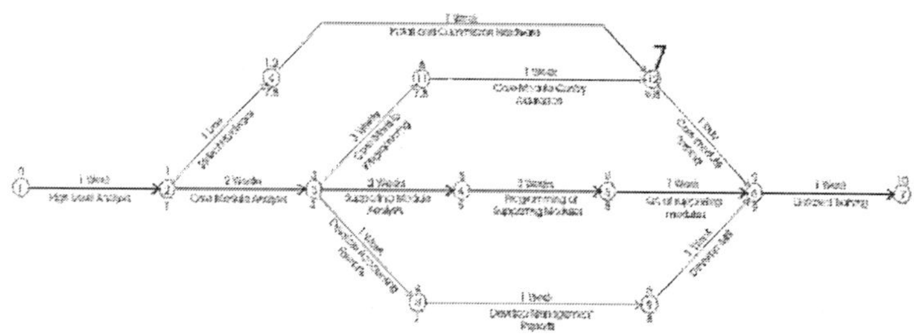

Figure 6: Critical Path Analysis for Example Computer Project

This shows all the activities that will take place as part of the project. Notice that each event circle has a figure below it as well as a figure above. This shows the latest time that it can be reached with the project still being completed in the minimum time possible. You can calculate this by starting at the last event (in this case number 7), and working backwards.

You can see that event 4 can be completed any time between 1.2 weeks in and 7.8 weeks in. The timing of this event is not critical. Events 1 to 2, 2 to 3, 3 to 4, 4 to 5, 5 to 6 and 6 to 7 must be started and completed on time if the project is to be completed in 10 weeks. This is the 'critical path'—these activities must be very closely managed to ensure that activities are completed on time. If jobs on the critical path slip, immediate action should be taken to get the project back on schedule. Otherwise completion of the whole project will slip.

'Crash Action'

You may find that you need to complete a project earlier than your Critical Path Analysis says is possible. In this case you need to take action to reduce the length of time spent on project stages. You could pile resources into every project activity to bring down time spent on each. This would probably consume huge additional resources. A more efficient way of doing this would be to look only at activities on the critical path.

As an example, it may be necessary to complete the computer project in Figure 6 in 8 weeks rather than 10 weeks. In this case you could look at using two analysts in steps '2 to 3' and '3 to 4', and two programmers instead of one in step '4 to 5'. This would shorten the project by two weeks, but would raise the project cost—doubling resources at any stage often only improves productivity by, say, 50%. This occurs as time spent on coordinating the project consumes time gained by increasing resource.

Note that in this example, shortening the project by two weeks brings activities '3 to 11', '11 to 12' and '12 to 6' onto the critical path as well.

As with Gantt Charts, in practice project managers tend to use software tools like Microsoft Project to create CPA Charts. Not only do these ease make them easier to draw, they also make modification of plans easier and provide facilities for monitoring progress against plans. Microsoft Project is reviewed at the top of our left hand title bar.

PERT (Programme Evaluation and Review Technique)

PERT is a variation on Critical Path Analysis that takes a slightly more skeptical view of time estimates made for each project stage. To use it, estimate the shortest possible time each activity will take, the most likely length of time, and the longest time that might be taken if the activity takes longer than expected.

Use the formula below to calculate the time to use for each project stage:

$$\frac{\text{Shortest time} + 4 \times \text{likely time} + \text{longest time}}{6}$$

This helps to bias time estimates away from the unrealistically short time-scales normally assumed.

Main Points

Critical Path Analysis is an effective and powerful method of assessing:

- What tasks must be carried out
- Where parallel activity can be performed
- The shortest time in which you can complete a project
- Resources needed to execute a project
- The sequence of activities, scheduling and timings involved
- Task priorities
- The most efficient way of shortening time on urgent projects.

An effective Critical Path Analysis can make the difference between success and failure on complex projects. It can be very useful for assessing the importance of problems faced during the implementation of the plan. PERT is a variant of Critical Path Analysis that takes a more skeptical view of the time needed to complete each project stage.

The Planning Cycle

Planning Process for Middle-Sized Projects

The planning cycle brings together all aspects of planning into a coherent, unified process.

By planning within this structure, you will help to ensure that your plans are fully considered, well focused, resilient, practical and cost-effective. You will also ensure that you learn from any mistakes you make, and feed this back into future planning and decision making.

Planning using this cycle will help you to plan and manage ongoing projects up to a certain level of complexity—this will depend on the circumstance. For projects involving many people over a long period of time, more formal methodologies and approaches are necessary. It is best to think of planning as a cycle, not a straight through process. Once you have devised a plan you should evaluate whether it is likely to succeed. This evaluation may be cost or number based, or may use other analytical tools. This analysis may show that your plan may cause unwanted consequences, may cost too much, or may simply not work.

In this case you should cycle back to an earlier stage. Alternatively you may have to abandon the plan altogether—the outcome of the planning process may be that it is best to do nothing! Finally, you should feed back what you have learned with one plan into the next.

Steges in Planning Cycle

Analysis of Opportunities

The first thing to do is to do is to spot what needs to be done. You will crystallize this into a formal aim at the next stage in the process.

One approach to this is to examine your current position, and decide how you can improve it. There are a number of techniques that will help you to do this:

SWOT Analysis

This is a formal analysis of your strengths and weaknesses, and of the opportunities and threats that you face.

Risk Analysis

This helps you to spot project risks, weaknesses in your organization or operation, and identify the risks to which you are exposed. From this you can plan to neutralise some risks.

Understanding Pressures for Change

Alternatively, other people (e.g., clients) may be pressing you to change the way you do things. Alternatively your environment may be changing, and you may need to anticipate or respond to this. Pressures may arise from changes in the economy, new legislation, competition, changes in people's attitudes, new technologies, or changes in government. The planning cycle is shown in Figure 7.

A different approach is to use any of a whole range of creativity tools to work out where you can make improvements. These creativity tools culminate in the powerful Simplex process.

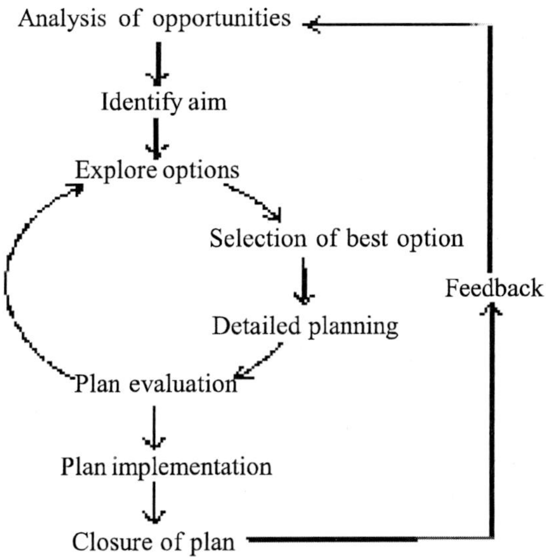

Figure 7: The Planning Cycle

Identifying the Aim of Your Plan

Once you have completed a realistic analysis of the opportunities for change, the next step is to decide precisely what the aim of your plan is. Deciding and defining an aim sharpens the focus of your plan, and helps you to avoid wasting effort on irrelevant side issues.

The aim is best expressed in a simple single sentence. This ensures that it is clear and sharp in your mind. If you are having difficulty in formulating the aim of your plan, ask yourself:

(1) What do I want the future to be?
(2) What benefit do I want to give to my customers?
(3) What returns do I seek?
(4) What standards am I aiming at?
(5) What values do I and my organisation believe in?

You can present this aim as a 'Vision Statement' or 'Mission Statement'. Vision statements express the benefit that an organisation will provide to its customers. For example, the vision statement for Mind Tools™ is: "To enrich the quality of our customers lives by providing the tools to help them to think in the most productive and effective way possible". While this is wordy, it explains what this site aims to do.

Mission statements give concrete expression to the vision statement, explaining how it is to be achieved. The mission statement for this site is: "To provide a well structured, accessible, concise survey of the best and most appropriate mind tools available".

Exploring Options

By this stage you should know where you are and what you want to do. The next thing to do is to work out how to do it. The creativity tools section of this site explains a wide range of powerful creativity tools that will help you to generate options.

At this stage it is best to spend a little time generating as many options as possible, even though it is tempting just to grasp the first idea that comes to mind. By taking a little time to generate as many ideas as possible you may come up with less obvious but better solutions. Just as likely, you may improve your best ideas with parts of other ideas.

Selecting the Best Option

Once you have explored the options available to you, it is time to decide which one to use. If you have the time and resources available, then you might decide to evaluate all options, carrying out detailed planning, costing, risk assessment, etc., for each. Normally you will not have this luxury.

Two useful tools for selecting the best option are Grid Analysis and Decision Trees. Grid Analysis helps you to decide between different options where you need to consider a number of different factors. Decision Trees help you to think through the likely outcomes of following different courses of action.

Detailed Planning

By the time you start detailed planning, you should have a good picture of where you are, what you want to achieve and the range of options available to you. You may well have selected one of the options as the most likely to yield the best results. Detailed planning is the process of working out the most efficient and effective way of achieving the aim that you have defined. It is the process of determining who will do what, when, where, how and why, and at what cost.

When drawing up the plan, techniques such as use of Gantt Charts and Critical Path Analysis can be immensely helpful in working out priorities, deadlines and the allocation of resources.

While you are concentrating on the actions that need to be performed, ensure that you also think about the control mechanisms that you will need to monitor performance. These will include the activities such as reporting, quality assurance, cost control, etc., that are needed to spot and correct any deviations from the plan. A good plan will:

- State the current situation
- Have a clear aim

- Use the resources available
- Detail the tasks to be carried out, whose responsibility they are, and their priorities and deadlines
- Detail control mechanisms that will alert you to difficulties in achieving the plan.

Identify risks, and plan for contingencies. This allows you to make a rapid and effective response to crises, perhaps at a time when you are at low ebb or are confused following a setback.

Consider transitional arrangements—how will you keep things going while you implement the plan?

Evaluation of the Plan and its Impact

Once you have worked out the details of your plan, the next stage is to review it to decide whether it is worth implementing. Here you must be objective—however much work you have carried out to reach this stage, the plan may still not be worth implementing.

This is frustrating after the hard work of detailed planning. It is, however, much better to find this out now than when you have invested time, resources and personal standing in the success of the plan. Evaluating the plan now gives you the opportunity to either investigate other options that might be more successful, or to accept that no plan is needed or should be carried out. Depending on the circumstances, the following techniques can be helpful in evaluating a plan:

PMI (Plus/Minus/Interesting)

This is a good, simple technique for 'weighing the pros and cons' of a decision. It involves listing the plus points in the plan in one column, the minus points in a second column, and the implications and points of uncertainty of the plan in a third column. Each point can be allocated a positive or negative score.

Cost/Benefit Analysis

This is useful for confirming that the plan makes financial sense. This involves adding up all the costs involved with the plan, and comparing them with the expected benefits.

Force Field Analysis

Similar to PMI, Force Field Analysis helps you to get a good overall view of all the forces for and against your plan. This allows you to see where you can make adjustments that will make the plan more likely to succeed.

Cash Flow Forecasts

Where a decision is has mainly financial implications, such as in business and marketing planning, preparation of a Cash Flow Forecast can be extremely useful. It allows you to assess the effect of time on costs and revenue. It also helps in assessing the size of the greatest negative and positive cash flows associated with a plan. When it is set up on a spreadsheet package, a good Cash Flow Forecast also functions as an extremely effective model of the plan. It gives you an easy basis for investigating the effect of varying your assumptions.

Thinking Hats

Thinking Hats is a very good technique to use to get a rounded view of your plan and its implications. It provides a context within which you can examine a plan rationally, emotionally, optimistically, pessimistically and creatively. Any analysis of your plan must be tempered by common sense.

If your analysis shows that the plan either will not give sufficient benefit, then either return to an earlier stage in the planning cycle or abandon the process altogether.

Implementing Change

Once you have completed your plan and decided that it will work satisfactorily, it is time to implement it. Your plan will explain how! It should also detail the controls that you will use to monitor the execution of the plan.

Closing the Plan

Once you have achieved a plan, you can close the project. At this point is often worth carrying out an evaluation of the project to see whether there are any lessons that you can learn. This should include an evaluation of your project planning to see if this could be improved.

If you are going to be carrying out many similar projects, it may be worth developing and improving an Aide Memoire. This is a list of headings and points to consider during planning. Using it helps you to ensure that you do not forget lessons learned in the past.

Main Points

The planning cycle is a process that helps you to make good, well-considered, robust plans.

The first step, the analysis of opportunities, helps you to base the plan firmly in reality. The second, definition of the aim, gives your plan focus.

The third stage is to generate as many different ways for achieving this aim as possible. By spending time looking for these you may find a better solution than the obvious one, or may be able to improve the obvious solution with parts of other ones.

Next select the best approach, and make a detailed plan showing how to implement it. Evaluate this plan to make sure that it will be worth implementing. If it is not, return to an earlier stage and either improve the plan or make a different one. If no plan looks like producing enough benefit to justify the cost, make no changes at all.

Once you have selected a course of action, and have proved that it is viable, carry it out. Once it is finished, examine it and draw whatever lessons you can from it. Feed this back into future planning.

Stakeholder Analysis & Stakeholder Management

As you become more successful in your career, the actions you take and the projects you run will affect more and more people. The more people you affect, the more likely it is that your actions will impact people who have power and influence over your projects. These people could be strong supporters of your work—or they could block it.

Stakeholder management is an important discipline that successful people use to win support from others. It helps them ensure that their projects succeed where others fail. Stakeholder analysis is the technique used to identify the key people who have to be won over. You then use stakeholder planning to build the support that helps you succeed.

The benefits of using a stakeholder-based approach are that:

(1) You can use the opinions of the most powerful stakeholders to shape your projects at an early stage. Not only does this make it more likely that they will support you, their input can also improve the quality of your project.

(2) Gaining support from powerful stakeholders can help you to win more resources—this makes it more likely that your projects will be successful.

(3) By communicating with stakeholders early and frequently, you can ensure that they fully understand what you are doing and understand the benefits of your project—this means they can support you actively when necessary.

(4) You can anticipate what people's reaction to your project may be, and build into your plan the actions that will win people's support.

Stakeholder Analysis

The first step in stakeholder analysis is to identify who your stakeholders are. The next step is to work out their power, influence and interest, so you know who you should focus on. The final step is to develop a good understanding of the most important stakeholders so that you know how they are likely to respond, and so that you can work out how to win their support—you can record this analysis on a stakeholder map.

After you have used this tool and created a stakeholder map, you can use the stakeholder planning tool to plan how you will communicate with each stakeholder.

The steps of stakeholder analysis are explained below:

Identifying Your Stakeholders

The first step in your stakeholder analysis is to brainstorm who your stakeholders are. As part of this, think of all the people who are affected by your work, who have influence or power over it, or have an interest in its successful or unsuccessful conclusion.

The table below shows some of the people who might be stakeholders in your job or in your projects:

Your boss	Shareholders	Government
Senior executives	Alliance partners	Trades associations
Your coworkers	Suppliers	The press
Your team	Lenders	Interest groups
Customers	Analysts	The public
Prospective customers	Future recruits	The community
Your family		

Remember that although stakeholders may be both organisations and people, ultimately you must communicate with people. Make sure that you identify the correct individual stakeholders within a stakeholder organisation.

Prioritise Your Stakeholders

You may now have a long list of people and organisations that are affected by your work. Some of these may have the power either to block or advance. Some may be interested in what you are doing, others may not care.

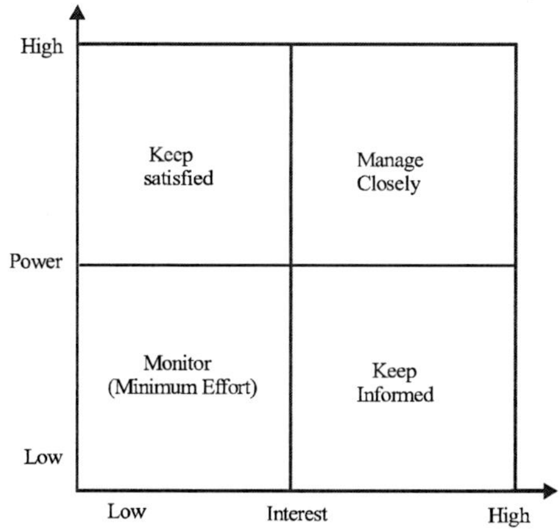

Figure 8: Stakeholders Interest Grid

Map out your stakeholders using the power/interest grid shown in Figure 8, and classify them by their power over your work and by their interest in your work. For example, your boss is likely to have high power and influence over your projects and high interest. Your family may have high interest, but are unlikely to have power over it.

Someone's position on the grid shows you the actions you have to take with them:

(1) *High power, interested people*—these are the people you must fully engage and make the greatest efforts to satisfy.

(2) *High power, less interested people*—put enough work in with these people to keep them satisfied, but not so much that they become bored with your message.
(3) *Low power, interested people*—keep these people adequately informed, and talk to them to ensure that no major issues are arising. These people can often be very helpful with the detail of your project.
(4) *Low power, less interested people*—again, monitor these people, but do not bore them with excessive communication.

Understanding your Key Stakeholders

You now need to know more about your key stakeholders. You need to know how they are likely to feel about and react to your project. You also need to know how best to engage them in your project and how best to communicate with them.

Key questions that can help you understand your stakeholders are:

(1) What financial or emotional interest do they have in the outcome of your work? Is it positive or negative?
(2) What motivates them most of all?
(3) What information do they want from you?
(4) How do they want to receive information from you? What is the best way of communicating your message to them?
(5) What is their current opinion of your work? Is it based on good information?
(6) Who influences their opinions generally, and who influences their opinion of you? Do some of these influencers therefore become important stakeholders in their own right?
(7) If they are not likely to be positive, what will win them around to support your project?
(8) If you don't think you will be able to win them around, how will you manage their opposition?

(9) Who else might be influenced by their opinions? Do these people become stakeholders in their own right?

A very good way of answering these questions is to talk to your stakeholders directly—people are often quite open about their views, and asking people's opinions is often the first step in building a successful relationship with them.

You can summarise the understanding you have gained on the stakeholder map, so that you can easily see which stakeholders are expected to be blockers or critics, and which stakeholders are likely to be advocates and supporters or your project. A good way of doing this is by color coding: showing advocates and supporters in green, blockers and critics in red, and others who are neutral in orange.

You can create your own example of stakeholder analysis at work—whether for your current role, a job you want to do or a new project. Conduct a full stakeholder analysis. Ask yourself whether you are communicating as effectively as you should be with your stakeholders. What actions can you take to get more from your supporters or win over your critics?

Main Points

As the work you do and the projects you run become more important, you will affect more and more people. Some of these people have the power to undermine your projects and your position. Others may be strong supporters of your work. Stakeholder management is the process by which you identify your key stakeholders and win their support. Stakeholder analysis is the first stage of this, where you identify and start to understand your most important stakeholders.

The first stage of this is brainstorm who your stakeholders are. The next step is to prioritise them by power and interest, and to plot this on a power/interest grid. The final stage is to get an understanding of what motivates your stakeholders and how you need to win them around.

Stakeholder Management and Planning

Having conducted a stakeholder analysis exercise, you will have most of the information you need to plan how to manage communication with your stakeholders. You will have identified the stakeholders in your job and in your projects, and will have marked out their positions on a stakeholder map.

The next stage is to plan your communication so that you can win them around to support your projects. Stakeholder planning is the process by which you do this. To carry out a stakeholder planning exercise, start with a stakeholder planning sheet. This is a table with the following column headings:

- Power
- Interest
- Stakeholder name
- Key interests and issues
- Current status—advocate, supporter, neutral, critic, blocker
- Desired support—high, medium or low
- Desired project role (if any)
- Actions Desired (if any)
- Messages needed
- Actions and communications.

Using this table, work through the planning exercise using the steps below:

(1) *Update the Planning Sheet with Power/Interest Grid Information*: Based on the power/interest grid you created in your stakeholder analysis, enter the stakeholders' names, their influence and interest in your job or project, and your current assessment of where they stand with respect to it.

(2) *Plan Your Approach to Stakeholder Management*: The amount of time you should allocate to stakeholder management depends on the size and difficulty of your projects and goals, the time you have available for communication, and the amount of help you need to achieve the results you want. Think through the help you need, the amount of time that will be taken to manage this and the time you will need for communication. Help with the project could include sponsorship of the project, advice and expert input, reviews of material to increase quality, etc.

(3) *Think Through What You Want from Each Stakeholder*: Next, work through your list of stakeholders thinking through the levels of support you want from them and the roles you would like them to play (if any). Think through the actions you would like them to perform. Write this information down in the 'Desired Support', 'Desired Project Role' and 'Actions Desired' columns.

(4) *Identify the Messages You Need to Convey*: Next, identify the messages that you need to convey to your stakeholders

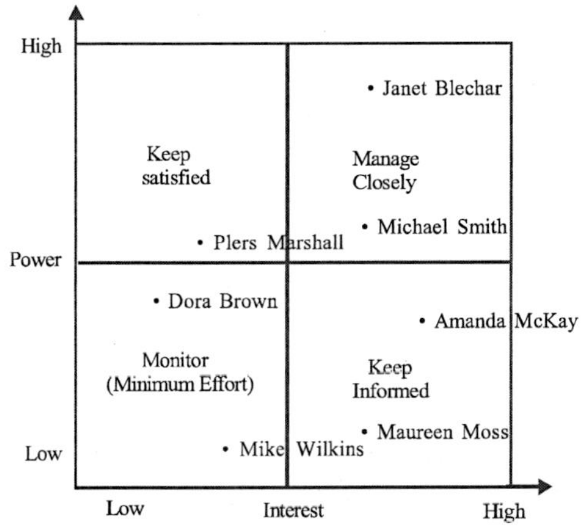

Figure 9: Stakeholders Management Grid

to persuade them to support you and engage with your projects or goals. Typical messages will show the benefits to the person or organisation of what you are doing, and will focus on key performance drivers like increasing profitability or delivering real improvements.

(5) *Identify Actions and Communications*: Finally, work out what you need to do to win and manage the support of these stakeholders. With the time and resource you have available, identify how you will manage the communication to and the input from your stakeholders.

Focusing on the high-power/high-interest stakeholders first and the low-interest/low-power stakeholders last, devise a practical plan that communicates with people as effectively as possible and that communicates the right amount of information in a way that neither under nor over-communicates.

Think through what you need to do to keep your best supporters engaged and on-board. Work out how to win over or neutralise the opposition of skeptics. Where you need the active support of people who are not currently interested in what you are doing, think about how you can engage them and raise their level of interest.

Also, consider how what you are doing will affect your stakeholders. Where appropriate, let people know as early as possible of any difficult issues that may arise, and discuss with them how you can minimise or manage any impact.

It is usually a good idea to manage people's expectations about likely problems as early as possible. This gives them time to think through how to manage issues, and preserves your reputation for reliability. Once you have prepared your stakeholder plan, all you need to do is to implement it. As with all plans, it will be easier to implement if you break it down into a series of small, achievable steps and action these one-by-one.

As the work you do and the projects you run become more important, you will affect more and more people. Some of these people have the power to undermine your projects and your position. Others may be strong supporters of your work. Stakeholder management is the process by which you identify your key stakeholders and win their support.

Stakeholder analysis is the first stage of this, where you identify and start to understand your most important stakeholders. The first step in this is brainstorm who your stakeholders are. The next is to prioritise them by power and interest, and to plot this on a power/interest grid. The final step is to get an understanding of what motivates your stakeholders and how you need to win them around.

Once you have completed your stakeholder analysis, the next stage is stakeholder planning. This is the process you use to plan how to manage your stakeholders and gain their support for your projects. Stakeholder planning can usefully be conducted using a planning sheet like the one described. To prepare your plan, go through the following steps:

- Update the planning sheet with information from the power/ interest grid
- Think through your approach to stakeholder management
- Work out what you want from each stakeholder
- Identify the messages you need to convey
- Identify actions and communications.

Good stakeholder management helps you to manage the politics that can often come with major projects. It helps you win support for your projects and eliminates a major source of project and work stress.

SWOT Analysis

SWOT Analysis (also known as TOWS analysis) is a powerful technique for understanding your Strengths and Weaknesses, and for looking at the Opportunities and Threats you face. Used in a business context, it helps you carve a sustainable niche in your market. Used in a personal context, it helps you develop your career in a way that takes best advantage of your talents, abilities and opportunities.

(1) *Business SWOT Analysis*: What makes SWOT particularly powerful is that, with a little thought, it can help you uncover opportunities that you are well placed to take advantage of. And by understanding the weaknesses of your business, you can manage and eliminate threats that would otherwise catch you unawares.

(2) *Personal SWOT*: More than this, by looking at yourself and your competitors using the SWOT framework, you can start to craft a strategy that helps you distinguish yourself from your competitors, so that you can compete successfully in your market.

Using the Tool

To carry out a SWOT Analysis write down answers to the following questions:

Strengths

- What advantages does your company have?
- What do you do better than anyone else?
- What unique or lowest-cost resources do you have access to?
- What do people in your market see as your strengths?

Consider this from an internal perspective, and from the point of view of your customers and people in your market. And be realistic: It's far too easy to fall prey to 'not invented here syndrome'. Also, if you are having any difficulty with this, try writing down a list of your characteristics. Some of these will hopefully be strengths!

In looking at your strengths, think about them in relation to your competitors—for example, if all your competitors provide high quality products, then a high quality production process is not a strength in the market, it is a necessity.

Weaknesses

- What could you improve?
- What should you avoid?
- What are people in your market likely to see as weaknesses?

Again, consider this from an internal and external basis: Do other people seem to perceive weaknesses that you do not see? Are your competitors doing any better than you? It is best to be realistic now, and face any unpleasant truths as soon as possible.

Opportunities

- Where are the good opportunities facing you?
- What are the interesting trends you are aware of?

Useful opportunities can come from such things as:

- Changes in technology and markets on both a broad and narrow scale
- Changes in government policy related to your field
- Changes in social patterns, population profiles, lifestyle changes, etc.

A useful approach to looking at opportunities is to look at your strengths and ask yourself whether these open up any opportunities. Alternatively, look at your weaknesses and ask yourself whether you could open up opportunities by eliminating them.

Threats

- What obstacles do you face?
- What is your competition doing?

- Are the required specifications for your job, products or services changing?
- Is changing technology threatening your position?
- Do you have bad debt or cash-flow problems?
- Could any of your weaknesses seriously threaten your business?

Carrying out this analysis will often be illuminating—both in terms of pointing out what needs to be done, and in putting problems into perspective.

Strengths and weaknesses are internal to your organisation. Opportunities and threats relate to external factors. For this reason the SWOT Analysis is sometimes called Internal-External Analysis and the SWOT Matrix is sometimes called an IE Matrix Analysis Tool.

You can also apply SWOT Analysis to your competitors. As you do this, you'll start to see how and where you should compete against them.

An Illustration

A start-up small consultancy business might draw up the following SWOT or TOWS matrix:

Strengths

(1) We are able to respond very quickly as we have no red tape, no need for higher management approval, etc.
(2) We are able to give really good customer care, as the current small amount of work means we have plenty of time to devote to customers.
(3) Our lead consultant has strong reputation within the market.
(4) We can change direction quickly if we find that our marketing is not working.
(5) We have little overhead, so can offer good value to customers.

Weaknesses

(1) Our company has no market presence or reputation.
(2) We have a small staff with a shallow skills base in many areas.
(3) We are vulnerable to vital staff being sick, leaving, etc.
(4) Our cash flow will be unreliable in the early stages.

Opportunities

(1) Our business sector is expanding, with many future opportunities for success.
(2) Our local council wants to encourage local businesses with work where possible.
(3) Our competitors may be slow to adopt new technologies.

Threats

(1) Will developments in technology change this market beyond our ability to adapt?
(2) A small change in focus of a large competitor might wipe out any market position we achieve.
(3) The consultancy may therefore decide to specialize in rapid response, good value services to local businesses. Marketing would be in selected local publications, to get the greatest possible market presence for a set advertising budget. The consultancy should keep up-to-date with changes in technology where possible.

Main Points

SWOT Analysis is a simple but powerful framework for analyzing your company's strengths and weaknesses, and the opportunities and threats you face. This helps you to focus on your strengths, minimise threats, and take the greatest possible advantage of opportunities available to you.

Risk Analysis

Almost everything we do in today's business world involves a risk of some kind: customer habits change, new competitors appear, factors outside your control could delay your project. But formal risk analysis and risk management can help you to assess theese risks and decide what actions to take to minimise disruptions to your plans. They will also help you to decide whether the strategies you could use to control risk are cost-effective.

Using the Tool

Here we define risk as 'the perceived extent of possible loss'. Different people will have different views of the impact of a particular risk—what may be a small risk for one person may destroy the livelihood of someone else.

One way of putting figures to risk is to calculate a value for it as:

risk = probability of event x cost of event

Doing this allows you to compare risks objectively. We use this approach formally in decision making with Decision Trees.

To carry out a risk analysis, follow these steps:

Identify Threats

The first stage of a risk analysis is to identify threats facing you. Threats may be:

(1) Human—from individuals or organisations, illness, death, etc.

(2) Operational—from disruption to supplies and operations, loss of access to essential assets, failures in distribution, etc.

(3) Reputational—from loss of business partner or employee confidence, or damage to reputation in the market.

(4) Procedural—from failures of accountability, internal systems and controls, organisation, fraud, etc.
(5) Project—risks of cost over-runs, jobs taking too long, of insufficient product or service quality, etc.
(6) Financial—from business failure, stock market, interest rates, unemployment, etc.
(7) Technical—from advances in technology, technical failure, etc.
(8) Natural—threats from weather, natural disaster, accident, disease, etc.
(9) Political—from changes in tax regimes, public opinion, government policy, foreign influence, etc.
(10) Others.

This analysis of threat is important because it is so easy to overlook important threats. One way of trying to capture them all is to use a number of different approaches:

(1) Firstly, run through a list such as the one above, to see if any apply.
(2) Secondly, think through the systems, organisations or structures you operate, and analyse risks to any part of those.
(3) See if you can see any vulnerabilities within these systems or structures.
(4) Ask other people, who might have different perspectives.

Estimate Risk

Once you have identified the threats you face, the next step is to work out the likelihood of the threat being realised and to assess its impact. One approach to this is to make your best estimate of the probability of the event occurring, and to multiply this by the amount it will cost you to set things right if it happens. This gives you a value for the risk.

Managing Risk

Once you have worked out the value of risks you face, you can start to look at ways of managing them. When you are doing this, it is important to choose cost effective approaches—in most cases, there is no point in spending more to eliminating a risk than the cost of the event if it occurs. Often, it may be better to accept the risk than to use excessive resources to eliminate it. Risk may be managed in a number of ways:

By Using Existing Assets

Here existing resources can be used to counter risk. This may involve improvements to existing methods and systems, changes in responsibilities, improvements to accountability and internal controls, etc.

By Contingency Planning

You may decide to accept a risk, but choose to develop a plan to minimise its effects if it happens. A good contingency plan will allow you to take action immediately, with the minimum of project control if you find yourself in a crisis management situation. Contingency plans also form a key part of Business Continuity Planning (BCP) or Business Continuity Management (BCM).

By Investing in New Resources

Your risk analysis should give you the basis for deciding whether to bring in additional resources to counter the risk. This can also include insuring the risk: Here you pay someone else to carry part of the risk—this is particularly important where the risk is so great as to threaten your or your organisation's solvency.

Reviews

Once you have carried out a risk analysis and management exercise, it may be worth carrying out regular reviews. These might involve formal reviews of the risk analysis, or may involve testing systems and plans appropriately.

Main Points

Risk analysis allows you to examine the risks that you or your organisation face. It is based on a structured approach to thinking through threats, followed by an evaluation of the probability and cost of events occurring.

Risk analysis forms the basis for risk management andcrisis prevention. Here the emphasis is on cost effectiveness. Risk management involves adapting the use of existing resources, contingency planning and good use of new resources.

PMI Weighing Pros and Cons of a Decision

Using Tool

PMI stands for 'Plus/Minus/Interesting'. It is a valuable improvement to the 'weighing pros and cons' technique used for centuries. PMI is an important decision making tool: the mind tools used so far in this section have focused on selecting a course of action from a range of options. Before you move straight to action on this course of action, it is important to check that it is going to improve the situation (it may actually be best to do nothing!) PMI is a useful tool for doing this.

To use PMI, draw up a table headed up with: 'Plus', 'Minus', and 'Interesting'. In the column underneath 'Plus', write down all the positive results of taking the action. Underneath 'Minus' write down all the negative effects. In the 'Interesting' column write down the implications and possible outcomes of taking the action, whether positive, negative, or uncertain.

By this stage it may already be obvious whether or not you should implement the decision. If it is not, consider each of the points you have written down and assign a positive or negative score to it appropriately. The scores you assign may be quite subjective.

Once you have done this, add up the score. A strongly positive score shows that an action should be taken, a strongly negative score that it should be avoided.

An Illustration

A young professional is deciding where to live. Her question is 'Should she move to the big city?'

She draws up the PMI table below:

Plus	*Minus*	*Interesting*
More going on (+5)	Have to sell house (-6)	Easier to find new job? (+1)
Easier to see friends (+5)	More pollution (-3)	Meet more people? (+2)
Easier to get places (+3)	Less space (-3)	More difficult to get own work done? (-4)
	No countryside (-2)	
	More difficult to get to work? (-4)	
+13	**-18**	**-1**

She scores the table as 13 (Plus) - 18 (Minus) - 1 (Interesting) = - 6

For her, the comforts of a settled rural existence outweigh the call of the 'bright lights'—it would be much better for her to live outside the city, but close enough to travel in if necessary.

PMI was codified by Edward de Bono in his book *Serious Creativity*.

Main Points

PMI is a good way of weighing the pros, cons and implications of a decision. When you have selected a course of action, PMI is a good technique to use to check that it is worth taking.

To use the technique, draw up a table with three columns headed Plus, Minus and Interesting. Within the table write down all the positive points of following the course of action, all the negatives, and all the interesting implications and possible outcomes. If the decision is still not obvious, you can then score the table to show the importance of individual items. The total score should show whether it is worth implementing the decision.

Cost/Benefit Analysis

Using Tool

You may have been intensely creative in generating solutions to a problem, and rigorous in your selection of the best one available. This solution may still not be worth implementing, as you may invest a lot of time and money in solving a problem that is not worthy of this effort.

Cost/Benefit Analysis is a relatively simple and widely used technique for deciding whether to make a change. As its name suggests, to use the technique simply add up the value of the benefits of a course of action, and subtract the costs associated with it.

Costs are either one-off, or may be ongoing. Benefits are most often received over time. We build this effect of time into our analysis by calculating a payback period. This is the time it takes for the benefits of a change to repay its costs. Many companies look for payback over a specified period of time, e.g., three years.

In its simple form, cost/benefit analysis is carried out using only financial costs and financial benefits. For example, a simple cost/benefit analysis of a road scheme would measure the cost of building the road, and subtract this from the economic benefit of improving transport links. It would not measure either the cost of environmental damage or the benefit of quicker and easier travel to work.

A more sophisticated approach to cost/benefit measurement models is to try to put a financial value on intangible costs and benefits. This can be highly subjective—is, for example, a historic water meadow worth Rs. 25,000, or is it worth Rs. 500,000 because if its environmental importance? What is the value of stress-free travel to work in the morning?

These are all questions that people have to answer, and answers that people have to defend. The version of cost/benefit analysis we explain here is necessarily simple. Where large sums of money are involved (for example, in financial market transactions), project evaluation can become an extremely complex and sophisticated art. The fundamentals of this are explained in *Principles of Corporate Finance* by Richard Brealey and Stewart Myers—this is something of a 'bible' on the subject.

Main Points

Cost/Benefit Analysis is a powerful, widely used and relatively easy tool for deciding whether to make a change. To use the tool, firstly work out how much the change will cost to make. Then calculate the benefit you will from it. Where costs or benefits are paid or received over time, work out the time it will take for the benefits to repay the costs.

Cost/Benefit Analysis can be carried out using only financial costs and financial benefits. You may, however, decide to include intangible items within the analysis. As you must estimate a value for these, this inevitably brings an element of subjectivity into the process.

Force Field Analysis

Using the Tool

Force Field Analysis is a useful technique for looking at all the forces for and against a decision. In effect, it is a specialized method of weighing pros and cons. By carrying out the analysis you can plan to strengthen the forces supporting a decision, and reduce the impact of opposition to it.

To carry out a force field analysis, follow these steps:

(1) List all forces for change in one column, and all forces against change in another column.
(2) Assign a score to each force, from 1 (weak) to 5 (strong).
(3) Draw a diagram showing the forces for and against change. Show the size of each force as a number next to it.

For example, imagine that you are a manager deciding whether to install new manufacturing equipment in your factory. You might draw up a force field analysis like the one in Figure 10:

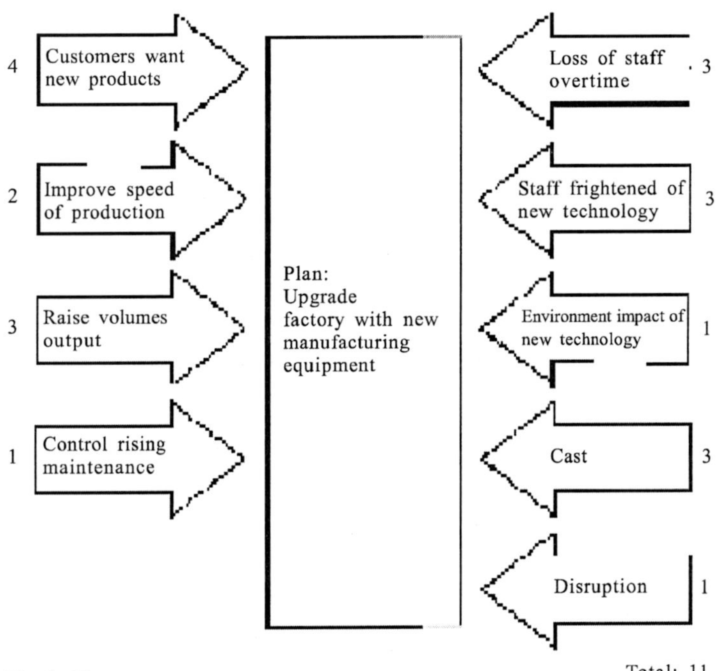

Figure 10: Force Field Analysis Example

Once you have carried out an analysis, you can decide whether your project is viable. In the example above, you might initially question whether it is worth going ahead with the plan.

Where you have already decided to carry out a project, force field analysis can help you to work out how to improve its probability of success. Here you have two choices:

- To reduce the strength of the forces opposing a project, or
- To increase the forces pushing a project.

Often the most elegant solution is the first: just trying to force change through may cause its own problems. People can be uncooperative if change is forced on them.

If you had to implement the project in the example above, the analysis might suggest a number of changes to the initial plan:

(1) By training staff (increase cost by 1) you could eliminate fear of technology (reduce fear by 2).

(2) It would be useful to show staff that change is necessary for business survival (new force in favor, +2).

(3) Staff could be shown that new machines would introduce variety and interest to their jobs (new force, +1).

(4) You could raise wages to reflect new productivity (cost +1, loss of overtime -2).

(5) Slightly different machines with filters to eliminate pollution could be installed (environmental impact -1).

These changes would swing the balance from 11:10 (against the plan), to 8:13 (in favour of the plan).

Main Points

Force field analysis is a useful technique for looking at all the forces for and against a plan. It helps you to weigh the importance of these factors and decide whether a plan is worth implementing. Where you have decided to carry out a plan, force field analysis helps you identify changes that you could make to improve it.

Six Thinking Hats

Using the Tool

'Six Thinking Hats' is an important and powerful technique. It is used to look at decisions from a number of important perspectives. This forces you to move outside your habitual thinking style, and helps you to get a more rounded view of a situation. This tool was created by Edward de Bono in his book '*6 Thinking Hats*'.

Many successful people think from a very rational, positive viewpoint. This is part of the reason that they are successful. Often, though, they may fail to look at a problem from an emotional, intuitive, creative or negative viewpoint. This can mean that they underestimate resistance to plans, fail to make creative leaps and do not make essential contingency plans.

If you look at a problem with the 'Six Thinking Hats' technique, then you will solve it using all approaches. Your decisions and plans will mix ambition, skill in execution, public sensitivity, creativity and good contingency planning.

You can use Six Thinking Hats in meetings or on your own. In meetings it has the benefit of blocking the confrontations that happen when people with different thinking styles discuss the same problem. Each 'Thinking Hat' is a different style of thinking. These are explained below:

White Hat

With this thinking hat you focus on the data available. Look at the information you have, and see what you can learn from it. Look for gaps in your knowledge, and either try to fill them or take account of them.

This is where you analyse past trends, and try to extrapolate from historical data.

Red Hat

'Wearing' the red hat, you look at problems using intuition, gut reaction, and emotion. Also try to think how other people will react emotionally. Try to understand the responses of people who do not fully know your reasoning.

Black Hat

Using black hat thinking, look at all the bad points of the decision. Look at it cautiously and defensively. Try to see why it might not work. This is important because it highlights the weak points in a plan. It allows you to eliminate them, alter them, or prepare contingency plans to counter them.

Black Hat thinking helps to make your plans 'tougher' and more resilient. It can also help you to spot fatal flaws and risks before you embark on a course of action. Black Hat thinking is one of the real benefits of this technique, as many successful people get so used to thinking positively that often they cannot see problems in advance. This leaves them under-prepared for difficulties.

Yellow Hat

The yellow hat helps you to think positively. It is the optimistic viewpoint that helps you to see all the benefits of the decision and the value in it. Yellow Hat thinking helps you to keep going when everything looks gloomy and difficult.

Green Hat

The Green Hat stands for creativity. This is where you can develop creative solutions to a problem. It is a freewheeling way of thinking, in which there is little criticism of ideas. A whole range of creativity tools can help you here.

Blue Hat

The Blue Hat stands for process control. This is the hat worn by people chairing meetings. When running into difficulties because ideas are running dry, they may direct activity into Green Hat thinking. When contingency plans are needed, they will ask for Black Hat thinking, etc.

A variant of this technique is to look at problems from the point of view of different professionals (e.g. doctors, architects, sales directors, etc.) or different customers.

An Illustration

The directors of a property company are looking at whether they should construct a new office building. The economy is doing well, and the amount of vacant office space is reducing sharply. As part of their decision they decide to use the Six Thinking Hats technique during a planning meeting.

Looking at the problem with the White Hat, they analyze the data they have. They examine the trend in vacant office space, which shows a sharp reduction. They anticipate that by the time the office block would be completed, that there will be a severe shortage of office space. Current government projections show steady economic growth for at least the construction period.

With Red Hat thinking, some of the directors think the proposed building looks quite ugly. While it would be highly cost-effective, they worry that people would not like to work in it.

When they think with the Black Hat, they worry that government projections may be wrong. The economy may be about to enter a 'cyclical downturn', in which case the office building may be empty for a long time. If the building is not attractive, then companies will choose to work in another better-looking building at the same rent.

With the Yellow Hat, however, if the economy holds up and their projections are correct, the company stands to make a great deal of money. If they are lucky, maybe they could sell the building before the next downturn, or rent to tenants on long-term leases that will last through any recession.

With Green Hat thinking they consider whether they should change the design to make the building more pleasant. Perhaps they could build prestige offices that people would want to rent in any economic climate. Alternatively, may be they should invest the money in the short term to buy up property at a low cost when a recession comes.

The Blue Hat has been used by the meeting's Chair to move between the different thinking styles. He or she may have needed to keep other members of the team from switching styles, or from criticising other peoples' points.

Main Points

Six Thinking Hats is a good technique for looking at the effects of a decision from a number of different points of view. It allows necessary emotion and skepticism to be brought into what would otherwise be purely rational decisions. It opens up the opportunity for creativity within decision-making.

The technique also helps, for example, persistently pessimistic people to be positive and creative. Plans developed using the 'Six Thinking Hats' technique will be sounder and more resilient than would otherwise be the case. It may also help you to avoid public relations mistakes, and spot good reasons not to follow a course of action before you have committed to it.

9

Conflicts Management

Friction in the workplace can be stressful and counterproductive for everyone involved. Learn to approach the person with whom you are struggling and resolve the situation.

Steps to be Taken

(1) Decide whether you want to confront the person who is bothering you. It is usually better to air grievances in the open than to let them fester.

(2) Speak to the other person calmly, politely and rationally. Focus on the situation and facts, avoiding gossip and personal attacks.

(3) Be careful not to express hostility in your posture, facial expression or tone. Be assertive without being aggressive.

(4) Listen to the other person carefully: What is she trying to say? Be sure you understand her position.

(5) Express interest in what the other person is saying. You can acknowledge her ideas without necessarily agreeing

or submitting. Saying, "I understand that you feel this way. Here's how I feel..." acknowledges both positions.

(6) Communicate clearly what you want, offering positive suggestions and recommendations. Be willing to be flexible.
(7) Speak to your supervisor if a problem with a difficult co-worker seriously threatens your work, but avoid whining.

Conflict occurs when individuals or groups are not obtaining what they need or want and are seeking their own self-interest. Sometimes the individual is not aware of the need and unconsciously starts to act out. Other times, the individual is very aware of what he or she wants and actively works at achieving the goal.

How to Deal with Conflict

Conflict

- Conflict is inevitable
- Conflict develops because we are dealing with people's lives, jobs, children, pride, self-concept, ego and sense of mission or purpose
- Early indicators of conflict can be recognised
- There are strategies for resolution that are available and work
- Although inevitable, conflict can be minimised, diverted and/or resolved.

Beginnings of Conflict

- Poor communication
- Seeking power
- Dissatisfaction with management style
- Weak leadership
- Lack of openness
- Change in leadership.

Conflict Indicators

- Body language
- Disagreements, regardless of issue
- Withholding bad news
- Surprises
- Strong public statements
- Airing disagreements through media
- Conflicts in value system
- Desire for power
- Increasing lack of respect
- Open disagreement
- Lack of candor on budget problems or other sensitive issues
- Lack of clear goals
- No discussion of progress, failure relative to goals, failure to evaluate the superintendent fairly, thoroughly or at all.

When Conflict Destructive

- Takes attention away from other important activities
- Undermines morale or self-concept
- Polarises people and groups, reducing cooperation
- Increases or sharpens difference
- Leads to irresponsible and harmful behaviour, such as fighting, name-calling.

When Conflict Becomes Constructive

- Results in clarification of important problems and issues
- Results in solutions to problems
- Involves people in resolving issues important to them
- Causes authentic communication
- Helps release emotion, anxiety, and stress
- Builds cooperation among people through learning more about each other

- joining in resolving the conflict
- Helps individuals develop understanding and skills

Techniques for Avoiding and/or Resolving Conflict

- Meet conflict head on
- Set goals
- Plan for and communicate frequently
- Be honest about concerns
- Agree to disagree—understand healthy disagreement would build better decisions
- Get individual ego out of management style
- Let your team create—people will support what they help create
- Discuss differences in values openly
- Continually stress the importance of following policy
- Communicate honestly—avoid playing 'gotcha' type games
- Provide more data and information than is needed
- Develop a sound management system.

Reaching Consensus through Collaboration

Groups often collaborate closely in order to reach consensus or agreement. The ability to use collaboration requires the recognition of and respect for everyone's ideas, opinions, and suggestions. Consensus requires that each participant must agree on the point being discussed before it becomes a part of the decision. Not every point will meet with everyone's complete approval. Unanimity is not the goal. The goal is to have individuals accept a point of view based on logic. When individuals can understand and accept the logic of a differing point of view, you must assume you have reached consensus.

Follow these guidelines for reaching consensus:

(1) Avoid arguing over individual ranking or position. Present a position as logically as possible.

(2) Avoid 'win-lose' statements. Discard the notion that someone must win.
(3) Avoid changing of minds only in order to avoid conflict and to achieve harmony.
(4) Avoid majority voting, averaging, bargaining, or coin flipping. These do not lead to consensus. Treat differences of opinion as indicative of incomplete sharing of relevant information, keep asking questions.
(5) Keep the attitude that holding different views is both natural and healthy to a group.
(6) View initial agreement as suspect. Explore the reasons underlying apparent agreement and make sure that members have willingly agreed.

Common Ground Approach

What is the Common Ground Approach? The Common Ground Approach is a means of navigating through conflict and identifying possibilities that are not apparent from an adversarial mind set. It is a set of principles and practices that, when utilised, causes a fundamental shift in people's relationship with conflict—away from adversarial approaches toward cooperative solutions. The Common Ground Approach—whether applied in a home, on the streets, or between ethnic groups—creates new possibilities of peaceful coexistence, drawing upon the strengths of diversity and interconnectedness.

What makes the Common Ground Approach effective is that is derived from over two decades of practical experience—it has been created from what works. We have found that people who become aware of the approach can begin to apply the principles and key practices immediately in their lives.

Core Principles

There are five core principles to the Common Ground Approach:

(1) *Conflict is neither Negative nor Positive:* Conflict isn't a bad thing in and of itself. It is the natural result of differences between people - religious, political, ethnic, or whatever they might be. Those differences can enrich us and can be as much at the root of peaceful progress as at the root of violence. Dealing with these differences constructively is a skill that can be developed.

(2) *Conflict can be Transformed:* Conflict transformation is not about ending conflict or even solving specific disputes—the goal is to shift the way individuals, communities and societies view and deal with their differences. What is important is how conflict is approached, to shift away from an adversarial stance toward a cooperative, problem-solving one. An essential step in transforming conflict is enabling people to communicate and have accurate information about each other.

(3) *Finding Common Ground*: Finding common ground is not the same as settling for the lowest common denominator—it's generating a new 'highest common denominator'. It's not about having two sides meet in the middle, but having them identify something together they can aspire to and work toward. When people who really care about an issue come together and bring their best thinking from their various perspectives, there is the potential for new options to be generated.

(4) *Peace is a Process*: There isn't a method for causing conflicts to transform instantaneously—it is not something you can achieve in a single event or by signing a peace accord—it is an on-going process of developing relationships of mutual respect and trust. Every peace process has its ups and downs. Making long-term commitments allows us to keep working on the underlying

causes of a conflict even during periods of increased intensity.

(5) *Humankind is Interdependent*: We are witnessing the impact of globalization on an unprecedented scale. Current problems—whether ethnic, environmental, or economic—are simply too complex and interconnected to be settled on an adversarial basis. The earth is running out of the space, resources and recuperative capacity to deal with wasteful conflict.

Key Practices

Although there are many practices that are useful in dealing with conflict constructively, we have identified four that we feel are essential:

(1) *Distinguish between Positions and Interests*: People naturally tend to take positions about issues, especially when in a conflict. Underlying these positions are generally broader interests, such as security and the well being of one's family. Interests usually relate to basic needs, while positions are opinions about how to achieve those needs. Positions may appear mutually exclusive, while interests tend to overlap.

(2) *Respect Each Other: Face Problems Together*: By making the distinction between problems and the people involved in a conflict, it is possible to help people shift their energies to focus on common concerns rather than seeing each other as the problem.

(3) *Listen to Understand*: When we focus our full attention on someone with the intention of improving understanding rather than winning an argument, it helps to create a relationship conducive to mutual problem solving.

(5) *Choose Your Approach*: While we may not always have a choice about the conflicts we find ourselves in, it is

possible to choose our response to them. Peace is generated by the moment-by-moment choices we make in how we deal with conflict in our relationships and community.

How do we apply the Common Ground Approach to societal problems?—The Common Ground Approach was developed while addressing societal challenges in the 17 different countries where Search for Common Ground works. Through this experience we developed the following operating practices:

(1) *Make Long-term Commitments*: Avoid parachuting—dropping into a conflict for a short visit. Use a continuing presence to develop a knowledge base and to build networks of relationships on all sides of the conflict.

(2) *Use an Integrated Approach*: Work simultaneously on multiple levels and on multiple fronts while striving for societal conflict transformation.

(3) *Become Engaged in Order to See the Possibilities*: Conflicts are extraordinarily complex, and it takes profound engagement to start to understand them. Although we conduct assessment missions before undertaking any new programme, we strive to remain flexible to adapt to the changing environments in which we operate.

(4) *Be Social Entrepreneurs*: Look for problem solvers and creative thinkers who, from a shared vision, can develop finite and achievable projects. Continuously develop new tools and approaches.

(5) *Become Immersed in Local Cultures*: Work with and build on individuals' and communities' knowledge, wisdom and creativity. Partner with local peace builders to strengthen their ability to transform their own conflicts.

(6) *Practice Cooperative Action*: Dialogue is a necessary but insufficient means to change attitudes and behaviours. Wherever possible, work with parties in conflict to help

them not only understand their differences but also to act on their commonalities.

Dialogue

Dialogue is derived from the ancient root *leg* which means to collect or speak, as well as from the Germanic word *lekjaz*—the one who speaks magic words—and most recently from the Greek *dia-logos* which translates into the flowing through of the word or meaning or relationship. The story of dialogue originated with small groups of hunter gatherers who formed in circles of conversation around the fires at night to share their stories and dances and songs.

The word conversation itself means 'to tum together', It involves a forgetting, or a surrendering, of oneself and a reciprocity with the other in order to create a collectively-held space through which another dimension of reality can emerge. A part of what is surrendered is our relationship to memory and conditioned knowledge. In its place, we begin to cultivate a more subtle intelligence that is focused on refining and inquiring into our moment-to-moment perceptions and experiences of what is.

With the exception of the arts, certain spiritual traditions, like the Quakers and cultures who have maintained close connections to their oral tradition, the practice of dialogue became too time consuming and it gradually dropped away. Dialogue is a fundamental aspect of who we are. In giving it up, we became separated from an essential aspect of ourselves.

We can awaken it again by slowing down our thinking and allowing ourselves to be more inclusive, fluid and tentative in our thoughts. This, in itself, creates the kind of peripheral vision that allows for the more improvisational and creative dimension of our thinking to emerge.

The practicality of this is implied by Gary Hamel when he says, "The critical lack in businesses today are not resources or strategies, but imagination". The imagination is revitalised by acknowledging the truth of what is real. The new leaders will be those who are able to create spaces and processes for skilful conversation. Through surfacing the underlying images and structures of our thinking, and making the implicit explicit, we create the possibility of re-imagining ourselves, our organisations, and the quality of our work.

Through such practices as listening openly to one another without resistance, of framing questions which lead us in the direction to the mystery rather than to the answers, of following the subtle impulse of our thinking and inquiry, by suspending, examining, and reconsidering the validity of our own assumptions and beliefs and examining many different points of view, and reclaiming our capacity for an immediate and first-hand experience through touch, taste, hearing and sight, we begin to establish a dialogic relationship with our world.

While we belong to organisations, we also belong to a story. The capacity for thinking together is one of those stories. It is both new and also very old. We need to connect again to the underlying narrative that gives form and vitality to our organisations. The stability we seek is not only in our technologies, structures and products, but in the quality of thinking and feeling that is beneath the stories, the images and the values and visions and the thoughts that form us.

10

Project Closeout

Introduction

The purpose of this phase is to assess the project and derive any lessons learned and best practices to bc applied to future projects. Project closeout begins with a post-implementation review. The review may start with a survey designed to solicit feedback on the project from the project team, customers, consumers and other stakeholders. Once feedback has been collected and evaluated, an assessment meeting is conducted to derive best practices and formulate lessons learned to inform future efforts. Ideally, the best practices and lessons learned should be stored in a centralised organisational repository, facilitating access and retrieval by managers of future projects. Project closeout ends with administrative closeout—providing feedback on project team members, updating the skills inventory, capturing key project metrics, and filing all pertinent project materials into the project repository.

Processes Involved

This phase consists of the following processes:

(1) *Conducting post-implementation review*—where the project manager assesses the results of the project by soliciting feedback from team members, customers and other stakeholders through the use of a survey to gather lessons learned, best practices and performance patterns or trends, and communicate those results in the form of a post-implementation Report.

(2) *Perform administrative closeout*—where the project manager formally closes the project by providing performance feedback to team members, and archiving all project information.

Role Performers

The following roles are involved in carrying out the processes of this phase.

- Project manager
- Project sponsor
- Project team member
- Customer
- Consumer
- Internal stakeholders
- External stakeholders
- Performing organisation management

Categories of Deliverables

The major outcome of this phase is the post-implementation report, which formalises the feedback received from all involved parties, and identifies best practices and lessons learned. The output from the tasks performed as part of conducting a post-implementation review serves as the building blocks for the report. Of even more importance is the transfer of lessons learned and best practices from the post-implementation report to an organisational repository of project management data. The final deliverable of this phase is the archived project repository. The following table lists all project closeout processes, tasks and their deliverables.

Conducting Post-implementation Review

A project is considered complete when it has been successfully implemented and transitioned to the performing organisation and approved by the project sponsor. At this point in the project management lifecycle, the responsibilities of the project manager are to assess how closely the project met customer needs, highlight what worked well, learn from mistakes made during the project, identify patterns and trends, derive ways to improve upon processes executed throughout the project, and, most importantly, communicate results. The purpose of this process is to gather the information required to meet those responsibilities, and to present the information in a post-implementation report.

Role Performers

- Project manager
- Project team members
- Project sponsor
- Customers
- Consumers.

Tasks to be Performed

Soliciting Feedback

The most important measures of the success of a project are whether the product was developed and delivered successfully and how well the needs of the customers have been met. The most effective way to determine these measures is to solicit feedback. The project manager should gather feedback using a survey appropriate to the project. Depending on the size and type of the project and the structure of the performing organisation, different surveys may be required for different stakeholder groups, and surveys will need to be distributed to the appropriate individuals. At a minimum, feedback should be solicited from the project sponsor and project team members who performed the tasks in the project schedule. The project manager should determine if surveys should also be given to customer representatives, consumers, or other stakeholders in order to collect sufficient information for assessing the success of the project in meeting its goals and their needs. The survey must also assess the outcome of the project and the performance of the project team and performing organisation. The project manager must stress to all survey participants the importance of their honest feedback as one of the primary mechanisms for assessing the project's performance. The written survey should be distributed, in either electronic or hard copy form, with a specific due date for its completion. The project manager should follow up if the survey is not returned on time. If distribution is extensive, it may be helpful to keep a list of to whom and when the survey was sent and returned. The project manager also has the option of conducting a survey in person or over the telephone. An interview survey can often be more effective than a written one. While those responding to a written survey are limited to answering the questions as they are written, an intuitive project manager will be able to expand upon the verbal responses of the survey participant, gathering information that might otherwise not be uncovered.

In some cases, however, participants may be reluctant to disclose information as honestly in person. The project manager may not be the appropriate person to administer the survey interview to some stakeholder groups. Each project is unique and questions should be tailored to address the specificproject and the intended audience. It is very important to solicit feedback from the project team. Because they have a different point of view from that of customers and consumers, project team members provide an 'inside look' at the way the project was executed. They are also an important resource for communicating lessons learned and best practices. It is also important to obtain feedback on the performance of the project manager! The project manager's immediate supervisor, or an individual in a similar capacity, needs to take responsibility for obtaining honest feedback from the project sponsor, customer, and project team. Once survey feedback has been collected, the project manager must review, analyse, and summarize the results for presentation at the project assessment meeting. The following is a suggested list of categories to use when compiling survey information:

- Product effectiveness
- CSSQ management
- Risk management
- Communications management
- Acceptance management
- Organisational change management
- Issues management
- Project implementation and transition
- Performance of performing organisation
- Performance of project team.

Summarised feedback will be used during the project assessment meeting as a starting point for identifying lessons learned and best practices to use in future projects. It will also be included in the post-implementation report created at the end of project closeout. A project may come in on time, under budget, and meeting all defined quality standards. Every deliverable may have been 100% error free and perfectly consistent with the project scope. But, if the customer is not satisfied with the outcome, the project cannot be considered a success!

Conducting Project Assessment

The goal of this task is for the project manager to meet with select members of the project team and stakeholder communityto present the summarized results of the feedback surveys, discuss all other aspects of the completed project, gain consensus on what was successful and what was not, and derive best practices and lessons learned. In addition to the project team, the project manager should consider inviting project managers from the performing organisation with experience on similar projects. Based on experience and prior knowledge, other project managers can provide information and insight on the assessment process. It is a good idea for the project manager to distribute the summarised survey results to each participant in advance of the project assessment meeting, to allow them to come prepared to address the contents. In order to provide the best possible products and services to customers, performing organisation management must strive to continuously improve. During the course of the assessment meeting, participants will consider the summarised feedback results and the experience of the project managers in attendance to discuss and assess the performance of the project. Based upon these discussions, the group will identify and agree upon lessons learned. These lessons will not only benefit the current project team, they will also help managers and team members of similar projects. The lessons may be positive or negative. Lessons learned must not simply be identified during the meeting. It is also important to document each one and develop an action plan describing when and how they might be implemented within the performing organisation. During the course of the project, the project manager, customer, and project team members most likely recognised certain procedures that, when exercised, improved the production of a deliverable, streamlined a process, or suggested ways to improve standardised templates. Best practices are documented as part of the project assessment meeting and later shared with other project managers so they can be repeated. In some cases, the outstanding 'successes' might be translated into new procedures to be followed by future projects.

Preparing Post-implementation Report

After the project assessment meeting, the project manager prepares a post-implementation report. In the report, the project manager distills information gleaned from the discussion and organizes it according to the feedback categories described above, adding information on key project metrics. The report documents the effectiveness of the product in meeting the needs of the customer, the effectiveness of project management and the project team, how well the performing organisation supported the project, lessons learned, best practices to be used in future projects, and the key project metrics that will enable the performing organisation to compare success measures across projects. It also contains recommendations for improvement to be used by other projects of similar size and scope. During perform administrative closeout, the report is archived in the project repository. The project manager must present or distribute the post-implementation report to members of the performing organisation. In performing organisations that undertake many projects, it is most effective to assign an individual or agency unit to take ownership of collecting and organising the information, teaching the lessons learned, and implementing the best practices throughout the organisation.

A central repository, owned and maintained by someone within your performing organisation, provides a place where lessons learned and best practices can be archived for use by all project managers in the organisation.

Performing Administrative Closeout

The purpose of this process is to perform all administrative tasks required to bring the project to an official close.

Role Performers

- Project manager
- Team leader.

Tasks to be Performed

Updating Skills Inventory and Provide Performance Feedback

During the course of the project, project team members most likely enhanced their current skills or obtained new ones. The investment made in improving an individual's skills should not be lost. In order to leverage skills on future projects, and to facilitate and encourage individual growth, the project manager should maintain a record of the skills developed and used on the project. If a skills inventory exists within the performing organisation, the project manager or team leader must be sure each project team member takes the time to update it with any skills newly developed and any new project roles that were assumed. An up-to-date inventory will become invaluable to future project managers when attempting to appropriately staff their projects. It can also be used as input for an individual's immediate supervisor when providing performance feedback. If no skills inventory exists within a performing organisation, the project manager should encourage the performing organisation to implement one. The inventory can be as simple as a hardcopy list, or as sophisticated as an electronic skills database, depending upon the needs and desires of the organisation.

The project manager and/or team leader must also take the time to document their feedback on the accomplishments and performance of each project team member. As the person most aware of the day-to-day activities performed by the project team, the team leader or project manager is the most appropriate person to provide honest and accurate feedback. Feedback documentation should be prepared and reviewed with the individual team members first. Following this performance discussion, the documentation is submitted promptly to each project team member's immediate supervisor to be used as input to performance appraisals. The performance feedback mechanisms (appraisal forms, project exit interviews, etc.) specific to the performing organisation should be used.

Archiving Project Information

Throughout the course of the project, the project manager maintained a project repository. As the project progressed, the purpose of the repository was to create a central point of reference for all project materials to be used by anyone involved in the project. Once the project comes to an official close, the repository provides an audit trail documenting the history and evolution of the project. During project closeout, the project manager should examinethe repository to ensure that all relevant project-related material, documents produced, decisions made, issues raised and correspondence exchanged have been captured. In addition, the post-implementation report should be included. When the project is officially closed, the project repository should include the following materials:

- Project supporting documentation, including the business case and project proposal
- Project description/definition documents such as the project charter and project plan
- Any working documents or informal documents defining cost, scope, schedule and quality of the project
- Project schedules—retain all copies electronically, but only include the baseline and final schedule in the hardcopy repository
- Project financials
- Project scope changes and requests log

- Project status reports
- Team member progress reports and timesheets
- Issues log and details (open and resolved)
- Project acceptance log by deliverable
- Project deliverable approval forms, with original signatures
- Risk management worksheets
- Audit results, if encountered
- Correspondence, including any pivotal or decision-making memos, letters, e-mail, etc.
- Meeting notes
- Final project acceptance form, with original signatures
- Post-implementation report.

A hard copy repository should be archived in a designated documentation area. It may be made available electronically at the discretion of the project sponsor in accordance with organisational records management policies.

Key Elements in Project Closeout

Project closeout may be perceived as the least important of all of the project phases, but its value to future projects cannot be underestimated. The knowledge gathered, the expertise developed, the lessons learned, the practices perfected—will remain locked temporarily in a few people's heads unless the post-implementation review is conducted promptly, documented thoroughly, and (most importantly) its results are disseminated appropriately throughout the performing organisation. What are some of the key elements of project closeout that require the most attention? The post-implementation review definitely stands out, and receives the most attention in the following table that identifies processes and tasks which have pitfalls highlighted in this section.

You Waited too Long to Get Feedback

Your project is a success! Everyone is walking on air! In your joy and celebration, you neglect to solicit immediate feedback from the project team and other stakeholders. ... Every project has its challenges, and everyone can learn from them. But people tend to forget the challenges they faced during the course of a project when the final outcome is a success. It is very important to solicit feedback as soon as project closeout begins so you get immediate, honest, and complete information regarding not only the project successes, but the failures. Then, the celebration can begin!

You aren't Sure You are Ready to Hear What They Really Think of the Project

(1) Your project was a miserable failure. Your team mutinied; your customers hate you; and you are in big trouble with your boss because the project came in months late and way over budget. You want to put this wretched experience behind you. The last thing you want to do is dredge up all the misery again. Why give everyone yet another opportunity to kick you?

(2) Your project went OK. You had a pretty good team (with just a few nuts and bolts); you are still on speaking terms with your customers; and the project was just a bit over, mostly because of someone who insisted on 'just one more thing'. You can probably even use this project as a resume-builder for future opportunities. So why jeopardise it by giving everybody a chance to bring up all the things that could have been done better? Let sleeping dogs lie!

(3) You are on top of the world. Your project was a success. The customers love the product. Your boss nominated you for an award because you delivered the project on time and under budget. So why are you still afraid to find out what everybody thinks about the experience? As you can see, whatever the outcome, the bias is always to 'close the chapter' and move on. And yet, for your personal

growth, for the benefit of your organisation, and for all the other project managers to come, you need to spend the time to review the project. You need to understand what you did right—and what you did wrong. You need to know how your behavior, your approach, and your techniques, really worked—not from your own skewed perspective, but from the objective standpoint of your team, your customers, and your management; if you think about it, from the only perspective that really matters, at least vis-à-vis your career.

You Decide to Play Facilitator

Since you are the one inviting the folks to your project assessment meeting, and it is your project they are reviewing, the temptation is to try to facilitate the meeting yourself. Bad idea for two reasons. First of all, you probably don't know how to do it right. A few project managers do happen to be talented facilitators; a lot more think they are, but in reality don't have a clue as to what's involved in getting meaningful output from a large group of disparate personalities. Remember, if you want a professional job, secure a professional. Many agencies have trained facilitators that are available for such meetings. Alternatively, you may consider hiring an outside consultant if it can be done expediently.

Secondly, even if you are a great facilitator, what do you want to concentrate on during this meeting? Remember what they say in the legal profession, "a lawyer representing himself has a fool for a client".

Likewise, it's a bad idea to play scribe, for the same reasons: you probably can't type as fast as people talk.

You Get Lost in the Feedback and Learn the Wrong Lessons

If you overcome your fears and invite a good cross-section of the project team to the project assessment meeting, and get a good facilitator to lead the session, you are going to get a lot of feedback—especially if, in preparation for the meeting, your facilitator asks the participants to list all the things that could have been handled better. Making sense of all the feedback will be tough. Here are some guidelines: first, concentrate on what's important. During the meeting, your facilitator should ask the group to prioritise their feedback, both positive and negative. What were the things that impeded the project the most? If there was a problem (corrected or not) with cost, scope, schedule, or quality—what contributed the most to it? The group should come to consensus on the top three or four or five things that affected the project the most. (How? That's why you get a professional facilitator!)

Second, select items that may be of use to other projects. If your locality had a flood for the first time in fifty years during the crucial phase of your project, and as a result your schedule got thrown off kilter, well, too bad for you—but nobody else really cares.

Third, 'genericise' your experience so it can be applicable to multiple projects. If one of your key team members developed a rare tropical disease and as a result you had to scramble to identify and secure another resource who could do the work while the expert recuperated, the lesson learned is not how to treat the rare tropical disease, but how to anticipate and prepare for the risk of a key member of the team being unavailable— for whatever reason.

You are too Modest

No matter how rotten everyone thinks you are at managing projects, you are guaranteed to have done at least something right. So along with getting all the negative feedback at the project assessment meeting, you also need to accentuate the positive. That is not difficult if your facilitator, in preparation for the meeting, asks the participants to list all the things that went right with the project.

Again, making sense of the feedback is possible if you follow the same guidelines: prioritise the comments, select those that are applicable to other projects, and make them generic and useful.

Don't be bashful about throwing things in that only you thought of. After all, who knows this project better than you? And be specific. If you came up with a better format for a progress report that suits your organisation or your project circumstances to a 'T'—include it, both as a template, and as a filledin example. If you followed an unorthodox issue escalation procedure, but it worked better than the tried-and-true chainof- command one, by all means, let the other folks have the benefit of your ingenuity and good fortune.

You Let it All Go to Waste

You complete a magnificent project, one that will be a feather in your cap for years to come. You survey half the world for their feedback. You hold a great project assessment Meeting, and come up with a host of brilliant strategies for other project managers to emulate, and a multitude of obstacles for them to avoid. You triumphantly record them all into your project repository, and file it away. Never to be seen again. That's because your organisation does not have a way to disseminate this hard-won knowledge throughout the workplace. There is no central repository of historical project data. There is no agency unit charged with taking ownership to collect, organise and make available information about other projects. There is nobody assigned to actively teach lessons learned, or faithfully implement best practices. There is no way to share organisational knowledge, other than by personal contact. But it doesn't have to be that way. You can change that, and you can benefit greatly by doing it. First, start accumulating the knowledge from your own projects and from others you are aware of. Second, publicize what you are doing, and create a track record of successful utilisation. Third, present the organisational knowledge repository idea to your management, and encourage them to take action. Someone at a management level needs to assign ownership to the appropriate individuals for implementing best practices and lessons learned throughout the performing organisation. By then, the organisation will have been exposed to the idea, will think it is fabulous, and will think you're fabulous for coming up with it. Let others learn from your experiences while you benefit by learning from theirs.

Completion is Anti-climactic

Your project ends successfully. People go their separate ways. You feel like the whole experience is now nothing more than a vague memory. Why? May be you didn't take the time to appropriately celebrate your success. Don't be afraid to approach your project sponsor to inquire about funds that may exist for hosting a celebration function. The function may be as simple as a cake and coffee meeting, or may be an agency-sponsored party or event. In any case, you want your project team to have good memories of their experiences on projects you manage, so they will be excited about having the opportunity to work with you again.

Index